Macroeconomics
as a Second Language

Macroeconomics as a Second Language

Martha L. Olney
University of California, Berkeley

WILEY

John Wiley & Sons, Inc.

VP & PUBLISHER	George Hoffman
ACQUISITIONS EDITOR	Lacey Vitetta
PROJECT EDITOR	Jennifer Manias
SENIOR EDITORIAL ASSISTANT	Emily McGee
ASSOCIATE DIRECTOR OF MARKETING	Amy Scholz
ASSISTANT MARKETING MANAGER	Diane Mars
PRODUCTION MANAGER	Janis Soo
ASSISTANT PRODUCTION EDITOR	Elaine S. Chew
CREATIVE DIRECTOR	Harry Nolan
SENIOR DESIGNER	Kevin Murphy
COVER DESIGNER	RDC Publishing Group Sdn. Bhd.

This book was set in 10/12 Times by Laserwords Private Limited, Chennai, India and printed and bound by Courier Westford. The cover was printed by Courier Westford.

Founded in 1807, John Wiley & Sons, Inc. has been a valued source of knowledge and understanding for more than 200 years, helping people around the world meet their needs and fulfill their aspirations. Our company is built on a foundation of principles that include responsibility to the communities we serve and where we live and work. In 2008, we launched a Corporate Citizenship Initiative, a global effort to address the environmental, social, economic, and ethical challenges we face in our business. Among the issues we are addressing are carbon impact, paper specifications and procurement, ethical conduct within our business and among our vendors, and community and charitable support. For more information, please visit our website: http://www.wiley.com/go/citizenship.

Evaluation copies are provided to qualified academics and professionals for review purposes only, for use in their courses during the next academic year. These copies are licensed and may not be sold or transferred to a third party. Upon completion of the review period, please return the evaluation copy to Wiley. Return instructions and a free of charge return mailing label are available at www.wiley.com/go/returnlabel. If you have chosen to adopt this textbook for use in your course, please accept this book as your complimentary desk copy. Outside of the United States, please contact your local sales representative.

To order books or for customer service please, call 1-800-CALL WILEY (225-5945).

Library of Congress Cataloging-in-Publication Data

Olney, Martha L., 1956- author.
    Macroeconomics as a Second Language / Martha L. Olney.
        p. cm
    Includes index.
    ISBN 978-0-470-50538-0 (pbk.)
    1. Macroeconomics. 2. Macroeconomics—Terminology. I. Title.
    HB172.5.O46 2010
    339—dc22

                                            2010047243

Printed in the United States of America

10 9 8 7 6 5 4 3 2 1

To my students
This one's for you!

About the Author

Martha L. Olney is an award-winning teacher of economics and the author of several economics textbooks. She is the recipient of Distinguished Teaching Awards from the University of California at Berkeley and the University of Massachusetts, Amherst; the Jonathan Hughes Prize for Excellence in Teaching Economic History from the Economic History Association; and was recognized in 2007 by the Stavros Center for Free Enterprise and Economics Education of Florida State University as one of the nation's Great Teachers of Economics.

Her previous textbooks include *Microeconomics as a Second Language* (Wiley, 2009), *Macroeconomics*, co-authored with Brad DeLong (McGraw-Hill, 2006), and *Essentials of Economics*, co-authored with Paul Krugman and Robin Wells (Worth, 2007).

She currently serves as Adjunct Professor of Economics at the University of California, Berkeley. Her open-access website includes course materials for Principles of Economics and other courses: *http://www.econ.berkeley.edu/~olney*.

Preface

Economics is all around us all the time. Much of it is quite intuitive. But you'd never know it if by some cruel turn of fate you were dropped into the middle of an "Intro to Econ" lecture at your local college or university. That's because the intuition gets lost in the language.

With apologies to *Through the Looking Glass* author Lewis Carroll, whom I paraphrase: Economists use words to mean exactly what we want them to mean. Words like "rational" have a perfectly fine dictionary meaning. Economists use "rational" in a different way, to mean "behavior that is consistent with trying to maximize something." Or, what about "market"? You might think that means a store, a place you go to buy something. Not to an economist. The "market for tomatoes" doesn't exist at your local farmer's market, or grocery store. A "market" is an idea, an abstraction, a collection of all the behavior and potential behavior of those who want to buy and those who want to sell something.

The key to "getting" economics is to view it as a second language. You need to become conversant in econ-speak just as you would in French or Japanese or any other new-to-you language. The ideas of economics are intuitive. The expression of economics is a second language.

ABOUT THIS BOOK

Macroeconomics as a Second Language "cuts to the chase." It zeroes in on the concepts, assumptions, and models that you need to learn. This book is a student study aid in the Principles of Macroeconomics. We take a bare-bones approach here. Our focus is the principles of macroeconomics and the language used to express them.

What if you're not currently enrolled in a macroeconomics course? This book is a good aid for you, too. Trying to pick up some economics concepts and language? This book will help you out. Trying to follow the news about the economy? This book is for you. Rather than wade through a 700–900 page principles textbook, *Macroeconomics as a Second Language* gives you the basics to get you up to speed quickly.

ORGANIZATION

Macroeconomics is a story, a rather long story at that. Think of it as a novel, with characters introduced in the early chapters, the action unveiled in the middle chapters, and the characters' experiences placed into a context in the final chapters. Reading just the first chapter won't give you a sense of the story. Jumping in at the middle creates confusion about who is who. Reading only the last chapter leaves you baffled as to how it all fit together.

For those who have studied microeconomics, the study of macroeconomics can be a bit of a jolt. Economists agree on what is to be taught in micro. In microeconomics, there is one story and one basic approach: start from supply and demand, then examine the various sources of market failure.

Macroeconomics enjoys little of that agreement. Pick up six textbooks at random and you'll probably find four—or more—different approaches to macroeconomics. Terminology accounts for some of the difference. But that's not all. What order should the material be presented in? What topics should be included—and omitted? What relationships should be emphasized?

While the companion volume *Microeconomics as a Second Language* can help you out in nearly any microeconomics class taught in any classroom, the same promise can't be made for this book. In *Macroeconomics as a Second Language*, I chose to present the material in the order and with the emphasis that makes sense to the thousands of students I have taught.

Part I contains the basics. An overview of macroeconomics is provided in Chapter 1. Economics principles are often expressed with equations and graphs, so Chapter 1 also presents the math and graphing tools you need. We dive into economics in Chapter 2 with the model of the Production Possibilities Frontier (PPF), which is about the choices we make in deciding what goods and services will be produced. Demand and Supply is the most often used model in economics; Chapter 3 helps you master it. How we measure the macroeconomy—output, unemployment, and inflation—is covered in Chapter 4.

Macroeconomics is the study of long-run growth and short-run fluctuations. Long-run growth—how does the standard of living change from generation to generation—is addressed in Chapter 5. The remainder of the book focuses on short-run fluctuations: Why do an economy's unemployment and inflation rates change from year to year?

Keynesian principles (Part III) are the basics of most macroeconomic analysis, even by people who assert "I'm not a Keynesian." Those principles are:

- The amount of output that firms produce depends upon the total (or, aggregate) demand for goods and services (Chapter 6).

- Total (or, aggregate) demand is the sum of consumption, investment, government, and net export spending (Chapter 7).

- Because consumption depends on income, any initial change in aggregate demand has a multiplied effect on total output (Chapter 8).

Policy is studied in Part IV, starting with an overview of fiscal and monetary policy in Chapter 9. Fiscal policy, government deficits and debt are covered in Chapter 10.

Monetary policy takes up the next three chapters. Money is *not* created by a government printing press; money is created by banks making loans (Chapter 11). The central bank—in the United States, the Fed—can change the amount of money in the economy, but must choose between pursuing a money supply target and an interest rate target (Chapter 12). Monetary policy changes interest rates, which affect aggregate demand (Chapter 13).

The determination and effect of price inflation are the focus of Part V. I'll let you in on a little secret: macroeconomists' understanding of why and how prices change is the weakest part of macroeconomics. They are better at explaining the *effects* of a change in prices than they are in explaining the *causes* of a change in prices.

For three decades, macro has been taught with the aggregate supply/aggregate demand (*AS/AD*) model (Chapter 14). The *AS/AD* model is useful for explaining the 1970s and early 1980s, a time when the model's critical assumption, that the central bank targets the money supply, was satisfied. More recently, macro has been taught with a monetary policy model (Chapter 15), also known as the Taylor Rule approach, or a monetary policy reaction function. This model starts from the assumption that the central bank sets an interest rate target based on current and future expected values of inflation and output. By the end of Chapter 15, you'll be able to analyze the Fed's behavior with the best of them.

An "open" economy is one in which exports and imports are not zero. Like most textbooks, this book concludes with a chapter on open economy macro. But the discussion of exports and imports is not confined just to Chapter 16. The determinants of exports and imports are in Chapter 7; the open economy multiplier is in Chapter 8; monetary policy's effects on exports and imports are in Chapter 13.

FEATURES

Each chapter begins with a list of the key terms and concepts, graphs, and equations covered in that chapter. The first use of each concept in the chapter is highlighted in **bold**. The index at the back of the book also contains all these key terms.

TIP

"TIP" notes in each chapter highlight tricks for remembering or common errors to avoid.

TRY

"TRY" questions give you the chance to test what you've learned. Answers to all "TRY" questions are at the back of the book.

HOW BEST TO LEARN ECONOMICS

Economics is not a novel to be read at the beach. (Though we welcome beach-goers to give this book a try!) Economics is best learned with pencil in hand. Don't just read a new term. Write it down. Don't just look at a graph. Draw it yourself. Jot notes and questions in the margins. Be actively engaged with what you are reading.

And then comes the key to truly learning econ. Breathe it. Everywhere you look, everything you read, every word you hear—think econ. Think about how you can explain it in the language of economics.

The world is rife with bloggers and pundits arguing over the effects of fiscal and monetary policy . . . break it down with the language of macroeconomics. Local communities are cutting spending and raising taxes . . . understand why with the language of macroeconomics. Family members struggle with unemployment . . . gain insight into their predicaments with the language of macroeconomics. A politician wants your vote . . . analyze the promises with the language of macroeconomics.

Economics is all around you. To become fully conversant in the language of economics, think econ. All the time. And now, let's begin.

Acknowledgments

Thank-yous are usually perfunctory. In this case, that's not so. My mother's descent into dementia and her eventual death necessitated a much greater than usual level of patience and understanding from the folks at Wiley. Judith Joseph believed in this project from the beginning, and I am truly grateful. Jennifer Manias stepped into the project and offered the right mix of understanding and urgency. Thank you. Very much.

In addition, I'd like to thank the reviewers who provided invaluable feedback on this manuscript—on one or more of its various drafts—I hope you are pleased with the final product: Fatma Wahdan Antar, Manchester Community College; Bruce C. Brown, Cal State Polytechnic University; Matthew P. Dudman, MBA/LL.M, Cal Maritime; Timothy S. Fuerst, Bowling Green State University; J. Robert Gillette, University of Kentucky; Chang Yong Kim, University of Oregon; Rajeev Goel, Illinois State University; Michael Lampert, Truckee Meadows Community College; Steven Pressman, Monmouth University; Virginia A. Reilly, Ocean County College; Mark Siegler, California State University, Sacramento; David M. Switzer, St. Cloud State University; and, William Walsh, University of St. Thomas. A special call-out goes to David Switzer, a Berkeley alumnus, who blended his experiences as a faculty member with his memories as my student to give first-rate and extensive feedback.

Last, but far from least, to my wife Esther Hargis and our son Jimmy: Being able to head to my study after dinner, without (too much) guilt, makes projects such as this possible. Your sacrifices so that I can write are not taken for granted. Thank you, thank you. And Jimmy, I think I now owe you a trip to Disneyland.

Contents

10. Fiscal Policy   169

11. Money Creation   183

12. The Money Market   202

13. Monetary Policy and Interest Rates   220

PART V   Inflation and Output   235

14. Inflation and Output: The *AS/AD* Approach   237

PART VI The Open Economy   283

PART I

Basics

Chapter 1

Economics Tools—Math and Graphing

Economics studies the behavior of the economy. Microeconomics studies the behavior of individuals within the economy; macroeconomics studies the economy as a whole. This book and its companion volume, *Microeconomics as a Second Language*, highlight the language of economics. Both books are designed to be supplements to standard principles textbooks. This chapter begins with an overview of macroeconomics, and also focuses on the mathematical tools used in studying economics.

KEY TERMS AND CONCEPTS

- Microeconomics
- Macroeconomics
- Aggregate
- Positive economics
- Normative economics
- Empirical evidence
- Social science
- Economic models
- Functional notation
- Variable
- Dependent variable
- Independent variable
- Δ means change
- Rate of change
- Two-dimensional graph
- Horizontal axis
- Vertical axis
- Truncated axis
- Curve
- Slope
- Directly (positively) related
- Inversely (negatively) related

- Straight line
- Linear curve
- Nonlinear curve
- Concave to the origin
- Convex to the origin
- Move along a curve
- Shift of a curve

INTRODUCTION TO ECONOMICS

Economics is divided into microeconomics and macroeconomics. **Microeconomics** deals with questions about the behavior of individuals: individual people, individual firms, individual markets. Questions in microeconomics include

- What determines the price of some product?
- How much output will a firm produce?
- What determines the wage rate in a labor market?

Macroeconomics deals with questions about the behavior of groups of people, about the entire economy. Economists sometimes use the phrase **aggregate** to describe any such group. Macroeconomics is usually applied to a national economy, such as that of the United States, but the tools of macroeconomics can be applied to any aggregate economy: a region, a state, a county, a city. Questions in macroeconomics include

- What determines the economy's inflation rate?
- What determines the economy's unemployment rate?
- What determines the total income of an economy?

Economic analysis—whether it is microeconomic or macroeconomic analysis—can be divided into two categories: positive economics and normative economics. **Positive economics** answers questions that are usually phrased as "How does this thing affect that thing?" How does a drop in spending by households affect the number of jobs in an economy? **Normative economics** answers questions that are usually phrased as "Should this action be taken?" Should the federal government raise taxes?

Most economic analysis is positive economic analysis. Positive economics requires analysis of a question, but no judgment as to what is best for society. Normative economics requires a value judgment. When offering a normative analysis—should this action be taken?—it is necessary to state what goal(s) we are trying to achieve. Disagreements among economists are almost always in the realm of normative economics. Disagreeing economists usually agree on the positive analysis: how will the policy affect the economy? But they disagree on the best goal: Is our goal to reduce inequality, or to enhance growth? Is it to lower inflation, or to create jobs? When you hear economists disagree, oftentimes their ultimate disagreement is over what goals they hold for society.

The use of **empirical evidence** is also an important part of economics. Empirical evidence means data—statistics, numbers—that can be used to support an argument. How much does spending for macaroni and cheese change when families have less money to spend? "How much" is an empirical question, a question that calls for a numerical (empirical) answer.

Economics is a **social science** that uses mathematical tools. It is a social science because it deals with the behavior of people. It uses mathematical tools because ideas and theories and models and empirical evidence about people's economic behavior are expressed mathematically.

OVERVIEW OF MACROECONOMICS

Macroeconomics helps us understand the news. "Unemployment rate up"—that's macroeconomics. "Inflation is at a 20-year high"—that's macro. "The economy is in recession"—macro. "The Fed announced an increase in interest rates"—macro. "Federal tax rebate checks are coming soon"—macro. "Household saving is at an all-time low"—macro. "A weaker dollar is boosting U.S. exports"—still macro! Every day, there is macroeconomic news.

Learning macroeconomics requires assembling a series of building blocks. Each piece builds on the previous piece. You can avoid feeling baffled only by mastering each piece before going on.

Macroeconomists are infamous for their tendency to disagree. An old joke goes something like this: get two economists in the room and you're likely to get at least four different opinions. Some people thus scoff at macroeconomists: "What good is someone who can't even tell me what will happen?"

True: macroeconomists cannot tell you with certainty what *will* happen in the future. But they can make informed guesses. And you can learn to make these guesses, too.

Macroeconomists *can* tell you the effect of a policy *all else constant*—when nothing but the policy and all of its effects changes. The challenge is that in the real world, "all else" is never constant.

What will happen when the Fed lowers interest rates? If "all else" was held constant and only interest rates changed, we could tell you. But out there in the real world, lots of other things change, too.

So what will the news tell us tomorrow? It's hard to say! One economist will predict one thing; another will predict something else. And each will follow his or her first prediction with "On the other hand, the effect could instead be . . . " Two economists. Four opinions. You too might wonder, "What good is someone who can't even tell me what will happen?"

A lot of good, actually. There are two keys to understanding macroeconomics and its relationship to the real world:

- The stories we tell in macro are all "if-then" stories. "*If* this happens, *then* that is the effect." But the conclusion—the "then"—rests on assumptions. Are business people optimistic about the future? When the Fed lowers interest rates, will banks also lower the interest rates they charge? Some assumptions are made explicit in the "if"—"If business people don't change their attitudes and the Fed lowers interest rates . . . " But some assumptions are implicit—important assumptions, but not spoken aloud. Whether explicit or implicit, changing an assumption can change the conclusion.

- Our observations about macroeconomics are all "real-world" observations. What we read in the news is what we're trying to explain. But the real world is messy and complicated. It doesn't allow us to "hold all else constant" in order to see a policy's effect. Truly *doing* macroeconomics is one part straightforward analysis—if this, then that—and one part tracking the multitude of things that are changing.

The economist who disagrees with herself is not incompetent. She is underscoring these two keys. Different assumptions about behavior lead to different conclusions. Different real-world messiness leads to different real-world results.

One other thing to keep in mind: macroeconomics is like a novel. It is not a short story that unfolds completely in 22 quick pages. Macro is all about the interaction of millions of us in many different roles. We need to set the stage, meet the characters, and watch the drama unfold.

We begin with three chapters from the companion volume, *Microeconomics as a Second Language*. These chapters review the math tools used throughout economics (Chapter 1), and then introduce two microeconomic models that show up quite often in macroeconomics: the production possibilities frontier model (Chapter 2) and the model of demand and supply (Chapter 3). Our tale of macroeconomics begins in Chapter 4.

ECONOMIC MODELS

Economic models are used to answer questions in economics. Economic models are almost never physical models such as a model airplane. Instead, **economic models** are the formal way economists answer questions and tell stories. Economic models are the stories we tell.

Every economic model consists of three things:

- A question
- Simplifications of and abstractions from the real world
- Assumptions about economic behavior

Change any one of these three things and you have a different model.

For example, if the question is "What determines the price of a pickle?" the model to use is the model of supply and demand (Chapter 3). But if the question is instead "What determines the level of unemployment?" we use a different model. Change the question and it's a different model, a different economic story.

Alternatively, one simplification of the complex world we live in is to divide it into four groups: households, businesses, government, and the rest of the world. When this simplification is made, we are using a macroeconomic model called the Keynesian model (which we'll cover in Chapter 6). But if we instead simplified the world into just two groups—capitalists and workers—then we would be using a different model. Change the simplification and it's a different model, a different economic story.

Or, if we assume that households determine their annual spending by considering how much they need to save to be able to live comfortably in their retirement years, we are using a model called the life-cycle model. But if instead we assume that households determine their annual spending by considering just that year's income, we are using a different model. Change an assumption and it's a different model, a different economic story.

Economic models are expressed in three ways:

- Words
- Mathematical equations
- Graphs

Most models are expressed in two ways (words and one other); some are expressed in all three.

If you don't understand the words, look at the graph. If a graph doesn't make sense, look at the equation or the words. All three ways of expressing a model should reinforce each other. Think of them as three languages all telling you the same thing. Eventually you should understand all three expressions of any model, and be able to move back and forth between them.

MATHEMATICAL TOOLS

In a Principles of Economics course, you need to be able to use a few mathematical tools. We cover the most commonly used math tools here. Graphing tools (covered in the next section) are perhaps more important to your success in studying economics. Be sure to refer back to this chapter often, until you are comfortable with these math and graphing tools.

Fractions and Decimals

In some parts of economics, we use fractions—in other parts, decimals. You want to be comfortable going back and forth between fractions and decimals. And you want to be comfortable reducing fractions:

$$\frac{30}{40} = \frac{3}{4} = 0.75$$

$$\frac{20}{40} = \frac{1}{2} = 0.5$$

$$0.6 = \frac{6}{10}, \ so \ \frac{1}{0.6} = \frac{10}{6} = \frac{5}{3}$$

Absolute Value

On a few occasions, economists use absolute value. The absolute value of any number is the distance that number is from zero (ignoring whether the number is above or below zero). The absolute value of a number is indicated with two straight lines: $|\ |$. So $|4| = 4$ and $|-4| = 4$.

Functional Notation

Much of economics is shorthanded with equations and symbols (or, notation). For example, an economist writes the simple sentence "How many sodas you want to buy depends primarily on the price of soda" as $q_D = f(p)$. Economists say they have expressed the relationship in an equation using **functional notation**. It is important to be able to "read" equations.

What words are in your head as you read "$q_D = f(p)$"? If you thought "q sub D equals f parentheses p," you'll have a lot of trouble in economics. You're in better shape if you read that equation as "q sub D equals a function of p." But to really *get* economics, you want to read "$q_D = f(p)$" as "quantity demanded depends upon price."

Success in reading equations depends on two things:

- Being able to translate the functional notation such as $f(\ )$ into words
- Knowing what the symbols (notation) stand for

To know what q_D, p, and more stand for, you must simply memorize their meanings. Memorizing will be easier if you use the same notation every time. Think of it as "txtng 4 economists."

TIP

Start by making a list of your book's notation. Then, every time your instructor says "price," write "p" in your notes. Every time she says "quantity," write "q." And so on.

Variables

Economists use the word "variable" over and over. This is one of many times when a commonly used word has a different and more technical meaning in the language of economics than in everyday conversation. A **variable** is something whose value *can* change. The price of a box of tissues at the nearby grocery store may have been the same for the last four months, but economists say price is a variable because its value *can* change. The variable is "price"; the notation we use for the variable "price" is p.

There are two types of variables: dependent and independent variables. The value of a **dependent variable** depends upon the values of the **independent variables**. How much a family spends in a month depends upon its income. Family spending is a dependent variable whose value depends upon the independent variable family income. Family spending and family income are both variables because the values of both *can* change. In any one relationship, there is only *one* dependent variable, but no limit to the number of independent variables.

Algebra

In macroeconomics, we often solve algebraic equations with one unknown. For example, what is the value of Y if

$$Y = 100 + 0.6Y$$

To solve this equation, first gather terms (remember, Y is the same as $1 \times Y$):

$$Y - 0.6Y = 100$$
$$0.4Y = 100$$

and then divide both sides of the equation in order to isolate Y:

$$\frac{0.4Y}{0.4} = \frac{100}{0.4}$$
$$Y = 250$$

Δ Means "Change"

Over and over in economics, we will talk about the change in the value of some variable. Economists use the uppercase Greek letter delta, Δ, to stand for change. Thus, Δx is read as "the change in x." ΔY is "the change in Y." Substituting Δ for "change in" is another shorthand you should start using as you take notes in class.

Calculating Rate of Change

In some cases, we need to calculate a variable's **rate of change**, or percentage change, between two values. For instance, if Q increases from 50 to 60, at what rate has Q increased?

The general formula for calculating rate of change is

$$\frac{new\ value - old\ value}{old\ value}$$

So when Q increases from 50 to 60, the rate of change is $(60 - 50)/50 = 10/50 = 0.2$, or 20%.

TRY   (*Answers to all "TRY" questions are at the back of the book.*)

Try your hand at these math problems.

1. Solve for Y: $Y = 350 + 0.3Y$.

2. What is the rate of change of income when income rises from 100 to 110?

3. What is the rate of change of income when income falls from 110 to 100?

GRAPHING TOOLS

Thumb through any economics principles textbook and you'll see lots of graphs. Comfort in drawing, interpreting, and analyzing graphs is essential when studying econ.

The Basics

Almost every economics graph is a **two-dimensional graph**—a graph that depicts what is happening with just two variables. A two-dimensional graph has a **horizontal axis** and a **vertical axis**. Where the two axes cross is called the origin. The values of the variable depicted on the horizontal axis range from negative values on the left of the origin to positive values on the right. The values of the variable depicted on the vertical axis range from negative values below the origin to positive values above it.

Any one point on the graph shows simultaneously the values of both variables. Let's make up an example: the variable d is measured on the vertical axis and the variable w is measured on the horizontal axis. Point A in Figure 1.1 represents a negative value of w (it is to the left of the origin) and a negative value of d (it is below the origin). Point B represents a positive value of w (it is to the right of the origin) and a negative value of d (it is below the origin).

The axes divide the graph into four areas called quadrants. Because most variables in economics take on only positive values, we almost always use just the upper right quadrant, so most graphs begin with axes like you see in Figure 1.2.

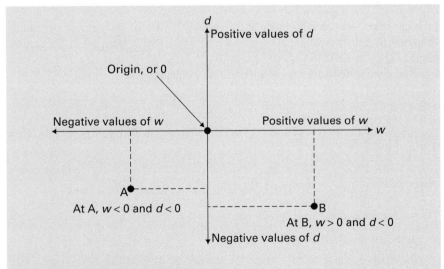

Figure 1.1 A Two-Dimensional Graph.

Two-dimensional graphs depict what is happening with two variables. The horizontal axis and vertical axis cross at the origin. Any point in the graph depicts two values simultaneously. Point A represents a negative value of w ($w < 0$) and a negative value of d ($d < 0$).

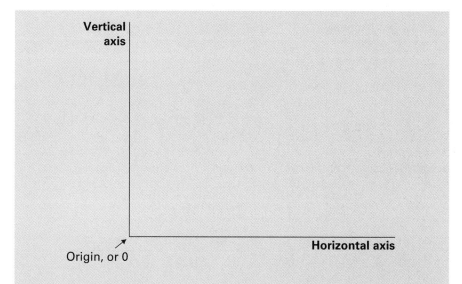

Figure 1.2 The Upper Right Quadrant.

Because most of the variables we measure in economics take on only positive values, most graphs in economics use just the upper right quadrant of a two-dimensional graph.

Borrowing from high school math classes, some books call the horizontal axis the *x-axis* and the vertical axis the *y-axis*. Be careful if you use that terminology. There are economics variables called X (usually for exports) and Y (usually income), but they are not always graphed on the *x-* and *y*-axes, respectively. You will not get confused if you always just use the terms "horizontal axis" and "vertical axis."

Plotting Data

If we have information (data) on two variables, we can plot that data on a graph. For example, suppose we find information on the average income people earned in 2007 sorted by the number of years of education completed. We could write the information down in a (cumbersome!) sentence: In 2007, people with a high school diploma earned, on average, $40,000 per year; people with a college degree earned $78,000; and people with a master's degree earned $91,000.

Or we could put the information in a table:

Table 1.1 Income Increases with Education

	Years of education	Average annual income in 2007
H.S. diploma	12	$40,000
College diploma	16	$78,000
Master's degree	18	$91,000

Source: U.S. Census Bureau, *Statistical Abstract of the United States: 2009*, Table 676.

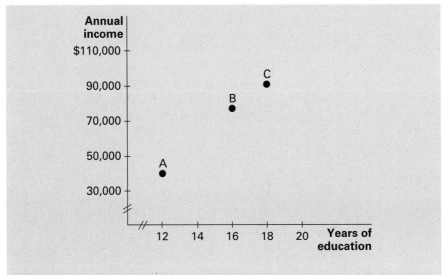

Figure 1.3 Plotting Data Points.
Each point on the graph represents one pair of values. Average income is measured on the vertical axis. Years of education is measured on the horizontal axis. Point A indicates that those with 12 years of education earned average annual income of $40,000.

It's certainly easier from the table than from the sentence to see that more education means higher income. But what about showing the same information in a graph?

To plot the data, put one variable on the horizontal axis and the other on the vertical axis. Often—though not always—in economics, the independent variable is put on the horizontal axis and the dependent variable on the vertical. (The independent variables are those that determine the values of the dependent variable.)

Each point on the graph in Figure 1.3 represents one pair of values. Point A indicates the average income of people with 12 years of education (measured on the horizontal axis) is $40,000 (measured on the vertical axis). Point C indicates that those with 18 years of education receive average income of $91,000.

Truncated Axes

Notice that the axes in our graph are truncated. A **truncated axis** omits values between 0 and some value. We use the two marks // near the origin to show that the axes are truncated. The horizontal axis is truncated between 0 and 12 years; the vertical axis, between $0 and $30,000.

Curves

Sometimes a relationship is depicted with a **curve** rather than individual points. The curve—an unbroken line that may or may not be straight—may connect actual data. In Figure 1.4, the data from Figure 1.3 are connected with a curve.

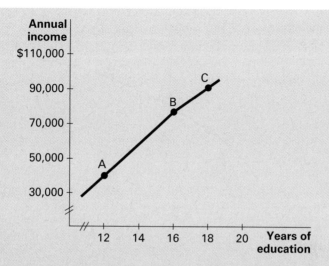

Figure 1.4 Connecting Data Points with a Curve.

A relationship between two variables can be depicted by a curve that connects known data points. Starting from the data in Table 1.1, the curve shows that average annual income increases with years of education.

Or the curve may depict a relationship without reflecting any actual data. Figure 1.5 indicates that spending by households is higher when household wealth is higher. In Figure 1.5, a point such as A represents values of spending and wealth. From A, dash over to the vertical axis to find the value of spending, and dash down to the horizontal axis to find the level of wealth. Point A represents the combination of wealth level A_1 and spending level A_2. Point B represents the combination of wealth level B_1 and spending level B_2.

Reading Graphs

It is as important to be able to "read" a graph as it is to be able to read an equation. When you look at Figure 1.5, what (if any!) words are in your head? One possibility is: "A graph with spending on the vertical axis and wealth on the horizontal axis is a curve that slopes up." This is correct, but doesn't help you much.

Another possibility is "Spending depends upon wealth." Again, correct but incomplete. The graph tells you much more than just that.

A good interpretation would be "Spending increases when wealth increases, but the increases in spending get smaller and smaller as wealth gets larger and larger."

Slope

Calculating the actual **slope** of a straight line or along a curve is sometimes necessary. Most of us learned in high school a formula for calculating slope: "slope

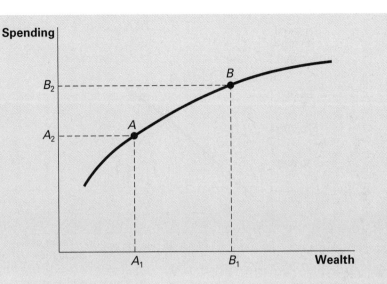

Figure 1.5 Graphs without Numbers.

Often, in economics, we draw graphs without using numerical values of the two variables. If we know that wealthier households spend more than poorer households, we can depict this relationship with a curve. This graph shows that spending increases when wealth increases, but that increases in spending get smaller and smaller as wealth gets larger and larger.

equals rise over run," or

$$slope = \frac{rise}{run}$$

That formula works here, too. The rise is the change between two points along the vertical axis. The run is the change between the same two points along the horizontal axis.

Between points A and B of Figure 1.6, the "rise" is $6 - 4 = 2$. The "run" is $3 - 2 = 1$. So the slope between A and B is

$$\frac{rise}{run} = \frac{\Delta y}{\Delta x} = \frac{6 - 4}{3 - 2} = \frac{2}{1} = 2$$

(Δ is the Greek uppercase letter "delta," and means "change.")

Positive or Negative Slope

When the slope is positive as in Figure 1.6, we say the two variables are **directly related**, or **positively related**, to each other. When the temperature rises (when x increases), more people drink lemonade (y increases). Economists say: temperature and lemonade consumption are directly related.

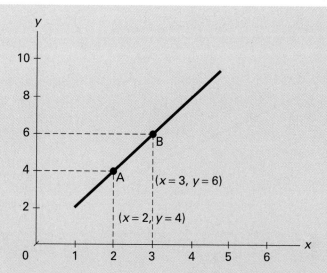

Figure 1.6 Calculating a Positive Slope.

The slope between any two points is equal to "rise over run." The rise is the change in values along the vertical axis. The run is the change in values along the horizontal axis. Between A and B, the value of y depicted on the vertical axis increases from 4 to 6. The rise equals $\Delta y = 6 - 4 = 2$. Between A and B, the value of x depicted on the horizontal axis increases from 2 to 3. The run equals $\Delta x = 3 - 2 = 1$. The slope between A and B is rise/run $= 2/1 = 2$.

TIP

Whenever you read about a relationship between two variables, sketch how it looks.

When the slope is negative, as in Figure 1.7, the two variables are **inversely related** (or, **negatively related**) to each other. When the temperature rises (when x increases), fewer people buy wool coats (y decreases). Economists say: temperature and sales of wool coats are inversely related.

TRY

4. What is the slope of the line in Figure 1.7?

A curve can be a **straight line**, sometimes called a **linear curve**. The slope along a straight line is the same no matter which two points you use. The slope is constant.

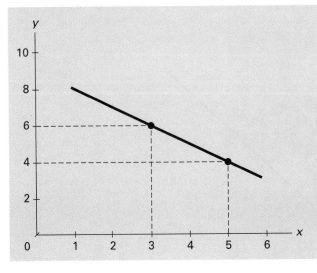

Figure 1.7 A Negative Slope.

When two variables are inversely or negatively related to each other, the relationship is depicted with a downward-sloping curve. As the variable measured on the horizontal axis increases, the variable measured on the vertical axis decreases.

Nonlinear Curve

A curve can also be, well, curvy—not a straight line. A curve that is not a straight line is sometimes called a **nonlinear curve**. The slope changes along a nonlinear curve. Figure 1.8a has a positive and increasing slope: y increases as x increases, and the increases in y get larger and larger as x increases. The slope between points C and D is greater than the slope between points A and B.

Figure 1.8b has a positive and decreasing slope: y increases as x increases and the increases in y get smaller and smaller as x increases. The slope between points C and D is smaller than the slope between points A and B.

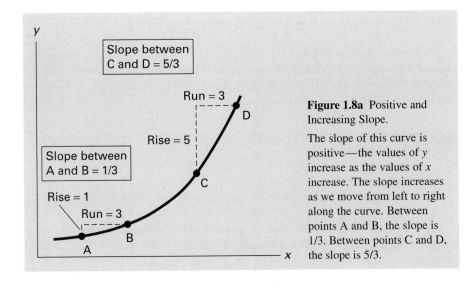

Figure 1.8a Positive and Increasing Slope.

The slope of this curve is positive—the values of y increase as the values of x increase. The slope increases as we move from left to right along the curve. Between points A and B, the slope is 1/3. Between points C and D, the slope is 5/3.

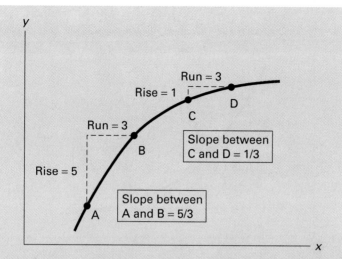

Figure 1.8b Positive and Decreasing Slope.

The slope of this curve is positive—the values of y increase as the values of x increase. The slope decreases as we move from left to right along the curve. Between points A and B, the slope is 5/3. Between points C and D, the slope is 1/3.

Figure 1.8c has a negative and increasing (in absolute value) slope: y decreases as x increases, and the decreases in y get larger and larger as x increases. Figure 1.8c is also sometimes called **concave to the origin**. The slope between points C and D is larger (in absolute value) than the slope between points A and B.

Figure 1.8d has a negative and decreasing (in absolute value) slope: y decreases as x increases, and the decreases in y get smaller and smaller as x increases.

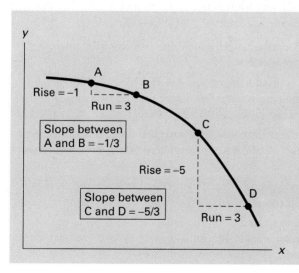

Figure 1.8c Negative and Increasing Slope.

The slope of this curve is negative—the values of y decrease as the values of x increase. The slope increases *in absolute value* as we move from left to right along the curve. Between points A and B, the slope is $-1/3$. Between points C and D, the slope is $-5/3$. Curves with negative and increasing slope are also sometimes called "concave to the origin."

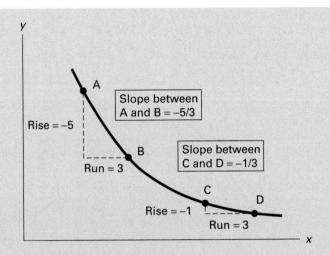

Figure 1.8d Negative and Decreasing Slope.

The slope of this curve is negative—the values of y decrease as the values of x increase. The slope decreases *in absolute value* as we move from left to right along the curve. Between points A and B, the slope is $-5/3$. Between points C and D, the slope is $-1/3$. Curves with negative and decreasing slope are also sometimes called "convex to the origin."

Figure 1.8d is also sometimes called **convex to the origin**. The slope between points C and D is smaller (in absolute value) than the slope between points A and B.

TRY

You need to be able to go back and forth between words and graphs. Try drawing a graph for each of the following statements:

5. Quantity demanded decreases as price increases (vertical axis: price; horizontal axis: quantity demanded).

6. Spending increases as wealth increases, but the increases in spending get smaller and smaller as wealth gets larger and larger (vertical axis: spending; horizontal axis: wealth).

7. As the number of workers increases, their marginal product first increases but then later decreases (vertical axis: marginal product; horizontal axis: number of workers).

8. Income always equals aggregate spending (vertical axis: aggregate spending; horizontal axis: income).

9. When the unemployment rate is low, the inflation rate is high, but when the unemployment rate is high, the inflation rate is low (vertical axis: inflation rate; horizontal axis: unemployment rate).

10. Quantity supplied increases as price increases (vertical axis: price; horizontal axis: quantity supplied).

11. For a monopolist, as quantity increases, marginal revenue has a steeper negative slope than average revenue (vertical axis: marginal revenue and average revenue; horizontal axis: quantity).

12. When the amount of butter produced is decreased from 2,000 to 1,900 units, the number of guns produced increases from 10 to 20 units. But when the amount of butter produced is decreased from 1,000 to 900 units, the number of guns produced increases from 80 to just 82 units (vertical axis: units of butter produced; horizontal axis: units of guns produced).

13. Quantity supplied is 13 when price is 5. But when price is 8, quantity supplied is 19 (vertical axis: price; horizontal axis: quantity supplied).

14. When price is 5, quantity demanded is 40. But when price is 10, quantity demanded is 30 (vertical axis: price; horizontal axis: quantity demanded).

Move Along versus Shift of a Curve

Economists are fond of the phrases **move along a curve** and **shift of a curve**. When we "move along" a curve, we are going between two points on an existing curve. In Figure 1.9a, if the price changes from p_A to p_B, quantity changes from q_A to q_B. We have moved along (or, in some books, slid along) the existing curve.

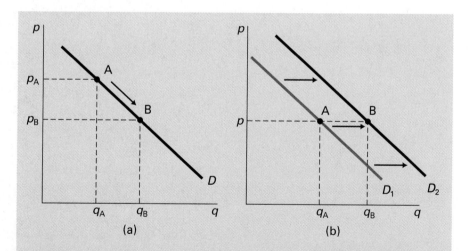

(a)   (b)

Figure 1.9 Moving along a Curve versus Shifting a Curve.

When we go between two points on an existing curve, we are "moving along" the curve. In Figure 1.9a, as price p decreases, we move along the curve from A to B to a higher quantity q. When there is an entirely new curve, we are "shifting" the curve. In Figure 1.9b, at *every* price p there is an increase in quantity q, so there is an entirely new curve D_2.

When the curve "shifts," the entire relationship between the two variables changes. In Figure 1.9b, if *at every price* there is an increase in quantity, the curve shifts from D_1 to D_2. In effect, the first curve D_1 ceases to exist. It sometimes helps to draw the new curve much darker than the initial curve.

An easy way to figure out whether we are moving along or shifting a curve is this: if an independent variable that is measured on one of the axes changes, we move along the existing curve. But if an independent variable that is *not* measured on one of the axes changes, the entire curve shifts.

CONCLUSION

This chapter has provided an overview of the mathematical tools used in economics. Refer back to this chapter as needed when tools are introduced and used. If you're still stuck, it might help to find a math book that provides more review. Now, we're ready to get into some of the meat of economics.

Chapter 2

Production Possibilities Frontier, Economic Growth, and Gains from Trade

$\mathbf{A}$ simple but powerful model of the economy is the production possibilities frontier (PPF) model. Economic growth and the gains from trade can also be illustrated with the PPF.

KEY TERMS AND CONCEPTS

- Production possibilities frontier
- Resources
- Scarce resources
- Trade-offs
- Opportunity cost
- Law of increasing opportunity cost
- Attainable
- Efficient
- Inefficient
- Unattainable
- Economic growth
- Productivity
- Gains from trade
- Ricardian model
- Theory of comparative advantage
- Absolute advantage
- Comparative advantage

KEY GRAPHS

- PPF
- Shifts of PPF
- Straight-line PPF

KEY EQUATION

• Calculation of opportunity cost

THE PRODUCTION POSSIBILITIES FRONTIER

The **production possibilities frontier** (PPF) is a model about the allocation of scarce resources. It can be applied to a person or a company, but it is most often applied to an entire economy. What are the possible production combinations that an economy can produce with the available resources in a given time frame?

Resources are those things used to produce goods and services. Resources are broadly defined:

• Labor or time

• Capital (machines and buildings)

• Land or natural resources

• Knowledge or technology

Resources are said to be **scarce** because at any moment in time, there is a fixed, finite quantity of each resource. There are only 24 hours in a day, only a certain number of available workers, a certain number of machines and buildings, a certain amount of natural resources, a certain level of knowledge.

Resources must be allocated because if a resource—you, for instance—is used for one activity, it cannot simultaneously be used for another. In the next minute, you can study economics or you can study chemistry. You can't do both. The land under the building under your feet can be used for farming or for buildings, but not for both. So our resources must be allocated.

The PPF makes a key simplifying assumption: there are only two types of output. We can say some useful things about scarcity and resource allocation, even when we make such an unrealistic assumption. And we don't lose much of our story by making this assumption. So we make the assumption: only two types of output.

TIP

The PPF model always considers two types of output—never more, never fewer.

Because resources can't do everything simultaneously, we face trade-offs or choices. Land can be used to produce food or produce machines. If more land is devoted to growing food, then less land must be devoted to producing machines. Why? Because there is a limited amount of land.

If you are going to use the next hour to study economics, you can't use the next hour to study chemistry. You face a choice—what economists call a **trade-off**.

Economists call these trade-offs **opportunity costs**. The opportunity cost of an activity is the next best alternative you forgo (don't undertake) in order to do the activity. If you weren't studying economics, what would you rather be doing? That's your opportunity cost of studying economics.

Because resources—labor or time, capital, land or natural resources, knowledge or technology—are limited, every activity has an opportunity cost. Every one. In the PPF model, where there are only two possible activities, the opportunity cost of one activity is measured by the amount of the other activity forgone (not undertaken).

The PPF is best illustrated with an example. The two outputs we'll use are guns (military items) and butter (nonmilitary items). If we use resources to produce guns, we are forgoing (not producing) butter. If our economy starts out producing, say, 10,000 guns per week and 50,000 pounds of butter per week, and we shift resources so that more guns are produced, then the *opportunity cost* of those additional guns will be the butter we can no longer produce.

One way to illustrate the point is by using numbers. With the available resources, the economy can produce any of the combinations of guns and butter shown in Table 2.1.

Table 2.1 Production Possibilities: Guns and Butter

Guns	0	5,000	10,000	15,000	20,000
Butter (lb)	75,000	65,000	50,000	30,000	0

How much butter do we forgo (not produce) when gun production is increased from 10,000 to 15,000? Look at the numbers in the highlighted section of the table. We forego $50,000 - 30,000 = 20,000$ pounds of butter. So economists say: the opportunity cost of increasing gun production from 10,000 to 15,000 guns is 20,000 pounds of butter.

TRY (*Answers to all "TRY" questions are at the back of the book.*)

1. Using the numbers in Table 2.1, what is the opportunity cost of increasing gun production from 15,000 to 20,000?

2. Using the numbers in Table 2.1, what is the opportunity cost of increasing butter production from 65,000 pounds to 75,000 pounds?

Resources are not equally well suited to producing everything. An acre of land that produces desert cactus is not well suited to producing rice. A skilled electrician is not as well suited to designing clothing. A car is not well suited to plowing fields. Resources do some things better than others. Economists sometimes say: resources are not ubiquitous.

Because resources are better suited to some activities than to other activities, the opportunity cost of switching resources is not constant. If the economy starts out producing 10,000 guns and 50,000 pounds of butter, which resources should be shifted to gun production if more guns are wanted? The smart (economists say efficient) thing to do is shift those resources away from butter production that are relatively worst at producing butter. That way, the best (economists say most efficient) resources are left producing butter.

But if each time we want to increase gun production, we shift the resources away from butter that are relatively worst at producing butter, as we go along, we start to move better and better butter producers over to gun production. And so we would have to give up more and more butter each time we shift resources from producing butter to producing guns. Economists call this the **law of increasing opportunity cost**.

The numbers in Table 2.1 illustrate this law. (When economists call something a "law," it means it is darn near always true.)

Shift resources so that we are producing 5,000 guns rather than 0, and the opportunity cost of those 5,000 guns is $75,000 - 65,000 = 10,000$ pounds of butter. But shift resources again so that now we are producing 10,000 guns rather than 5,000, and now the opportunity cost of that second batch of 5,000 guns is $65,000 - 50,000 = 15,000$ pounds of butter.

Table 2.2 shows the opportunity cost of shifting resources toward gun production.

Table 2.2   Opportunity Cost of Shifting from Butter to Gun Production

Guns	0		5,000		10,000		15,000		20,000
Butter forgone		10,000		15,000		20,000		30,000	

The opportunity cost of producing 5,000 additional guns rose from 10,000 to 15,000 to 20,000 to 30,000 pounds of butter. Because these numbers rise, the example illustrates the law of increasing opportunity cost.

When we draw a production possibilities frontier, all of these concepts are illustrated in one simple curved line.

Table 2.3   Plotting a Production Possibilities Frontier

Guns	0	5,000	10,000	15,000	20,000
Butter (lb)	75,000	65,000	50,000	30,000	0
Label	A	B	C	D	E

Figure 2.1 shows the five points and connects the points with a smooth curve. That smooth curve is what we call the **production possibilities frontier**.

The PPF is drawn on a simple set of axes because there are just two types of output. The axes are the amount of each product produced in some time period. In our example, we have the number of guns and the amount of butter produced

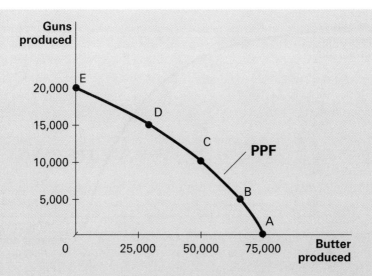

Figure 2.1 Production Possibilities Frontier for Guns and Butter.

The production possibilities frontier shows the combinations of output that can be produced with the available resources. Point A represents a combination of 75,000 pounds of butter and 0 guns. Point C represents a combination of 50,000 pounds of butter and 10,000 guns. Point E represents a combination of 0 pounds of butter and 20,000 guns.

per week. The particular time period doesn't matter. What does matter is that you know that the PPF is drawn for some particular finite time period.

The PPF shows tradeoffs by sloping down (it has a negative slope). The PPF shows the law of increasing opportunity costs by being curved (it is nonlinear). Economists often say the PPF is bowed out, or concave to the origin.

TIP

It doesn't matter which good is on which axis. Swap guns and butter. The PPF will still have the same shape—bowed out from the origin.

TRY

For the next two problems, use these numbers:

Rice (bu.)	0	5,000	8,000	10,000	11,000
Corn (bu.)	20,000	15,000	10,000	5,000	0

3. Draw the production possibilities frontier, putting corn on the vertical axis and rice on the horizontal axis.
4. Do these numbers illustrate the law of increasing opportunity cost?

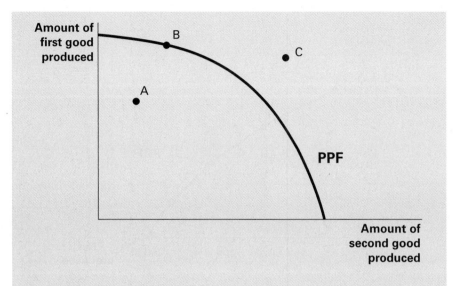

Figure 2.2 Production Possibilities Frontier.
The production possibilities frontier (PPF) is downward-sloping, because every activity has an opportunity cost. There are trade-offs. If more of the second good is produced, less of the first good can be produced. The PPF is nonlinear. It is bowed out, or concave to the origin. The opportunity cost of producing more of the second good is forgone production of the first good. As more of the second good is produced, the opportunity cost rises.

Figure 2.2 shows what a PPF looks like in general, when we don't have any numbers to start from. It is downward-sloping (higher on the left, lower on the right), because every activity has an opportunity cost. Producing more of one good requires producing less of the other. It is nonlinear (not a straight line) and bowed out, concave to the origin, because of the law of increasing opportunity costs. Resources are not equally well suited to all tasks.

Any point between the axes and the PPF (such as point A in Figure 2.2) or on the PPF (such as point B) represents a combination of output that can be produced with the available resources; economists say these combinations are **attainable**. Any point *on* the PPF (such as B) is a combination of output that uses all the available resources; economists call those combinations **efficient**. Any point inside but not on the PPF (between the axes and the PPF, such as A) represents a combination of output that is not using all the available resources; those combinations are called **inefficient**. Any combination of output outside of the PPF (above or to the right, such as C) represents a combination of output that cannot be produced with the available resources; economists call those points **unattainable**.

TRY

5. Draw a PPF. Label these four points on your graph:
   a. A combination of output that is attainable
   b. A combination of output that is efficient
   c. A combination of output that is inefficient
   d. A combination of output that is unattainable

6. Can a combination of output be simultaneously efficient and unattainable?

ECONOMIC GROWTH

The combinations of output outside of the current PPF can be attained if there is **economic growth**. Economic growth is defined here as an increase in the total amount of output that an economy can produce. (Growth will be defined at other times as an increase in the total amount of output per person: output divided by population.) Economic growth can occur two ways: more resources or more productive resources.

More resources—more people, more capital, more land, more natural resources—allows more output to be produced. The PPF shifts out. Usually the new PPF is pretty much parallel to the old one, as shown in Figure 2.3.

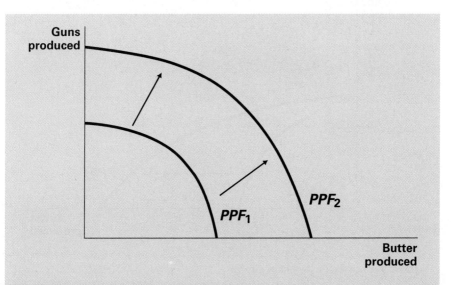

Figure 2.3 Economic Growth.

Economic growth is shown by a shifting out of the production possibilities frontier. More resources means more of both guns and butter can be produced. The new production possibilities frontier PPF_2 is above and to the right of the original production possibilities frontier PPF_1.

A decrease in available resources such as might happen in a natural disaster or drought or famine has the opposite effect. The PPF shifts in, toward the axis, because if there are fewer available resources, then less output can be produced.

If resources are able to produce more output, economists say there has been an increase in **productivity**. Workers can produce more output in an hour if they have better training. Machinery can produce more output in an hour if it is engineered to do so. Land can produce more output per acre if crops are rotated. Increased productivity allows for economic growth: more output is produced.

If the increase in productivity affects all types of output equally, the PPF will shift out as in Figure 2.3. For example, more education could increase labor productivity across the board.

But sometimes an increase in productivity will impact one type of output more than another. For instance, suppose a new technology for producing butter is developed. It increases the maximum amount of butter that can be produced if all resources are used to produce butter, but has no effect on the maximum amount of guns if all resources are used to produce guns. Figure 2.4 shows the new PPF. It starts at the same point on the "guns" axis but ends at a new point on the "butter axis."

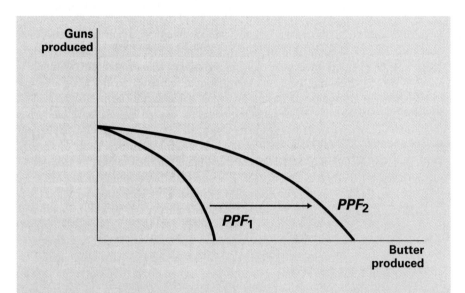

Figure 2.4 Asymmetric Economic Growth.

Sometimes economic growth affects some output but not others. A productivity increase that affects only butter (but not guns) means that more butter can be produced but that the maximum amount of guns able to be produced does not change. The end point of the PPF on the butter axis shifts to the right, but the end point on the guns axis does not change. Connect the two new end points to get the new production possibilities frontier, PPF_2.

GAINS FROM TRADE

Another way to attain the unattainable—to have combinations of output that are beyond an economy's production possibilities frontier—is through trade. The idea of the **gains from trade** is that collectively, more output can be produced if we specialize in producing the good we are relatively good at producing and then trade for other goods.

TIP

Some textbooks postpone this topic until the chapter on international trade. Others include it in the chapter on the production possibilities frontier.

When we all specialize, more output will be produced collectively than if we all try to be self-sufficient. Economists call this result the gains from trade. The idea is attributed to David Ricardo, a nineteenth-century British economist. Some economists call what we are about to do the **Ricardian model**. Others refer to it as the **theory of comparative advantage**.

Gains from trade exist even if one economy is better than the other economy at producing everything. When one economy (or person) can produce some output with fewer resources than another, economists say the first economy has an **absolute advantage**.

It takes 20 hours of labor for Miranda to sew a dress but it takes only 8 hours of labor for Michael to sew the same dress. Economists say: Michael has the absolute advantage in the sewing of dresses. In this example, absolute advantage is determined by looking at the input required (hours of labor) to produce a certain output (a sewn dress).

Instead, we could just as easily look at the amount of output (number of sewn dresses) produced with a certain amount of inputs (a week of labor). In 40 hours, Miranda could sew 2 dresses and Michael could sew 5. This is the same example. Again, because Michael can produce more output with the same inputs, economists say: Michael has the absolute advantage in the sewing of dresses.

We do not care about absolute advantage when showing the gains from trade. To demonstrate that specialization and trade produces more output than self-sufficiency, we instead look at a concept economists call "comparative advantage." Comparative advantage depends on opportunity cost. Let's start there.

To show the gains from trade, we need some simplifications and an assumption. Simplifications:

- There are only two countries (or two people, or two states . . . the key is *two*).
- There are only two types of output.

Because of these simplifications, some economists say: we are looking at a 2 by 2 matrix of countries and outputs. What they mean is that if we were to construct a table—a matrix—with the countries down the side and the outputs along the top, we would have a table that is 2 cells wide and 2 cells high. For example, if Kern County and Taft County are the economies and corn and wheat are the outputs, we could put all of the information we need in a table like Table 2.4.

Table 2.4   An Output Table

	Corn	Wheat
Kern County	Kern County's production of corn	Kern County's production of wheat
Taft County	Taft County's production of corn	Taft County's production of wheat

Assumption:

• Opportunity costs are constant.

We ignore the law of increasing opportunity costs when showing the gains from trade. We can ignore this law because the results we will get—that there are gains from trade—are the same whether we do or don't have increasing opportunity costs. Our task is simpler if we let opportunity costs stay constant. Any assumption that makes our task simpler and doesn't change our conclusion is an assumption worth making!

The existence of gains from trade can really only be seen with an example. Our two economies are Kern County and Taft County. Our two outputs are corn and wheat. In a year, an acre of land in Kern County can produce 200 bushels of corn or 150 bushels of wheat. In a year, an acre of land in Taft County can produce 100 bushels of corn or 50 bushels of wheat. Economists usually present this information in a table such as Table 2.5:

Table 2.5   Maximum Annual Production per Acre

	Corn	Wheat
Kern County	200 bu.	150 bu.
Taft County	100 bu.	50 bu.

TRY

Use Table 2.5 to answer these two questions.

7. Which economy has the absolute advantage in the production of corn?

8. Which economy has the absolute advantage in the production of wheat?

With the information in Table 2.5, we can calculate the opportunity costs for each economy. An acre of land can be used *either* for corn *or* for wheat, but not for both. The opportunity cost of corn is the amount of wheat forgone (not produced). The opportunity cost of wheat is the amount of corn forgone (not produced). We use the information on production possibilities to calculate the opportunity costs.

$$Opportunity \ cost \ of \ good \ A = \frac{maximum \ production \ of \ other \ good}{maximum \ production \ of \ good \ A}$$

In Kern County, the opportunity cost of 200 bushels of corn is 150 bushels of wheat. Divide by 200 to get the opportunity cost of 1 bushel of corn. The opportunity cost of 1 bushel of corn in Kern County is 150/200 = 0.75 bushels of wheat.

In Kern County, the opportunity cost of 150 bushels of wheat is 200 bushels of corn. Divide by 150: the opportunity cost of 1 bushel of wheat in Kern County is 200/150 = 4/3 or 1.33 bushels of wheat.

TIP

Notice that the opportunity cost of one good (wheat) is just the reciprocal of the opportunity cost of the other good (corn).

In Taft County, the opportunity cost of 100 bushels of corn is 50 bushels of wheat. Divide by 100: the opportunity cost of 1 bushel of corn in Taft County is 100/50 = 2 bushels of wheat.

Flip it over: The opportunity cost of 1 bushel of wheat in Taft County is 1/2 = 0.5 bushels of corn.

Economists usually present this information in a table such as Table 2.6.

Table 2.6   Opportunity Costs of 1 bushel of...

	...Corn	...Wheat
Kern County	150/200 = 0.75 bu. of wheat per bu. of corn	200/150 = 1.33 bu. of corn per bu. of wheat
Taft County	50/100 = 0.5 bu. of wheat per bu. of corn	100/50 = 2 bu. of corn per bu. of wheat

---

TIP

To be sure you get the right ratio, it helps to include the entire phrase such as "bushels of wheat per bushel of corn." In this case, the numerator has "bushels of wheat"; the denominator has "bushels of corn."

Opportunity costs are used to determine comparative advantage. The economy with the lower opportunity cost has what economists call the **comparative advantage** in the production of that good.

To produce a bushel of corn, Kern County gives up 0.75 bushels of wheat but Taft County gives up only 0.5 bushels of wheat. So economists say: Taft County has the comparative advantage in the production of corn.

To produce a bushel of wheat, Kern County gives up 1.33 bushels of corn and Taft County gives up fully 2 bushels of corn. Economists would say: Kern County has the comparative advantage in the production of wheat.

To determine the total possible production of corn and of wheat, we need to know how many acres are available in each economy. Let's assume there are 300 available acres in Kern County and 300 available acres in Taft County. The total maximum possible production is shown in Table 2.7.

Table 2.7   Maximum Annual Production per Economy

	Corn	Wheat
Kern County	200 bu. per acre × 300 acres = 60,000 bu.	150 bu. per acre × 300 acres = 45,000 bu.
Taft County	100 bu. per acre × 300 acres = 30,000 bu.	50 bu. per acre × 300 acres = 15,000 bu.

TIP

Confusion alert! The table is saying that Kern County can produce a maximum of 60,000 bushels of corn *or* 45,000 bushels of wheat. *Or*—not *and*.

The production possibilities can be shown in a graph. Each economy gets its own graph. In Kern County, 60,000 bushels of corn *or* 45,000 bushels of wheat *or* any combination of corn and wheat in between can be produced. In Taft County, 30,000 bushels of corn *or* 15,000 bushels of wheat *or* any combination of corn and wheat in between can be produced. Figure 2.5 shows these production possibilities. The PPFs are straight lines because we assume that the opportunity costs shown in Table 2.6 do not change.

The graphs can be used to calculate opportunity costs. Say the same thing another way: the slope of the production possibilities frontiers is the opportunity cost. The slope of the PPF is rise/run, or $\Delta wheat/\Delta corn$. In Kern County, the slope of the PPF is 45/60 = 0.75. This is the opportunity cost of a bushel of corn in Kern County.

The slope of the PPF in Taft County is 15/30 = 0.5. This is the opportunity cost of a bushel of corn in Taft County.

TIP

You simply have to memorize that the slope is the opportunity cost of the good on the horizontal axis (the denominator of the slope equation), measured in units forgone of the good on the vertical axis (the numerator of the slope equation).

Now we need to choose some current level of production for both Kern and Taft Counties. Typically economists choose a point somewhere near the middle of

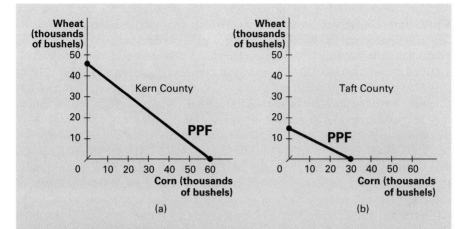

Figure 2.5 Production Possibilities Frontiers for Kern and Taft Counties.

In Kern County, the production possibilities are 45,000 bushels of wheat and no bushels of corn, 60,000 bushels of corn and no bushels of wheat, or any combination in between. In Taft County, the production possibilities are 15,000 bushels of wheat and no bushels of corn, 30,000 bushels of corn and no bushels of wheat, or any combination in between. Because we assume constant opportunity costs, the production possibilities frontiers are straight lines.

the PPF of each economy. Let's assume that Kern County is producing 18,000 bushels of corn and 31,500 bushels of wheat, a point on its PPF. And let's assume that Taft County is producing 6,000 bushels of corn and 12,000 bushels of wheat.

TIP

Showing the gains from trade requires that you (or your book, or your instructor) make assumptions like these about each economy's production possibilities and current levels of production.

Total worldwide production is just the sum of production in each economy. See Table 2.8.

Table 2.8   Total Production without Specialization

	Corn	Wheat
Kern County	18,000	31,500
Taft County	6,000	12,000
Total Production	24,000	43,500

Each economy should specialize in producing the good in which it has the comparative advantage. Kern County has the lower opportunity cost—the comparative advantage—in producing wheat, so it should use all of its resources to produce wheat. Kern County will produce 45,000 bushels of wheat (see Table 2.7).

Taft County has the lower opportunity cost—the comparative advantage—in producing corn. So Taft County should use all of its resources to produce corn. Taft County will produce 30,000 bushels of corn.

Total production of wheat has increased! Without specialization, Kern and Taft Counties were together producing 43,500 bushels of wheat. With specialization, they are producing 45,000 bushels of wheat. There is a gain of 1,500 bushels of wheat.

Total production of corn has also increased! Without specialization, Kern and Taft Counties were together producing 24,000 bushels of corn. With specialization, they are producing 30,000 bushels of corn. There is a gain of 6,000 bushels of corn.

Kern and Taft Counties can now trade wheat for corn. The result is that both can consume more corn and wheat, with specialization and trade, than they could when each economy was self-sufficient. Economists say: this result demonstrates the gains from trade.

TRY

9. When economists say there are "gains from trade," what is being gained?

10. There are two people, Robin and Marian. Marian is relatively better than Robin at gardening. Robin is relatively better than Marian at cooking. But Robin is better than Marian at doing everything. Will Robin and Marian gain from trading? Who should do what?

Chapter 3

Demand and Supply

The model of demand and supply is used to determine the price of a product. It is the most used model in economics. Success in economics depends upon mastering the model of demand and supply.

KEY TERMS AND CONCEPTS

- Model of demand and supply
- Good
- Service
- Market
- Demand
- Supply
- Equilibrium price
- Equilibrium quantity
- Quantity demanded
- Market demand
- Individual demand
- Demand schedule
- Demand curve
- Move along a curve
- Shift of a curve
- Complementary goods
- Substitute goods
- Income
- Normal good
- Inferior goods
- Wealth
- Tastes and preferences
- Quantity supplied
- Market supply
- Individual supply
- Supply schedule
- Supply curve
- Substitutes in production

- Complements in production
- Market equilibrium
- Market shortage
- Market surplus

KEY GRAPHS

- Equilibrium in a market
- Shift of demand
- Shift of supply

OVERVIEW OF MODEL OF DEMAND AND SUPPLY

The **model of demand and supply** is used over and over in economics. This model answers the question: What determines the price and quantity sold in the market for a product? The product may be a **good**, a tangible product such as a pen, house, book, or shirt, or it may be a **service**, an intangible such as a doctor's appointment, a haircut, computer repair, or DVD rental. A **market** is not a physical place; it is the collection of the actions of the buyers and sellers of a product.

Demand captures the behavior of buyers. There are many factors that may influence the quantity or amount of a product that we wish to purchase. Economists usually identify five factors that influence buyer demand:

- The item's price
- The prices of other items we could use with or instead of this product
- Our income
- Our wealth
- Our tastes or preferences

Supply captures the behavior of sellers. As with demand, there are many factors that may influence the quantity of a product that sellers wish to sell. Economists usually identify four factors that influence seller supply:

- The item's price
- Costs of inputs
- Productivity of inputs
- The prices of other items that could be produced with the same inputs

The item's price matters to both buyers and sellers. The interaction of demand and supply determines the **equilibrium price** and **equilibrium quantity** of the product. At the equilibrium price, the quantity of the product buyers wish to purchase (called quantity demanded) equals the quantity of the product sellers wish to sell (called quantity supplied). Economists often say: prices depend upon supply and demand.

DEMAND

We focus first on price. **Quantity demanded** is the quantity associated with any one particular price. The many combinations of possible price and related quantity demanded make up the demand for the product. Demand refers to all the combinations of price and quantity demanded. **Market demand** for a product is the sum of everyone's **individual demand**.

How does a change in price affect the quantity of a product that buyers wish to buy? When prices rise, buyers don't want to buy as much. Economists say: an increase in price lowers quantity demanded. When the price of a product falls, buyers want to buy more. Economists say: a decrease in price raises quantity demanded.

TIP

"Demand" and "quantity demanded" are different. It is very important that you not mix up the two.

The relationship between price and quantity demanded can be depicted in a table that economists often call a **demand schedule**. Let's suppose that we survey all potential buyers of spiral notebooks. We ask each person: How many 100-page one-subject spiral notebooks will you purchase in a semester if spiral notebooks cost 50 cents each? What if they cost $1.00 each? $1.50 each? $2.00 each? $2.50 each? We add up the individual demand (each person's response) at each price. This gives us the market demand, shown in Table 3.1.

Table 3.1   Demand Schedule

Price	50¢	$1.00	$1.50	$2.00	$2.50
Quantity demanded	10,000	8,000	6,000	4,000	2,000
Label	A	B	C	D	E

Demand can also be depicted in a graph. Price is always shown on the vertical axis. Quantity is always shown on the horizontal axis. You may be bothered by this. You may want to argue that since we said that price determines quantity demanded, price should be shown on the horizontal axis. Don't. Everyone, everywhere, plots price on the vertical axis and quantity on the horizontal axis.

TIP

For the supply and demand model, price is *always* shown on the vertical axis. Quantity is *always* shown on the horizontal axis. Memorize this.

Figure 3.1a shows the **demand curve** for spiral notebooks. Each combination of price and quantity demanded in Table 3.1 is plotted and labeled. A smooth curve

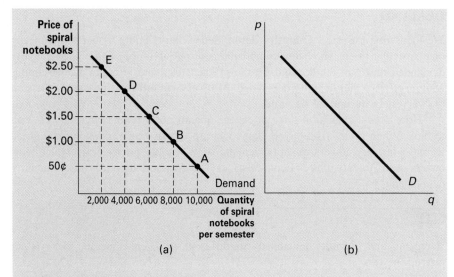

Figure 3.1 Demand Curves Slope Down.

The demand curve for spiral notebooks in Figure 3.1a is based on the combinations of price and quantity demanded in Table 3.1. In general, a demand curve is a downward-sloping curve, as shown in Figure 3.1b.

connects the five points. This is our demand curve. It slopes down. The demand curve has this negative slope because there is an inverse relationship between price and quantity demanded. In general, demand curves are downward-sloping—when you draw a demand curve, you start from the upper left and go down to the lower right—as shown in Figure 3.1b.

TIP

Economists say: demand curves slope down (have a negative slope) because there is an inverse relationship between price and quantity demanded. This means that demand curves slope down because when the price is lower, quantity demanded is higher.

If the price of the product changes, we **move along** the demand curve. Different price? Go to a different point on the same demand curve. But if any of the other four factors that affect demand changes, then the entire demand curve will **shift**. That is, at each possible price of the product, there will be a change in the quantity demanded. There will be a whole new curve. Figure 3.2 illustrates.

Prices of Other Products

Items that we use *with* the product are called **complementary goods**. Pens are complements to spiral notebooks. In general, when the price of a complementary

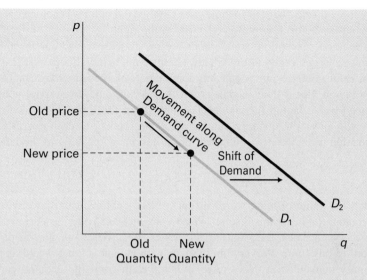

Figure 3.2 Movement along vs. Shift of a Demand Curve.

A movement along the demand curve occurs when the good's price changes. When the price changes from the "old price" to the "new price," we move along the demand curve D_1 from the "old quantity" to the "new quantity." But if something *other than the good's price* changes, the entire demand curve shifts. At every price, there is a new quantity demanded, which is shown as a second demand curve D_2.

good rises, we buy less of both the complement and the initial product. If pens triple in price, some people will start taking class notes on a laptop rather than in a spiral notebook, lowering the quantity demanded of spiral notebooks at each possible price. The entire demand curve for spiral notebooks shifts to the left. Economists say: when the price of a complement (the pen) rises, demand for the primary product (the spiral notebook) falls.

Items we use *instead* of the product are called **substitute goods**. Loose-leaf filler paper and binders are substitutes for spiral notebooks. In general, when the price of a substitute good rises, we buy more of the initial product. If binders triple in price, some people will stop using loose-leaf filler paper and binders and will instead start taking class notes in a spiral notebook, raising the quantity demanded of spiral notebooks at each possible price. The entire demand curve for spiral notebooks shifts to the right. Economists say: when the price of a substitute (binder and paper) rises, demand for the primary product (the spiral notebook) rises.

Income

Income is what we receive for working. When our income rises, we can afford to buy more of everything. In general, increased income raises the quantity demanded of a product at each possible price. If we want to buy more of a good when our income rises, economists call the good a **normal good**. Regardless of the price, we will buy more music after our income rises than we did before. When income rises, the demand curve for a normal good shifts to the right.

There is one exception: some goods are purchased because our income is so low that we can't currently afford what we really want to buy. Economists call these goods **inferior goods**. Some people buy spiral notebooks because they cannot afford to buy a laptop. But if their incomes rose, they would buy fewer spiral notebooks and instead buy a laptop for taking class notes. For these people, an increase in income will lower the quantity demanded of the product at each possible price. When income rises, the demand curve for an inferior good shifts to the left.

Wealth

Wealth is the value of what we own (our assets)—houses, cars, jewelry, stocks, bonds, mutual funds, cash and so on. Wealth can increase either because we obtain more assets or because the value of our assets rises. When our wealth rises, we can afford to buy more of everything. So, as with income, higher wealth increases the quantity demanded at every price. When wealth rises, the demand curve for the product shifts to the right.

Tastes or Preferences

Apart from prices, income, and wealth, sometimes we just *like* a product and want to buy it. Sometimes we learn of a product through advertising and decide to buy it. Or a friend plays some music and we decide to download it, too. Economists call this the influence of tastes or preferences. **Tastes and preferences** is a catch-all phrase that captures the multitude of reasons other than prices, income, and wealth that we may decide we want more or less of a product. If our tastes shift in favor of an item, at every possible price there is a higher quantity demanded. The demand curve shifts to the right. If our tastes shift away from the item, demand shifts to the left.

Size of the Market

One additional factor that shifts the market demand curve is the size of the market. If college enrollment increases, more individuals will want to purchase spiral notebooks. The market demand curve will shift to the right.

SUPPLY

Sellers' behavior is captured with the supply curve. **Quantity supplied** is the quantity associated with any one particular price. The many combinations of price and quantity supplied make up the supply of the product. **Market supply** of a product is the sum of every seller's **individual supply**.

When the price of an item rises, sellers want to sell more of that item. Economists say: an increase in price raises quantity supplied. When the price of the item falls, sellers want to sell less. Economists say: a decrease in price lowers quantity supplied.

TIP

"Supply" and "quantity supplied" are different. Do not mix them up.

As with demand, the relationship between price and quantity supplied can be depicted in a table that economists call a **supply schedule**. Let's suppose we survey all the potential sellers of spiral notebooks. We ask each seller: how many 100-page one-subject spiral notebooks will you want to sell in a semester if you can sell spiral notebooks for 50 cents each? What if you can sell them for $1.00 each? $1.50 each? $2.00 each? $2.50 each? We add up the individual supply (each firm's responses) at each price. This gives us the market supply, shown in Table 3.2.

Table 3.2   Supply Schedule

Price	50¢	$1.00	$1.50	$2.00	$2.50
Quantity supplied	4,000	5,000	6,000	7,000	8,000
Label	V	W	X	Y	Z

Supply can also be depicted in a graph. Price is again on the vertical axis. Quantity is on the horizontal axis. Figure 3.3 shows the **supply curve** for spiral

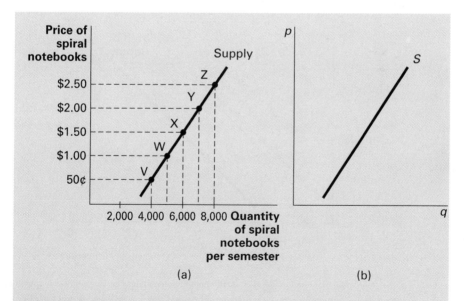

(a)   (b)

Figure 3.3 Supply Curves Slope Up.

The supply curve for spiral notebooks in Figure 3.3a is based on the combinations of price and quantity supplied in Table 3.2. In general, a supply curve is upward-sloping, as shown in Figure 3.3b.

notebooks. Each combination of price and quantity supplied in Table 3.2 is plotted and labeled in Figure 3.3a. A smooth curve—the supply curve—connects the five points.

A general supply curve is shown in Figure 3.3b. The supply curve slopes up. When you draw the supply curve, you start from the bottom left and go to the upper right. The supply curve has a positive slope because there is a direct relationship between price and quantity supplied. When price is higher, quantity supplied is higher. When price is lower, quantity supplied is lower.

TIP

Here's a trick to help remember which curve is which. **D**emand slopes **D**own. **Sup**ply slopes **up**.

If the price of the product changes, we move along the existing supply curve to a different quantity supplied. But if either of the other two factors that affect supply changes, the entire supply curve shifts. At each possible price, due to a change in one of these factors, there will be a change in quantity supplied. There is a whole new supply curve. See Figure 3.4.

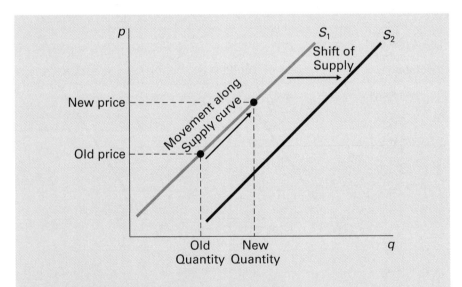

Figure 3.4 Movement along vs. Shift of a Supply Curve.

A movement along the supply curve occurs when the good's price changes. When the price changes from the "old price" to the "new price," we move along the supply curve S_1 from the "old quantity" to the "new quantity." But if something *other than the good's price* changes, the entire supply curve shifts. At every price, there is a new quantity supplied, which is shown as a second supply curve S_2.

Costs of Inputs

When it costs more to produce an item, sellers will not want to sell as much output at each possible price. If higher wages are paid to employees in the spiral notebook factory, sellers of spiral notebooks will not want to produce and sell as many notebooks, lowering the quantity supplied at every possible price of spiral notebooks. The entire supply curve of spiral notebooks will shift to the left. Economists say: supply decreased.

Another way to get the same result is this. When it costs more to produce an item, sellers will want to charge a higher price. Any particular quantity supplied will be associated with a higher price as a result of the increased cost of inputs. The supply curve shifts up, which looks the same as the supply curve shifting left.

One reason we don't typically explain the impact of higher input costs this way is that it is too easy to get confused. The new supply curve is *above* the old supply curve. The supply curve has moved *up*. But at every price, there is a *lower* quantity supplied. Economists say: when the costs of inputs rises, supply of the product goes *down*.

TIP

Here's one way to be sure your shift of the supply curve is drawn correctly. Draw the first (old) supply curve. Then draw an arrow *that is parallel to the horizontal axis* to show which way to shift the supply curve. If you are increasing supply, your arrow will point to the right. If you are decreasing supply, your arrow will point to the left. Finally, draw the second (new) supply curve at the end of your arrow. If your arrows go left or right (never up or down, never on the diagonal), you'll never be in the wrong!

Productivity of the Inputs

When inputs are more productive, producing more for each input, the costs of producing the output fall. If the machines that bind the notebooks can run at a faster pace so that more notebooks are produced per hour, sellers of spiral notebooks will be willing to supply a greater quantity at every possible price of spiral notebooks. The entire supply curve of spiral notebooks shifts to the right. Economists say: increased productivity increases supply.

Prices of Related Output

Items that can be produced *instead* of the current output but using the same inputs are called **substitutes in production**. Lined paper is a substitute in production for spiral notebooks—it can be produced *instead* of spiral notebooks with many of the same inputs. In general, when the price of a substitute in production rises, firms will want to produce more of that item and less of the initial output. They will shift their inputs to producing the now-higher-priced substitute in production, and will produce less of the initial product. If lined paper doubles in price, many firms will produce fewer spiral notebooks and more lined paper. At every possible price of spiral notebooks, the quantity supplied will decline. The entire supply curve of spiral notebooks will shift to the left. Economists say: when the price of a substitute in production (lined paper) rises, supply of the primary product (spiral notebooks) falls.

Items that can be produced *with* the current output and using the same inputs are called **complements in production**, or by-products. Paper confetti is a complement in production to spiral notebooks—all those three holes punched out of each sheet become confetti! In general when the price of a complement in production rises, firms will want to produce more of both the complement and the initial output. If confetti triples in price, spiral notebook producers will want to produce more confetti *and* more spiral notebooks. At every possible price of spiral notebooks, the quantity supplied will rise. The entire supply curve will shift to the right. Economists say: when the price of a complement in production (confetti) rises, supply of the primary product (spiral notebooks) rises.

Size of Market

One additional factor that shifts the supply curve is the number of sellers in the market. If more office supply stores open in the community, more sellers will want to sell spiral notebooks at each price. The entire supply curve shifts to the right.

EQUILIBRIUM

Market equilibrium occurs when the market finds the price where quantity demanded equals quantity supplied. At that price, every buyer who is willing to purchase the item is able to do so. And at that price, every seller who is willing to sell the item is able to do so. There are no buyers and no sellers unable to do what they are willing to do. Economists say: the market is in equilibrium when quantity demanded equals quantity supplied.

We can use the demand and supply schedules to find equilibrium. Table 3.3 combines the information from Tables 3.1 and 3.2.

When spiral notebooks sell for $1.50, quantity demanded and quantity supplied both equal 6,000 spiral notebooks per semester. The equilibrium price in this market

Table 3.3 Demand and Supply Schedules

Price	50¢	$1.00	$1.50	$2.00	$2.50
Quantity demanded	10,000	8,000	6,000	4,000	2,000
Quantity supplied	4,000	5,000	6,000	7,000	8,000
Shortage or surplus or equilibrium?	Shortage of 6,000	Shortage of 3,000	Equilibrium	Surplus of 3,000	Surplus of 6,000

is $1.50 per spiral notebook. The equilibrium quantity is 6,000 spiral notebooks per semester.

When the price is below the equilibrium price, quantity demanded exceeds quantity supplied. Economists call this difference between quantity demanded and quantity supplied a **market shortage**. When spiral notebooks are priced at $1.00 each, quantity demanded of 8,000 notebooks exceeds quantity supplied of 5,000 notebooks. The market shortage is 3,000 spiral notebooks per semester. A market shortage puts upward pressure on prices.

When the price is above the equilibrium price, quantity supplied exceeds quantity demanded. Economists call this difference a **market surplus**. When spiral notebooks are priced at $2.50 each, quantity supplied of 8,000 notebooks exceeds quantity demanded of 2,000 notebooks. The market surplus is 6,000 spiral notebooks per semester. A market surplus puts downward pressure on prices.

When the market is in equilibrium, there is no market shortage and no market surplus. Quantity demanded equals quantity supplied. There is no pressure for price to change.

Market equilibrium is most often shown with a graph. Figure 3.5a shows the market for spiral notebooks. The equilibrium point is where the demand and supply curves cross (or, intersect). If the price is above the equilibrium price, the market surplus is the horizontal distance between the demand curve and the supply curve at that too-high price. If the price is below the equilibrium price, the market shortage is the horizontal distance between the demand curve and the supply curve at that too-low price. In general, Figure 3.5b shows how economists use supply and demand curves to find the equilibrium price and equilibrium quantity.

CHANGES OF EQUILIBRIUM

The power of the model of demand and supply comes from its ability to predict how equilibrium price and equilibrium quantity will change when one of the many factors that affect demand or supply changes. Here it is especially important to keep straight the difference between a movement along and a shift of a curve. If the price changes, we move along an existing curve. If some other factor changes, a curve will shift.

Shift of Demand

When there is a change in prices of related goods, income, wealth, tastes or preferences, or the size of the market, the demand curve shifts. There is a new quantity demanded associated with each possible price. The old equilibrium price and quantity will no longer clear the market. Equilibrium price and equilibrium quantity will change.

When demand increases as in Figure 3.6a, the entire demand curve shifts to the right. At the initial price, there is now a market shortage. Prices rise. As prices rise, sellers *move along* their supply curve, increasing quantity supplied. The market will settle at a new equilibrium with a higher equilibrium price and higher equilibrium quantity. Economists say: an increase in demand causes both prices and quantities to increase.

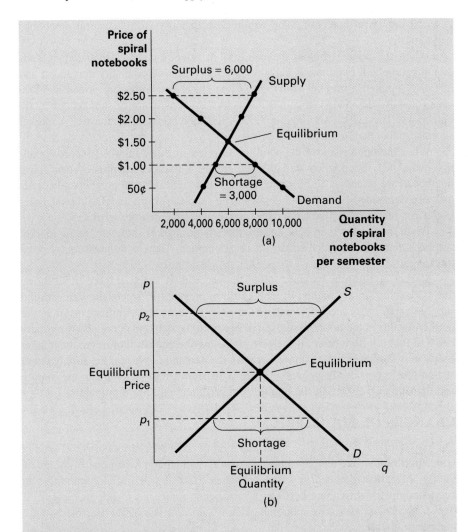

Figure 3.5 Market Equilibrium.

Equilibrium in the market for spiral notebooks in Figure 3.5a occurs at a price of $1.50 and quantity of 6,000. In general, market equilibrium occurs where the demand and supply curves intersect. When price is above the equilibrium price, there is a market surplus. When price is below the equilibrium price, there is a market shortage.

When demand decreases as in Figure 3.6b, the entire demand curve shifts to the left. At the initial equilibrium price p_1, there is now a market surplus. Because the demand curve shifted, quantity demanded is now less than quantity supplied at the old equilibrium price. Prices fall. As prices fall, sellers *move along* their supply curve, and quantity supplied falls. The market will settle at a new equilibrium with a

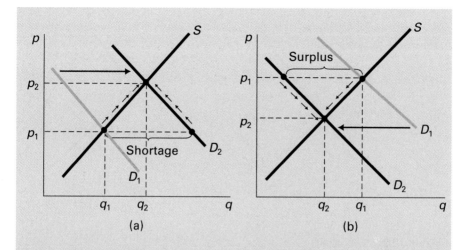

Figure 3.6 Shift of Demand.

In Figure 3.6a, demand increases from D_1 to D_2. At the initial price p_1, there is a market shortage. Equilibrium price rises to p_2 and equilibrium quantity rises to q_2. In Figure 3.6b, demand decreases from D_1 to D_2. At the initial price p_1, there is a market surplus. Equilibrium price falls to p_2 and equilibrium quantity falls to q_2.

lower equilibrium price and lower equilibrium quantity. Economists say: a decrease in demand causes both prices and quantities to decrease.

Shift of Supply

When there is a change in costs of inputs, productivity, the prices of related output, or the number of sellers, the supply curve shifts. There is a new quantity supplied associated with each possible price. The old equilibrium price and quantity will no longer clear the market. Equilibrium price and equilibrium quantity will change.

When supply increases as in Figure 3.7a, the entire supply curve shifts to the right. At the initial price, there is now a market surplus. Prices fall. As prices fall, buyers *move along* their demand curve, increasing quantity demanded. The market will settle at a new equilibrium with a lower equilibrium price and higher equilibrium quantity. Economists say: an increase in supply causes prices to decrease and quantities to increase.

When supply decreases as in Figure 3.7b, the entire supply curve shifts to the left. At the initial equilibrium price p_1, there is now a market shortage. Because the supply curve shifted, quantity supplied is now less than quantity demanded at the old equilibrium price. Prices rise. As prices rise, buyers *move along* their demand curve, and quantity demanded falls. The market will settle at a new equilibrium with a higher equilibrium price and lower equilibrium quantity. Economists say: a decrease in supply causes prices to rise and quantities to decrease.

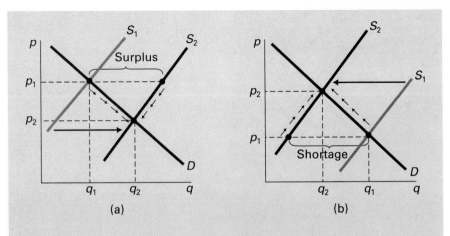

Figure 3.7 Shift of Supply.

In Figure 3.7a, supply increases from S_1 to S_2. When supply increases, the supply curve shifts to the right. At the initial price p_1, there is a market surplus. Equilibrium price falls to p_2 and equilibrium quantity rises to q_2. In Figure 3.7b, supply decreases from S_1 to S_2. When supply decreases, the supply curve shifts to the left. At the initial price p_1, there is a market shortage. Equilibrium price rises to p_2 and equilibrium quantity falls to q_2.

TRY   *(Answers to all "TRY" questions are at the back of the book.)*

Use a graph of supply and demand to determine how each event affects equilibrium price and equilibrium quantity.

1. In the market for laptops, buyer income rises.

2. In the market for pens, wages of pen manufacturers rise.

3. In the market for hybrid cars, buyer preferences shift toward hybrids.

4. In the market for SUVs, the price of gasoline rises.

5. In the market for restaurant meals, more restaurants open in town.

6. In the market for crude oil, hurricanes destroy dozens of oil rigs.

7. In the market for a town's rental apartments, the town's population increases.

8. In the market for brownies, the price of chocolate truffle cookies (which can be made with the same ingredients as brownies) increases.

Chapter 4

Measuring the Macroeconomy

Before we can tell stories about the macroeconomy, we need to know what is happening in it. What terms do economists use to describe the macroeconomy? How are those things measured? How has the U.S. economy performed over the last century? In this chapter, we focus on these questions.

KEY TERMS AND CONCEPTS

- National Income and Product Accounts (NIPA)
- Output
- Income
- Expenditure
- Employed
- Unemployed
- Gross domestic product (GDP)
- Nondurable goods
- Services
- Durable goods
- The underground economy
- Gross national product (GNP)
- Nominal GDP
- Real GDP
- Trend rate of growth
- Long-run growth
- Short-run fluctuations
- Standard of living
- Real GDP per capita
- Growth
- Stagnation
- Decline
- Recession
- Recovery
- Trough

- Peak
- Growth recession
- Depression
- Civilian labor force
- Out of the labor force
- Marginally attached to the labor force
- Discouraged worker
- Unemployment rate
- Labor force participation rate
- Frictional unemployment
- Structural unemployment
- Cyclical unemployment
- Full employment
- Seasonal unemployment
- Seasonally adjusted
- Natural rate of unemployment
- Non-accelerating inflation rate of unemployment (NAIRU)
- Inflation
- Hyperinflation
- Deflation
- Consumer price index (CPI)
- Market basket
- Laspeyres index
- GDP deflator
- Paasche index
- Disinflation
- Stagflation

KEY EQUATIONS

- Rate of change
- Unemployment rate
- Labor force participation rate
- Consumer price index
- GDP deflator

SOME HISTORY OF MACROECONOMICS

The worst economy of modern times occurred during the 1930s, in what we now call the Great Depression. Millions of people could not find work. Families lost their houses. Workers lost their jobs. Bankers lost their banks. It was worse than you or I can probably imagine. And yet the big question was "Why?" Why was this happening? Why were so many people out of work, hungry, poor? That is the key question of macroeconomics. At the time, there was no widely accepted answer.

In many ways, macroeconomic theory began in 1936 with the publication of *The General Theory of Employment, Interest, and Money* by John Maynard Keynes. (Keynes rhymes with "brains.") Keynes, a British economist, offered an explanation for the dire straits in which economies found themselves during the Great Depression. Paraphrasing:

> To understand why so many are out of work, we need to understand why so few people have jobs. People have jobs when there is output to produce. There is output to produce when someone wants to buy that output. So if lots of people are out of work, then there must be insufficient spending.

The most powerful stories are the simplest stories. Economics at its best is very intuitive. Keynes's story was simple, intuitive, and powerful. But did Keynes's story explain the real world?

To answer that question, economists needed to measure the concepts in Keynes's *General Theory*. What is output? Is everything output? What does it mean to be employed or unemployed? How are prices measured?

The result of many years of work in the 1930s and 1940s is a detailed system for counting what is produced in an economy, who receives income from producing it, and who buys it. That system is called the **National Income and Product Accounts (NIPA)**.

Several key ideas from Keynes's story show up in the NIPA.

- Output and employment are linked. **Output** is "produced" in the economy if someone has a paying job producing it. A beautiful sunset is not output, because no one is employed to produce it. A Hawaiian sunset cruise sold to vacationers is output, because people are employed to provide the cruise.

- **Income** is what we receive for producing goods and services. Your grand-mother's monthly Social Security check is not income, because it's not a payment for a government job. A nurse's monthly paycheck is income, because it's a payment for nursing services.

- Four groups in the economy purchase output. Spending, or what economists call **expenditure**, is done by households, businesses, government agencies, and the rest of the world.

- Someone is **employed** if he or she is being paid for producing output. People who are **unemployed** are those who are not employed *and* who want to be employed. A stay-at-home parent who is not working outside the home and who isn't looking for work outside the home is neither employed nor unemployed.

In the next few sections, we define output, employment, and inflation in careful detail. If you get confused—and it can be easy to do so, because there is a lot of new vocabulary coming—come back and re-read those four bullets. Much of what we're about to do condenses down to just those four bullets.

TRY   (*Answers to all "TRY" questions are at the back of the book.*)

1. What is the difference between "output" and "income"?

2. Who wrote *The General Theory*?

3. When was the Great Depression?

OUTPUT

The goods and services produced in an economy are together called output. Something is "output" if someone had a job producing it. That job could be a paid job, or it could be working for your family-owned business.

Economists call the total amount of output produced in an economy in a year the **gross domestic product**, or **GDP**. U.S. GDP in 2008 was $14,400 billion ($14.4 trillion, or $14,400,000,000,000). During 2008, $14,400 billion worth of goods and services were produced in the United States.

Where is most of that output now? Most of it is gone. Think about the things you bought in the last 48 hours. Most of them are probably gone. The cup of coffee? Drank it down. The ticket to a movie? Saw it. The tank of gas for the car? Used up. The hour of Wi-Fi access? Long gone. Most of what is produced in a year is gone well before that year is over.

However, some of that $14,400 billion worth of goods and services still exists. The new bus bought by a local transit agency? Still picking up passengers. The new kitchen added to the house up the block? Still in the house. The pickup truck purchased by the construction company? Still being driven.

Those things that are gone soon after they are produced are called either **nondurable goods** or **services**. Nondurable goods are things that you can touch, things that exist in some physical sense. Services are things that are produced but that do not exist in a physical sense—a haircut, an hour with an attorney, a nurse's assistance, a day at an amusement park. You can't pick services up, put them in your bag, and take them home.

Goods that are produced and exist for some time are called **durable goods**. How long is "some time"? Officially, the cutoff is 3 years. Something that typically lasts for 3 years or more is called a "durable good"; something that lasts for less than 3 years is a "nondurable good." A car is a durable good; a tank of gas is a nondurable good.

Understanding Gross Domestic Product

Remember: the definition of GDP helps flesh out Keynes's story. GDP measures the total amount of output produced in an economy in a year. Does something count as "output"? The answer depends on whether someone was currently employed to produce it.

Out of that principle come several observations about what isn't in GDP.

- Used goods are not part of GDP. You bought a used 1999 Chevy in 2009. No one was employed in 2009 to produce that used good. Production of your 1999 Chevy was included in GDP in 1999, when someone had a job manufacturing that car.

- Most work in the home is not part of GDP. If someone is paid to do the work, then the output is part of GDP. But if you make your own lunch, raise your own kids, clean your own house, and do your own laundry, that's terrific . . . but not in GDP.

- Volunteer work is not part of GDP. The time you spend in the Gulf Coast building houses with Habitat for Humanity or cleaning beaches is not part of GDP. It's volunteer work. You're not being paid.

Then there are a couple of rules about what isn't in GDP that have nothing to do with the principle that links output and employment. Instead, these rules reflect measurement challenges.

- Illegal activity is not counted in GDP. Street drug sales, prostitution, and illegal gambling all generate employment and income, but people who provide illegal services tend not to report that income to the government. Because there is no government record of illegal activity, it is not included in GDP.

- Unreported cash transactions are not counted in GDP. Babysitting for the family down the street was perfectly legal. But did you report the income on your taxes? I thought not—few teenagers do. Because some cash transactions are not reported to the government, the unreported cash transactions are not counted in GDP.

Illegal activity and unreported cash transactions are called, together, **the underground economy**. The U.S. underground economy is 5–20% as large as the "aboveground" economy. If we could count illegal activity and unreported cash transactions, U.S. GDP in 2008 would have been between $15.1 and $17.3 trillion, not $14.4 trillion.

Gross domestic product, or GDP, is *one number* that measures the *total* amount of output produced in an economy in a year. GDP is expressed in dollars, not in numbers. We do not add up the number of cars produced, plus the number of banana splits, plus the number of anvils. We add up the dollar value of the cars produced, plus the dollar value of the banana splits, plus the dollar value of the anvils—and so on.

Gross domestic product or GDP measures the total amount of output produced in an economy *in a year*. Why in a year? Why not month, or a quarter? Just because, that's why. Because that's the way it's done.

GDP tells us the *annual* amount of output produced. Even when the numbers are reported for a quarter (three months, which is a fourth or a quarter of a year), GDP is reported annually. U.S. GDP for the third quarter of 2008 was $14.5 trillion. That does *not* mean that $14.5 trillion worth of goods and services was produced in that three-month period from July 1 to September 30, 2008. It means: "If the economy had continued along at the pace it set in the third quarter of 2008, then over the course of a year the economy would produce $14.5 trillion worth of output." Somewhere around one-fourth of $14.5 trillion worth of output was actually produced in 2008:III (that's how we write the third quarter of 2008—the year, then a colon, then the number of the quarter in Latin numerals).

Gross domestic product or GDP measures the total amount of output produced *in an economy* in a year. When we measure U.S. GDP, what matters is *where* the output is produced. Is it produced within the United States? Then it's part of U.S. GDP. Is it produced outside the United States? Then it's part of some other country's GDP. Location—*domicile*—matters for GDP.

There is an older measure of output not often used anymore: **gross national product**, or **GNP**. Gross *national* product measures the total amount of output produced *by an economy* in a year. When we measure U.S. GNP, what matters is *who owns* the resources where the output is produced. Is the factory owned by a U.S. corporation? Then its output is part of U.S. GNP. Is the factory owned by a French corporation? Then its output is part of France's GNP. Ownership—nation—matters for GNP.

TRY

4. Give two examples of each of the following (six examples total): nondurable good, service, and durable good.

5. When you are trying to determine whether something is "output" and therefore part of GDP, what is a principle or rule you can use as a guide?

6. Why is the underground economy not counted in GDP?

7. U.S. GDP in 2007:II was $14.0 trillion. Approximately how much output (in dollars) was actually produced between April 1 and June 30, 2007?

8. What is the difference between GDP and GNP?

Real versus Nominal GDP

Gross domestic product or GDP measures the total amount of output produced in an economy in a year. The Bureau of Economic Analysis (BEA, http://bea.gov) is responsible for estimating GDP for the United States. Essentially, the BEA multiplies prices and quantities for everything produced, then adds all that up. Restating that in an equation,

$$\text{GDP} = (price_A \times quantity_A) + (price_B \times quantity_B) + (price_C \times quantity_C) + \cdots$$

or

$$GDP = \sum_{all\ output} (price \times quantity)$$

The symbol $\sum$, the upper-case letter sigma, means "the sum of." So the equation is read this way: "GDP equals the sum, over all output of goods and services, of price times quantity for each good or service produced."

GDP is price times quantity, added up for all the goods and services produced. If prices rise, then GDP rises—even if quantities didn't change. If quantities rise, then GDP rises—even if prices didn't change. So GDP can increase either because prices increase or because quantities increase.

That's a bit of a problem. Output and employment are supposed to be linked. More output is supposed to mean more jobs. An increase in quantities—an increase in GDP—does mean that more output is produced, so more people have jobs producing output. But an increase in prices—again, an increase in GDP—doesn't mean that more people have jobs. When GDP rises because prices have risen, the link between output and employment is broken.

How can we preserve the link between output and employment? The answer comes from thinking about the prices we use. **Nominal GDP** uses the prices and quantities from the same year. Nominal GDP for 1968 equals prices from 1968 times quantities produced in 1968. Nominal GDP for 2008 equals prices from 2008 times quantities produced in 2008. Nominal GDP will increase from one year to the next if prices rise, or if quantities rise. Economists sometimes call nominal GDP "GDP in current dollars."

Real GDP uses the prices from some base year. A base year is some specific year that someone in the government has selected. Calculations of real GDP for any year then use prices from that base year. Real GDP for 1968 equals prices from the base year times quantities produced in 1968. Real GDP for 2008 equals prices from the base year times quantities produced in 2008. Because prices don't change when comparing real GDP of one year with real GDP of the next year, real GDP will increase from one year to the next *only if* quantities rise. Economists sometimes call real GDP "GDP in constant dollars."

TIP

In macroeconomics, "real" means "holding prices constant." Don't think of any other meaning of the word "real"—real versus pretend, real versus unreal.

News about the economy always references real—not nominal—GDP. "The economy has expanded" means that real GDP has increased. "The economy is contracting" means that real GDP has fallen.

Using prices from just one particular base year is a problem when new goods are introduced after the base year. If the base year is 1968, what price do we use for an MP3 player? To incorporate new products, the government now has a very complicated way of measuring real GDP using what they call "chained dollars." Think of a daisy chain—a little bit of an old daisy's stem overlaps each newer daisy. So economists sometimes call real GDP "GDP in chained dollars." Very few people need to know how "chained dollars" are determined. What's important is this: whether using base-year prices or chained dollars, real GDP increases or decreases *only if* there are changes in the quantities of output produced.

Rate of Change of Real GDP

The rate of change of real GDP is the percentage change of real GDP between one year and the next.

$$Rate\ of\ change\ of\ real\ GDP = \frac{new\ value\ of\ GDP - old\ value\ of\ GDP}{old\ value\ of\ GDP}$$

Real GDP in 2007 was $13,229 billion. Real GDP in 2006 was $12,976 billion. So the rate of change between 2006 and 2007 was

$$Rate\ of\ change\ of\ real\ GDP = \frac{13,229 - 12,976}{12,976} = \frac{253}{12,976} = 0.019$$

Rates of change are always expressed in percent form. So multiply by 100 and add the word "percent."

$$Rate\ of\ change\ of\ real\ GDP = 0.019 = 1.9\ percent$$

Real GDP increased by 1.9% between 2006 and 2007.

When the new value is greater than the old value, the rate of change is positive. When the new value is smaller than the old value, the rate of change is negative.

Real GDP in 2009 was $12,881 billion. Real GDP in 2008 was $13,229 billion. The rate of change between 2008 and 2009 was

$$Rate\ of\ change\ of\ real\ GDP = \frac{12,881 - 13,229}{13,229}$$
$$= \frac{-348}{13,229} = -0.026 = -2.6\ percent$$

TRY

9. What is the key difference between nominal GDP and real GDP?

10. What can you conclude has happened if real GDP remains constant while nominal GDP rises?

11. Real GDP (chained 2005 dollars) was $5,987.2 billion in 1981, $5,870.9 billion in 1982, and $6,136.2 billion in 1983. What was the rate of change of real GDP between 1981 and 1982? Between 1982 and 1983?

Pattern of U.S. Real GDP

Figure 4.1 shows the pattern of U.S. real GDP since 1900. Time is plotted on the horizontal axis. Real GDP is on the vertical axis.

TIP

Time is always on the horizontal axis when we draw a graph that shows how something has changed over time.

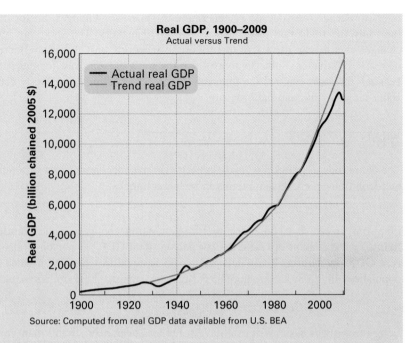

Figure 4.1 U.S. Real GDP, 1900–2009.

Real GDP for the United States has increased, though not at a steady pace, throughout the twentieth and twenty-first centuries. The Great Recession of 2007–2009 is clearly visible in the graph.

What do you notice when you look at the graph? Three things jump out.

- Real GDP has generally—though not always—increased since 1900.
- Real GDP is almost 40 times greater today than it was in 1900.
- The pattern of real GDP is not smooth.

The smooth, solid line in Figure 4.1 is what economists call the trend line. If real GDP had increased at a constant rate between 1900 and 2009, it would have followed that smooth line. The average rate of growth of real GDP between 1900 and 2009 was 3.5%. Economists call this the **trend rate of growth**. Adding the trend line helps us know three things:

- The trend over a century-plus is clearly for U.S. real GDP to increase.
- In the 1930s and early 1940s, real GDP was far away from trend.
- Even before the Great Recession of 2007–2009 began, U.S. real GDP was below its century-long trend.

GROWTH, STAGNATION, RECESSION, RECOVERY, AND MORE

Real GDP is used to tell us whether the economy is growing. Economists talk of **long-run growth** and **short-run fluctuations**. In macroeconomics, the long run refers to decade-over-decade or generation-to-generation changes. So for the long run, only the trend rate of growth of real GDP matters. The short run refers to changes over a year, or two, or three. For the short run, only the actual fluctuations of real GDP matter. Some textbooks use the term medium run for the period in between the short run and the long run. But macroeconomists generally care only about the short run and the long run.

TIP

The definitions of "short run" and "long run" in macroeconomics are different from the definitions of these same terms in microeconomics.

Long-run growth is about generation-to-generation changes in the **standard of living**, or the amount of real GDP per person. Real GDP per person is also called **real GDP per capita**. Real GDP per person is equal to real GDP divided by the population. In 2008, U.S. real GDP per person (chained 2005 dollars) was

$$Real\ GDP\ per\ capita\ in\ 2008 = \frac{\$13,229\ billion}{304.1\ million} = \$43,502$$

Long-run growth asks: Will you have a higher standard of living than your parents did? Will your children have a higher standard of living than you have today?

Economies experience either **growth, stagnation**, or **decline** in the long run. When the trend rate of growth of real GDP per capita is positive, there is economic growth. When the trend rate of growth is zero, the economy is stagnating. When the trend rate of growth is negative, the economy is declining. Figure 4.2 illustrates.

Short-run fluctuations are about year-to-year or even quarter-to-quarter changes in real GDP. Was more output produced this year than last year? Will output next year be greater than it was this year?

In the short run, economies experience **recession** and **recovery**. When real GDP decreases, economists say the economy is in recession. When real GDP increases, economists say the economy is in recovery. The point where the economy hits bottom is called the **trough**. The **peak** is the point where the economy hits the top and goes into a recession. Figure 4.3 illustrates the cycles of recession and recovery.

TIP

The rule of thumb: two or more consecutive quarters of decline in real GDP constitutes a recession.

An economy that is in recovery may still be worse off than it was before the recession began. Recovery means only that real GDP is now increasing. But, at least initially, the economy will still be worse off than it was before the recession began. Recovery is not the same thing as "recovered."

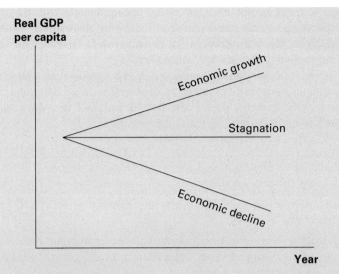

Figure 4.2 Growth, Stagnation, and Decline.

When the long-run trend rate of growth is positive, there is economic growth. When the long-run trend rate of growth is zero, there is stagnation. When the long-run trend rate of growth is negative, there is economic decline.

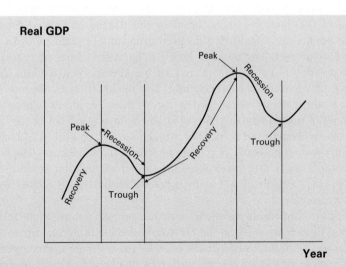

Figure 4.3 Recession and Recovery.

When real GDP is increasing in the short run, the economy is in recovery. The point where real GDP begins to decline is called the peak. When real GDP is decreasing in the short run, the economy is in recession. The point where real GDP begins to rise again is called the trough.

Because many people associate rising unemployment with the word "recession," economists coined a new phrase in the 1990s: **growth recession**. A growth recession occurs when the economy is growing—real GDP is increasing—but it is growing so slowly that unemployment is rising.

What about **depression**? "Depression" is not an official economic term. There is no economic measure of whether an economy is in a depression. A very bad recession may be termed a depression. But "depression" is a word more likely to be bandied about by journalists than by economists.

TRY

12. In macroeconomics, what are the definitions of "long run" and "short run"?
13. Associate each term that follows with the appropriate time frame, long run or short run: decline, depression, growth, growth recession, peak, recession, recovery, trough.

UNEMPLOYMENT

Once a month, the U.S. government releases an estimate of the number of Americans unemployed. These numbers come from a monthly household survey of about 60,000 households conducted by the Bureau of Labor Statistics (BLS, http://bls.gov), a division of the federal government's Department of Labor. Those households surveyed are asked a series of questions about each person in the household who is age 16 and over: Last week, were you working for pay? If not, have you looked for work in the last 4 weeks? If not, why not? From the answers to these questions (and a few more), the government is able to estimate the number of people who are employed, unemployed, and out of the labor force.

Someone is **employed** if she or he worked for pay, or worked 15 hours or more in a family-owned business. If you are on vacation, out sick, on temporary leave, or temporarily away from work for some similar reason, you are also counted as employed. In 2008, about 145 million people in the United States, ages 16 and over, were employed.

Someone is **unemployed** if she or he had no job, wanted a job, and had done something to look for a job in the previous 4 weeks. In normal times, about 7 or 8 million people in the United States, ages 16 and over, are unemployed. During a recession, more people are unemployed. Near the height of the recession in 2009, over 15 million people were unemployed.

Someone is in the **civilian labor force** if she or he is either employed or unemployed. In the United States in 2008, the civilian labor force was about 155 million people.

The labor force increases each year because more people enter the labor force than leave it. People enter the U.S. labor force when they leave school and look for their first job, when they re-enter the labor force, or when they migrate to the United States. People leave the U.S. labor force when they retire, stop working and don't look for another job, or emigrate from the United States.

Someone is **out of the labor force** if she or he is not employed and not unemployed. Most—but not all—people who are out of the labor force are retired, homemakers, or students. In 2008, about 80 million people in the United States, ages 16 and over, were out of the labor force.

Someone who wants a job but who has not done anything in the last 4 weeks to look for work is officially out of the labor force. But because these folks want work, the BLS calls them **marginally attached to the labor force**. Someone who wants a job but who has done nothing in the last 4 weeks to look for work because she or he believes there's no point in looking is called a **discouraged worker**. Of the 80 million people who were out of the labor force in 2008, about 5 million wanted a job but hadn't looked for work in the previous 4 weeks.

TIP

Everyone who is at least 16 years old falls into one—and only one—of these three categories: employed, unemployed, or out of the labor force.

The **unemployment rate** is the proportion or percentage of the labor force that is unemployed. The unemployment rate equals the number of people unemployed divided by the number of people in the labor force.

$$Unemployment\ rate = \frac{\#\ unemployed}{\#\ in\ labor\ force} = \frac{\#\ unemployed}{\#\ unemployed + \#\ employed}$$

In July 2008, the unemployment rate was 5.7%.

$$Unemployment\ rate = \frac{8{,}784{,}000}{8{,}784{,}000 + 145{,}819{,}000}$$

$$= \frac{8{,}784{,}000}{154{,}603{,}000} = 0.057 = 5.7\ percent$$

By October 2009, the unemployment rate had risen to 10.2%.

$$Unemployment\ rate = \frac{15{,}700{,}000}{15{,}700{,}000 + 138{,}275{,}000}$$

$$= \frac{15{,}700{,}000}{153{,}975{,}000} = 0.102 = 10.2\ percent$$

Normally the unemployment rate falls as real GDP rises, and the unemployment rate rises as real GDP falls. But sometimes the rise in real GDP is so gradual that the increase in the number of jobs is smaller than the increase in the labor force. That describe a growth recession: when real GDP is rising (and thus the economy is growing) but the unemployment rate is not falling. The number of employed rises. But the number of unemployed rises faster because of the entrants into the labor force.

The **labor force participation rate** (LFPR) is the proportion or percentage of the population ages 16 and over that is in the labor force.

$$LFPR = \frac{Labor\ Force}{Population(16\ and\ over)}$$

In July 2008, the labor force participation rate was 66.1%.

$$LFPR = \frac{54{,}603{,}000}{233{,}864{,}000} = 0.661 = 66.1\ percent$$

TRY

14. In 1982, 10.7 million people were unemployed, 99.5 million were employed, and 62.1 million people ages 16 and over were out of the labor force. What was the unemployment rate? What was the labor force participation rate?

Pattern of Unemployment

Unemployment generally rises in recessions and falls in recoveries. Figure 4.4 shows the U.S. unemployment rate since 1900. The Great Depression of the 1930s jumps out. Unemployment exceeded 25% in early 1933. Since World War II, there were two periods of particularly high unemployment: in the early 1980s

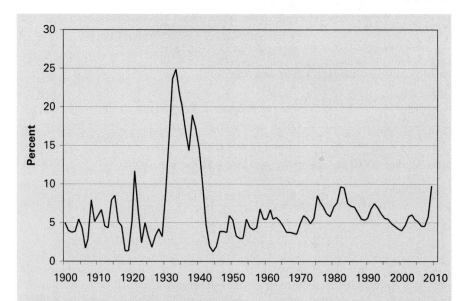

Figure 4.4 U.S. Unemployment Rate, 1900–2009.

Unemployment soared in the Great Depression of the 1930s. In the early 1980s and again in late 2009, the unemployment rate was over 10%. During the intervening quarter-century, the unemployment rate ranged generally between 4 and 8%.

and during the Great Recession of 2007–2009. In both cases, in some months the unemployment rate passed 10%.

Full Employment

The unemployment rate never goes to zero. It won't go to zero, because there are always some people who are voluntarily in-between jobs. Economists call this sort of unemployment **frictional unemployment**. It is considered healthy for an economy. Frictional unemployment occurs because you take time to find the right job for your education and experience, rather than taking the first job listed in the help-wanted ads.

People can also be unemployed because their skills have become obsolete or because their employers relocated to another part of the country. Economists call this sort of unemployment **structural unemployment**. It results from changes in the structure of the economy. Technological change rendered the skills of telephone operators obsolete. Telephone operators were laid off and, until they found another job, were part of structural unemployment.

When production of output temporarily falls and then rises—whether "temporarily" means a few months or a couple of years—that is part of the business cycle of recession and recovery. People who lose their jobs as part of the business cycle are experiencing **cyclical unemployment**.

Full employment is not the same as zero unemployment. When the labor force is fully employed, there is still frictional and structural unemployment. Full employment means that there is no cyclical unemployment. For the U.S., estimates of the unemployment rate at full employment vary between 4 and 6%.

TIP

The terms frictional, structural, and cyclical unemployment appear in some, but not all, principles of macroeconomics courses.

Seasonal unemployment is not reported in the monthly unemployment data, because that data is **seasonally adjusted** to remove the influence of changes that occur with the seasons, year after year. Someone is seasonally unemployed if his or her usual line of work is tied to the seasons of the year and he or she is looking for work in the off-season.

TRY

15. For each person below, identify the sort of unemployment being experienced.
    a. A new college grad is searching for a job but has not yet found one
    b. A ski lift operator is looking for work in April, after the ski season has ended

c. Due to declining sales, a sales clerk at Wal-Mart is laid off
d. A worker in San Francisco is looking for work because her company relocated from California to North Carolina

Natural Rate of Unemployment

How low can the unemployment rate go? We know it won't go to zero. But how low *can* unemployment go? The concept of the **natural rate of unemployment**, or NRU, captures how low the unemployment rate can go without causing other problems. There is more than one definition of the "natural rate of unemployment." Some economists use the phrase to mean the unemployment rate consistent with being on the production possibilities frontier. Others use "natural rate of unemployment" to mean the unemployment rate that occurs in a healthy economy with full employment. Other economists use the phrase as synonymous with the **non-accelerating inflation rate of unemployment**, or **NAIRU**, which means the lowest rate of unemployment consistent with a low and stable inflation rate.

TIP

There is nothing particularly "natural" about the natural rate of unemployment. It is not the rate of unemployment somehow given by nature.

The unemployment rate announced by the Bureau of Labor Statistics is an actual number. It reflects people who are actually unemployed. The unemployment rate in June 2008 was 5.5%. In June 2008, 5.5% of the labor force was unemployed.

The natural rate of unemployment is different. It is not a number that is calculated from people's actual experience. Instead the NRU is hypothetical, pretend. Think of it as a goal, or an ideal. An analogy: your weight today is what the scale says it is, but your "ideal weight" is the weight you and your doctor think would be best for you. You can't get on the scale and see your ideal weight. You can measure your actual weight. You can figure out the difference between your actual weight and your ideal weight. But you can't measure your ideal weight.

In the same sense, the natural rate of unemployment is an ideal. What is that rate? Answers vary. Even when economists agree about the definition of NRU, there is not one accepted value for the NRU. To know the value of the natural rate of unemployment requires knowing how low the unemployment rate can fall before inflation is triggered. But until we live through a period of low unemployment without rising inflation, we can't know for sure how low unemployment can go. Generally, though, the natural rate of unemployment is thought to be between 4 and 6%.

The NRU affects policy. How low should policy makers push unemployment? The answer depends on the value of the NRU. If the NRU is 6%, then pushing unemployment below 6% will trigger increased inflation—an undesired result. But if the NRU is 4%, then policy makers can push the unemployment rate down to 4% before inflation is triggered. Is the difference between 4 and 6% a big deal? In the United States, it's a difference of 3 million people. If the unemployment rate is 6% rather than 4%, an additional 3 million people are unemployed.

TRY

16. What is the definition of the natural rate of unemployment?

INFLATION

Inflation is a general rise in prices. When prices, on average, are increasing from one month to the next, there is inflation. If prices are rising very rapidly, say 20% or more per month, economists say there is **hyperinflation**. **Deflation** is a general fall in prices. When prices, on average, are decreasing from one month to the next, there is deflation.

Inflation, hyperinflation, and deflation are all statements about the average level of prices. So even when there is inflation, some prices might be falling. Computers are less expensive now than they were ten years ago. The price of computers has been falling. But many other things are more expensive now than they were ten years ago. On average, even with computer prices declining, prices have been rising. There has been inflation over the last decade.

What *is* the average level of prices? There are several different ways that the government calculates the "average price." Two ways are most often mentioned: the consumer price index and the GDP deflator.

Consumer Price Index

Prices paid by consumers for the goods and services we buy are averaged with the **consumer price index** or **CPI**. Not all goods and services are included in the average. Instead, the Bureau of Labor Statistics (BLS) uses what economists call a **market basket** of goods and services—a selection of items that a typical urban family of four buys in a month. The market basket does not change from month to month or year to year. The items are always the same.

The BLS has a base year for the consumer price index. The base year is currently actually a base period of three years, 1982–1984. Prices today are compared with prices in the base period.

The CPI is the ratio of the total amount paid for the market basket today to the total amount paid for the market basket during the base period. For ease of presentation, the ratio is multiplied by 100. For instance, the CPI for 1996 is

$$CPI_{1996} = \frac{\sum_i (base\ year\ quantity)_i \times (1996\ price)_i}{\sum_i (base\ year\ quantity)_i \times (base\ year\ price)_i} \times 100$$

Because the CPI is calculated using quantities from a base year, it is an example of what is called a **Laspeyres index**.

The CPI is calculated monthly. The CPI for 1982–1984 equals 100. The CPI in July 2008 equaled 220.

GDP Deflator

Prices paid by everyone for everything produced are averaged using the **GDP deflator**, or what is sometimes called the implicit price deflator for GDP. All goods and services produced are included in the average. The Bureau of Economic Analysis (BEA) calculates the GDP deflator. The items included in the GDP deflator change from quarter to quarter or year to year, as the items that are produced change. Because the GDP deflator is calculated using quantities from the current period, it is an example of what is called a **Paasche index**.

The GDP deflator is the ratio of the total value of what is produced today evaluated with today's prices to the total value of what is produced today evaluated using the prices of some base year. The ratio is multiplied by 100 for ease in presentation. The BEA is currently using the year 2005 as the base year.

The GDP deflator for the third quarter of 2007 is

$$GDP\ deflator = \frac{\sum_i (2007:\text{III } quantity)_i \times (2007:\text{III } price)_i}{\sum_i (2007:\text{III } quantity)_i \times (base\ year\ price)_i} \times 100$$

This is equivalent to something much simpler!

$$GDP\ deflator = \frac{nominal\ GDP}{real\ GDP} \times 100$$

The GDP deflator is calculated quarterly. The GDP deflator for 2005 equals 100. The GDP deflator for 2007:III was 107.

GDP Price Index

The GDP price index is very similar to the GDP deflator. The GDP price index incorporates chain-weighting, which is the BEA's way of taking into account goods and services that exist in one period but not in another. It should be sufficient to know that the GDP price index also uses current-period quantities, and looks at all goods and services produced (not just at a market basket of consumer goods and services).

TRY

17. What are the differences between the consumer price index on the one hand, and the GDP deflator or GDP price index on the other?

Rate of Change of Prices

The CPI and the GDP deflator are used to calculate the rate of change of prices. The rate of change is the percentage change, usually expressed annually, in prices.

$$Rate\ of\ change = \frac{new\ value - old\ value}{old\ value}$$

The CPI in July 2007 was 208.3. The CPI in July 2008 was 220.0. So the rate of change between July 2007 and July 2008 was

$$Rate\ of\ change = \frac{220.0 - 208.3}{208.3} = \frac{11.7}{208.3} = 0.056$$

This is a percent change. So multiply the result by 100 and put the word "percent" behind it:

$$Rate\ of\ change = 0.056 = 5.6\ percent$$

Consumer prices were, on average, 5.6% higher in July 2008 than they had been in July 2007.

Deflation, Inflation, and More

When prices on average are falling, the rate of change is negative. Economists say: the economy is experiencing deflation. The rate of change is then called the deflation rate. The United States experienced price deflation in 1955, and again in 2009.

When prices are rising, the rate of change is positive. Economists say: the economy is experiencing inflation. The rate of change is called the inflation rate.

When prices are rising but the inflation rate is falling, economists say there is **disinflation**. The inflation rate fell from 7.6% in February 1982 to 6.8% in March 1982. Economists say: there was disinflation between February and March 1982. There is no common term to describe periods when the inflation rate is rising.

When the inflation rate is very high, economists say the economy is experiencing hyperinflation. There are several definitions of how high the inflation rate needs to be in order for it to be called hyperinflation. A good rule of thumb is that an inflation rate of 20% or more *per month* is hyperinflation. The United States experienced hyperinflation during the Revolutionary War.

Stagflation is a term coined in the 1970s to refer to those periods when the economy is simultaneously experiencing a recession and high inflation rates. It is a blend of the words "stagnation" and "inflation."

TRY

18. The CPI was 172.2 in 2000 and 177.1 in 2001. What was the inflation rate between 2000 and 2001?

Pattern of Inflation

The United States has experienced inflation since 1950. The inflation rate rose above 10% in the 1970s, an experience many termed double-digit inflation.

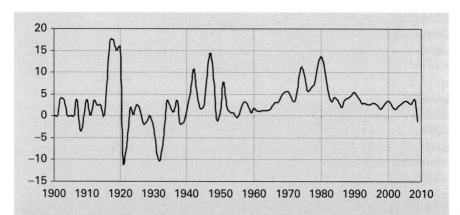

Figure 4.5 U.S. Inflation Rate, 1900–2009.

Before World War II, the U.S. experienced both inflation and deflation. But since the mid-1950s until very recently, the U.S. economy has experienced only inflation. The high inflation rates of the late 1970s were broken in the early 1980s. From then until prices fell during the Great Recession of 2007–2009, inflation remained between 2 and 4%.

Figure 4.5 shows the inflation rate for 1900 to the present. Notice that price deflation used to be relatively common in the United States but no longer is. Looking just at the post–World War II years, the inflation rate was around 2–4% throughout much of the 1960s, and again from the mid-1980s until 2008. The high inflation of the 1970s stands out as a post-war anomaly.

WHAT'S AHEAD

Now that we have defined many of the terms that we need in macroeconomics, we are ready to begin the story. First, we will look at the question of long-run growth. Then, we will turn to the determination of short-run fluctuations.

PART II

The Long Run

Chapter 5

Long-Run Economic Growth

Why are some nations rich and others poor? Why do standards of living sometimes rise quickly and other times slowly . . . or not at all? Economists answer these questions with models of economic growth. Economies can produce more output—become richer—when there are more inputs or when the inputs' productivity rises.

KEY TERMS AND CONCEPTS

- Growth
- Growth rate of the economy
- Rule of 70
- Aggregate production function
- Capital-labor ratio
- Constant returns to scale
- Scale of production
- Economies of scale
- Increasing returns to scale
- Diseconomies of scale
- Decreasing returns to scale
- Growth accounting
- Residual growth
- Total factor productivity (TFP)
- Labor productivity
- Capital productivity
- Capital stock
- Investment
- Depreciation rate
- Human capital
- Property rights
- Intellectual property rights
- Productivity growth slowdown
- Productivity growth resurgence

KEY EQUATIONS

- Real GDP per capita
- Rate of change
- Aggregate production function

KEY GRAPH

- Aggregate production function

WHAT IS GROWTH?

Economists use the word "growth" in two different contexts: short-run and long-run contexts. For macroeconomists, the short run is a period of a few months to a few years. Macroeconomists who focus on the short run use the term **growth** to refer to changes in real GDP from quarter to quarter, or year to year. Some use the phrase "growing the economy" to refer to policies or events that make real GDP increase over the short run.

The long run is a period of a decade or a generation. Long-run growth refers to changes from decade to decade, or generation to generation. Changes in what? Unfortunately for students, there are two answers. Some economists and textbooks use one definition of long-run growth; others use the other. Long-run growth can be

- Increases in real GDP, or

- Increases in real GDP per capita

Real GDP per capita is the phrase economists use for real GDP per person.

$$Real\ GDP\ per\ capita = \frac{Real\ GDP}{Population}$$

Real GDP per capita is also sometimes called the standard of living.

Production Possibilities Frontier

Economists sometimes use the model of the production possibilities frontier (PPF) to capture the idea of economic growth. Remember from Chapter 2 that the PPF shows the possible combinations of output that can be produced with the economy's available inputs. An increase in available inputs or an improvement in productivity allows more to be produced. The study of long-run growth focuses on what can increase the available inputs or increase productivity, shifting out the economy's production possibilities frontier.

Measuring Economic Growth

The key question of long-run growth is: What factors determine the growth rate of the economy? The **growth rate of the economy** is the annual rate of change of real GDP or of real GDP per capita.

$$Annual\ rate\ of\ change = \frac{value\ in\ some\ year - value\ in\ previous\ year}{value\ in\ previous\ year}$$

Real GDP in 2001 was $11,347 billion. Real GDP in 2002 was $11,553 billion. (Both figures are chained [2005] dollars). The annual rate of change in real GDP between 2001 and 2002 is

$$Annual\ rate\ of\ change = \frac{11,553 - 11,347}{11,347} = \frac{206}{11,347}$$

$$= 0.018 = 1.8\ percent$$

Because the study of long-run growth focuses on changes over long periods of time, the trend line is more important than the quarter-to-quarter or year-to-year movements in real GDP. One way to calculate the average annual rate of growth between two years that are more than one year apart is to compute the annual rate of change between each pair of years, and then compute the average of those rates of change.

The annual rates of change of real GDP from 1992 to 2002 are 2.9, 4.1, 2.5, 3.7, 4.5, 4.4, 4.8, 4.1, 1.1, and 1.8%. The average of these values is 3.39%. Economists say: the average growth rate of real GDP between 1992 and 2002 was 3.39%.

The study of long-run economic growth asks why some economies grow quickly and others grow slowly. Small differences in annual rates of growth add up to big differences over time. One way economists make this point is by using the **Rule of 70** (or, in some textbooks, the Rule of 72). The Rule of 70 is a math trick that allows us to figure out how many years it takes something to double if we know the annual rate of growth.

$$\frac{70}{annual\ rate\ of\ growth} = number\ of\ years\ to\ double$$

If the economy is growing 1.5% annually, it will take about 47 years for real GDP to double, because 70/1.5 equals about 47. If instead the economy is growing 2.0% per year, it will take only 35 years—over a decade less—for real GDP to double.

TRY (*Answers to all "TRY" questions are at the back of the book.*)

1. Suppose a country had the following values for real GDP (these are made-up numbers). Values are *billions* of constant (2000) dollars.

	1998	1999	2000	2001	2002
Real GDP	6,000	8,000	8,400	8,600	9,000

    a. What are the annual rates of change between each pair of years?
    b. Calculate the average annual rate of change.

2. Population in each year in the same country, in *millions*, was

	1998	1999	2000	2001	2002
Population	400	415	425	430	435

    a. Use the real GDP data from question 1. In each year, what is the value of real GDP per capita (or, the standard of living)? *Notice!* Real GDP is in billions, but population is in millions.
    b. Calculate the average annual rate of change in real GDP per capita.

3. If the standard of living is increasing 8.4% per year, how many years will it take for the standard of living to double? If instead the standard of living is increasing 2.0% per year, how many years will it take for the standard of living to double? If, instead, the standard of living is increasing 1.0% per year, how many years will it take for the standard of living to double?

What's Not Considered

We measure economic growth with real GDP or real GDP per capita. And we slide seamlessly between the terms real GDP per capita and standard of living. If real GDP per capita rises, economists say "The economy is better off." If real GDP per capita falls, economists say "The economy is worse off."

But remember that real GDP does not count everything that matters to people. Real GDP counts the goods and services produced in a year. It does not count environmental destruction, political instability, educational opportunity, freedom of choice, and more.

One irony of focusing only on real GDP is that a natural disaster can make a country "better off." How so? Rebuilding destroyed buildings contributes to real GDP, but the destruction itself may have no direct effect on real GDP.

AGGREGATE PRODUCTION FUNCTION

Economic growth looks at the macroeconomy—the entire economy at once. It is not about whether one industry or another will profit and grow. Economic growth is about the whole economy. How much is total output growing? What factors can enhance growth of output?

Output is all the goods and services counted in GDP. Don't start thinking about specific output such as cars and doctor's appointments and egg foo yung. Think of output all at once, in one thought, as lots and lots of goods and services.

Output—all the goods and services counted in GDP—is produced with inputs. Don't start thinking about specific inputs such as metal and plastic and eggs. Think of inputs in their broadest possible groupings: labor, physical capital, and natural resources. Output (GDP) is produced with inputs (labor, capital, and natural resources).

Capital does *not* mean money. Capital means physical capital—buildings (or structures) and equipment (or machinery).

Those inputs—labor, capital, and natural resources—are combined by producers using the available knowledge (which includes technology) about how to combine inputs to produce output. So we could say

output is produced with inputs and knowledge

But an economist says it with an equation. Instead of saying "is produced with," the economist says is a function of: output is a function of inputs and knowledge. And economists write that sentence with an equation:

$$\text{output} = F(\text{inputs, knowledge})$$

Economists call this equation the **aggregate production function**. It is a *function* because it's a mathematical statement that says how one thing (output) is related to other things (inputs and knowledge). It is a *production* function because it's a statement about the production of output. It is an *aggregate* production function because it's a statement about the entire economy, the aggregate economy, thought about all at once.

The inputs are labor, capital, and natural resources. Economists use the uppercase L to stand for labor and the uppercase K to stand for capital. There is not one accepted shorthand for natural resources (and not all textbooks include natural resources in the aggregate production function). Use NR to stand for natural resources. So our aggregate production function becomes

$$\text{Output} = F(L, K, NR, \text{knowledge})$$

Not everyone includes natural resources in their aggregate production function. It's just as common to include only labor and capital as the inputs.

Knowledge is very broad. It includes technical knowledge and nontechnical knowledge. Everything we've learned about how and everything that impacts how inputs are combined to produce output is included in what is called "knowledge."

Another way to write the aggregate production function pulls out "knowledge" and puts it alone before the F. There's no logic to the shorthand: the uppercase A is used to stand for knowledge or technology. So our aggregate production function becomes

$$\text{Output} = A \cdot F(K, L, NR)$$

Output increases if there is an increase in A (knowledge), or in the quantities of our inputs, K, L, and NR.

When economists express the aggregate production function this way, a slight change gives us an equation that helps us think about output per capita, or the standard of living. For reasons you learn in an intermediate micro theory course, the aggregate production function Output $= A \cdot F(K, L, NR)$ is equivalent to

$$\frac{\text{Output}}{L} = A \cdot F\left(\frac{K}{L}, \frac{NR}{L}\right)$$

Output per worker depends upon knowledge (A), the amount of capital per worker, and the natural resources per worker. Economists call the amount of capital per worker the **capital-labor ratio**. Think of it as the number of machines each worker has to work with. Output per worker increases if there is an increase in knowledge (A), the capital-labor ratio, or the amount of natural resources per worker.

Output per person and output per worker are not the same thing. But so long as the labor force participation rate—the ratio of workers to population—is constant, figuring out what makes output per worker increase rapidly or slowly is the same thing as figuring out what makes output per capita increase rapidly or slowly. Economists make this slide between output per worker and output per person with ease.

TRY

---

4. What are the inputs in the production function?
5. Output is produced with labor (L) and capital (K) and knowledge (A). What is the aggregate production function for output?
6. What is—and isn't—included in "capital"?

Diminishing Marginal Returns

One important concept from microeconomics shows up here: the law of diminishing marginal returns. As the quantity of one input increases while holding constant the quantity of the other inputs, there is more output produced. *But!* But each time we increase the quantity of that one input, the increases in output get smaller and smaller.

This law of diminishing marginal returns impacts the shape of the aggregate production function. As always, the graph is in just two dimensions. (You will never see a three-dimensional graph in introductory economics!) The quantity of output goes on the vertical axis. The quantity of one input—let's choose labor—goes on the horizontal axis. The curve in Figure 5.1 looks at how the quantity of output changes as we change the quantity of one input *holding constant the quantities of the other inputs and the amount of knowledge*.

A graph that shows how output per worker depends on the capital-labor ratio—*holding constant the natural resources-to-labor ratio and the amount of knowledge*—would have the same shape. A constant increase in the capital-labor ratio would yield ever smaller increases in output per worker.

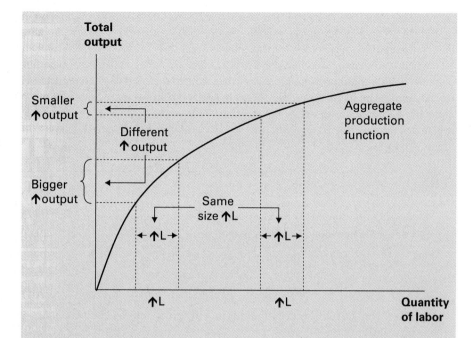

Figure 5.1 Aggregate Production Function.

The graph of the aggregate production function shows how the quantity of output varies with changes in one of the inputs, holding constant the quantities of the other inputs and the amount of knowledge. The curve is upward-sloping, because more labor produces more output. The curve gets flatter and flatter because of the law of diminishing returns: the increases in output get smaller and smaller as more and more labor is used.

Economies of Scale

Diminishing marginal returns occur when only one input is increased and, importantly, all other inputs are held constant. But what happens if all inputs are increased at once? Double all the inputs—twice as much labor, capital, and natural resources—and does output double? Does it more than double? Does it increase, but not to the point of doubling?

When *all* inputs are doubled and as a result there is twice as much output—double the inputs produces double the output—economists say the economy exhibits **constant returns to scale**. The inputs are the **scale of production**. When there are constant returns to scale, the return to increasing the scale is 1: double the inputs produces double the output; 1.7 times the inputs produces 1.7 times the output.

When *all* inputs are doubled and as a result there is *more* than twice as much output—double the inputs produces *more* than double the output—economists say the economy exhibits **economies of scale** or **increasing returns to scale**. When there are economies of scale, the return to increasing the scale of production is more than 1: double the inputs produces more than double the output; 1.7 times the inputs produces more than 1.7 times the output.

When *all* inputs are doubled and as a result there is *less* than twice as much output—double the inputs produces *less* than double the output—economists say the economy exhibits **diseconomies of scale** or **decreasing returns to scale**. When there are diseconomies of scale, the return to increasing the scale of production is less than 1: double the inputs produces less than double the output; 1.7 times the inputs produces less than 1.7 times the output.

TRY

7. Suppose the aggregate production function is Output $= 3 \cdot K^{1/2} \cdot L^{1/2}$. For each pair below, calculate output.

$K = 100, \ L = 1,000,$ so Output $= $ _____
$K = 100, \ L = 2,000,$ so Output $= $ _____
$K = 100, \ L = 3,000,$ so Output $= $ _____

Have you just illustrated diminishing marginal returns, or economies of scale?

8. Suppose the aggregate production function is Output $= 40 \cdot K^{1/3} \cdot L^{2/3}$. For each pair below, calculate output.

$K = 100, \ L = 4,000,$ so Output $= $ _____
$K = 200, \ L = 8,000,$ so Output $= $ _____
$K = 360, \ L = 14,400,$ so Output $= $ _____

Have you just illustrated diminishing marginal returns, or economies of scale? In this case, are there constant, increasing, or decreasing returns to scale?

SOURCES OF GROWTH

The aggregate production function helps us think about the sources of growth. Either form of the aggregate production function will do:

$$\text{Output} = F(K, L, NR, \text{knowledge})$$

or

$$\frac{\text{Output}}{L} = A \cdot F\left(\frac{K}{L}, \frac{NR}{L}\right)$$

Here's what the equations tell us.

- Increases in the quantity of inputs—K, L, and NR—will increase output.
- Increases in knowledge will increase output.

Economists use the phrase **growth accounting** to describe the exercise of figuring out—accounting for—which of these factors caused an economy to grow.

Sometimes economists will say things like "Output in the economy grew at an average annual rate of 5%. A larger labor force (that's L) accounts for half of that growth. More capital (K) accounts for another one-fourth, or 25%. More natural resources (NR) account for another 10%. And the remaining 15% of the growth in output must be attributable to increases in knowledge (A)."

How do economists measure knowledge? They don't. Growth accountants have ways of figuring out what share of economic growth is attributable to growth in each of the inputs, L, K, and NR. And then they *assume* that any growth they have not accounted for—what economists call **residual growth**—is attributable to other factors that are together called "knowledge."

What's left over—the residual, this thing called "knowledge"—is something that makes all the inputs produce more output. So economists also call it **total factor productivity**, or **TFP**. It's called "total factor" productivity because it isn't specific to any one factor. **Labor productivity** is the amount of output per worker, but not the amount of output per dollar of capital, nor the amount of output per dollar of natural resources. **Capital productivity** is the amount of output per dollar of capital, but not the amount of output per worker, nor the amount of output per dollar of natural resources. But total factor productivity is an increase in output that's not attributable *just* to labor or *just* to capital or *just* to natural resources.

Again, economic growth results from two primary forces:

- Increases in the quantity of inputs
- Increases in knowledge (total factor productivity)

Let's consider each of these forces in turn.

More Inputs

An increase in the quantity of inputs will increase the quantity of output. More inputs produce economic growth. Output increases if there is more capital (K), labor (L), or natural resources (NR).

- More K → more output
- More L → more output
- More NR → more output

Output per worker increases if there is a higher capital-labor ratio (K/L) or there are more natural resources per worker (NR/L). But if both capital and labor increase in such a way that the capital-labor ratio is unchanged, then there's no change in output per worker. And if both natural resources and labor increase in such a way that natural resources per worker is unchanged, then there's no change in output per worker.

- More K/L → more output per worker
  But more K and more L, in such a way that K/L is unchanged → no change in output per worker

- More NR/L → more output per worker
  But more NR and more L, in such a way that NR/L is unchanged → no change in output per worker

Increases in Labor Force

Increases in the labor force will increase the amount of output. But increases in the labor force alone will not increase output per worker. What can increase the labor force?

- Higher labor force participation rate → more L
  An increase in the share of the population that is working will increase the labor force. Starting around 1960, married women in the United States increased their labor force participation rate, which increased the potential of the U.S. economy to produce output.
- Population growth → more L
  Population increases from two sources: natural population growth and immigration.
      Natural population growth refers to the balance of births and deaths. An increase in births or a decrease in deaths will increase population. The U.S. baby boom of 1946–1964 saw increased births and larger family size. The development and mass distribution of penicillin in the 1930s and 1940s lowered the death rate by increasing life expectancy, the average number of years people live. A higher natural population growth rate ultimately increases the labor force, with about a 20-year delay.
      Immigration refers to the entry into a nation of people born in a different nation. Economic conditions and immigration laws are important determinants of the pattern of immigration. More immigration increases the labor force.

Increases in Capital

Increases in capital will increase the amount of output. And increases in capital will increase the capital-labor ratio, which will increase output per worker and the standard of living. The quantity of capital is called the **capital stock**. Think of it as the existing usable quantity of machinery and buildings. What can increase the economy's capital stock?

- More purchases of equipment or construction of buildings → more K
  When businesses purchase more equipment, there is more physical capital. When more buildings are constructed, there is more physical capital. Economists call purchases of equipment and construction of buildings **investment**. So more investment yields more capital.
- Less depreciation of capital → more K
  Equipment wears out. Economists call the wearing out of equipment depreciation. The faster equipment wears out, the higher its **depreciation rate** is. The longer equipment lasts, the lower its depreciation rate is. So less depreciation means capital lasts longer, which increases the capital stock.

TIP

Remember: capital refers to machines or equipment, and buildings or structures. Capital does *not* mean "money." And investment refers to purchases of machines or construction of buildings. Investment does *not* mean "making money" on the stock market or elsewhere.

Increases in Natural Resources.

Natural resources refers to land, minerals, oil, and so on. Increases in natural resources will increase the amount of output. And increases in natural resources will increase natural resources per worker, which will increase output per worker and the standard of living. What can increase the economy's natural resources?

- Land Acquisition → More *NR*
  Countries can acquire land in a number of ways. Purchase and annexation are two ways. The United States increased its land holdings with the Louisiana Purchase in 1803 and with the Texas Annexation in 1845. War is another way a country can increase its land holdings. Colonization, however accomplished, is another. Land acquisition increases the quantity of natural resources available.

- Mining and Discoveries → More *NR*
  Natural resources are more than just land. Mining can increase the quantity of minerals. Discoveries of oil, for instance, can increase the available quantity of oil. Mining and discoveries increase a nation's natural resources.

To return to the key questions: Why do some economies grow quickly and others grow slowly? One answer: Because of how quickly their inputs are growing. Faster growth of inputs generates faster growth of output. Faster growth of the capital-labor ratio or the amount of natural resources per worker generates faster growth of output per worker, or the standard of living. Some economies grow faster than others because the quantities of their inputs are growing faster than others.

Why are some nations rich and others poor? One answer: Because of how many inputs they have. More inputs produce more output. More machines per worker or more natural resources per worker produce more output per worker. Some nations are richer than others because they have more inputs than others.

Higher Productivity

Inputs are just half of the story. The other half of the story is knowledge, or total factor productivity. Faster growth of knowledge leads to faster growth. More knowledge allows an economy to produce more output and more output per worker.

But what is included in knowledge? What is it that increases total factor productivity? The answer is at once frustrating and exhilarating. What increases TFP? Answer: Lots!

- *Education*. More educated workers are more productive. Literacy rates low? Teach reading to children, and the country's economy will ultimately grow.

Wondering why average incomes are higher in Minnesota than they are in Mississippi? Take a look at the educational attainment of the people. And it's not just liberal arts college educations that matter: high-quality technical training provides workers with high productivity. Economists use the phrase **human capital** to describe the amount of education and skills that individuals have. Increase educational attainment and improve the quality of educational institutions, and an economy will grow.

- *Research and Development*. Technological developments matter. Who can doubt that the advances in computer technology have transformed economies? Scientific research and development can enhance economic growth.

- *Financial Institutions*. Better financial institutions move funds from savers to borrowers more efficiently, and at lower cost. If businesses can't get loans to buy physical capital, the financial institutions may be at fault. Financial institutions must do a good job of assessing risk. Savers must trust the financial institutions before they will entrust them with their savings. Better, stronger, safer financial institutions generate more growth than weak, untrusted ones.

- *Transportation Networks*. Roads burdened with potholes? Highways narrow, or non-existent? Bridges falling down? Waterways impassable? Then it will be hard—and expensive—for goods to be transported from the least-cost producers to the most interested consumers. Quality transportation networks generate more growth than bad or missing ones.

- *Political Institutions*. A nation's political institutions—how its leaders are selected, what happens when power is transferred from one leader to the next, who controls the nation's purse strings, how the government's decisions are made—are important. Think of the extreme. If a new set of leaders in a country refuses to pay off their predecessors' debt, then few will be willing to lend to that country. If "friends" of the nation's leader can get private loans canceled, then few will be willing to lend to those friends. The more others can trust the stability, continuity, and fairness of a political system, the stronger the growth of that country.

- *Property Rights*. The laws that govern what you can do with property you own are called **property rights**. When property rights give owners confidence that the benefits of property improvements will indeed accrue to them, owners are more willing to make those improvements. When, instead, the property rights system states that some or all of the benefits of property improvement will accrue to others, owners are less willing to make improvements. The same is true of **intellectual property rights**, the laws that govern who owns the ideas and knowledge someone comes up with. A good property rights system can enhance economic growth.

- *Judicial System*. The judicial system enforces contracts. Contracts are agreements between two individuals or two parties. When you sign papers to take out a student loan, you have entered into a contract with the lender.

The lender is willing to lend you money in part because of faith the judicial system will enforce the contract—it will force you to pay or otherwise endure the consequences spelled out in the contract. A reliable judicial system that enforces contracts fairly and consistently can enhance economic growth.

These are all big-think things. And they all matter—a lot—to the pace of growth in economies. Improvements show up as an increase in "knowledge" or "total factor productivity" (TFP). But improvements are difficult, if not impossible, to measure. That is why the contributions of improvement in knowledge are calculated as the residual, as what's left over after the contributions of labor, capital, and natural resources have been accounted for.

Back to the key questions: Why do some economies grow quickly and others grow slowly? One answer was because of the pace at which their inputs are growing. The second answer: because of the pace at which knowledge or TFP grows. Faster growth of knowledge generates faster growth of output. Some economies grow faster than others because their knowledge, or total factor productivity, is growing faster than others.

Why are some nations rich and others poor? One answer was because of their quantity of inputs. The second answer: because of the nation's level of knowledge or total factor productivity (TFP). More and better education, research and development, financial institutions, transportation networks, political institutions, property rights laws, and judicial systems all can enhance a nation's standard of living.

TRY

9. What are the two primary causes of increases in output and in output per worker?
10. What can lead to an increase in the labor force (L)?
11. What can lead to an increase in the capital stock (K)?
12. What can lead to an increase in natural resources (NR)?
13. What can lead to an increase in total factor productivity (A)?

THE PRODUCTIVITY GROWTH SLOWDOWN AND RESURGENCE

One way of measuring productivity is to calculate labor productivity: output per worker. Wait, you say—isn't "output per worker" the way economists measure the standard of living? Yes, it is. The calculation of labor productivity—output per worker—is the same as the calculation of the standard of living. So the pace of change in labor productivity tells us a lot about the pace of change of the standard of living.

For this reason, economists keep an eye on the economy's labor productivity growth rate. How much is labor productivity rising? Notice that the question is *not*: Is productivity rising? Almost always, the answer to that question is yes.

Rather, by how *much* is labor productivity rising? Remember that the Rule of 70 tells us that small changes in the annual growth rate can have a big effect on the number of years it takes for labor productivity to double. Labor productivity rising at 1.5% per year means that labor productivity (and the standard of living) will double in 47 years. One percentage point more—a labor productivity growth rate of 2.5%—makes labor productivity (and the standard of living) double in 28 years. Twenty years is considered to be a generation. So a difference of 1 percentage point—between 1.5 and 2.5%—means that the standard of living doubles one generation faster.

Small changes in the labor productivity growth rate can have big effects. So when labor productivity growth in the United States slowed down, economists were understandably concerned. As Figure 5.2 shows, the average U.S. labor productivity growth rate from 1950 to 1972 was 2.8%. Starting in the mid-1970s, labor productivity grew more slowly. From 1973 to 1995, the average labor productivity growth rate was only 1.5%. Economists call this drop in the labor productivity growth rate the **productivity growth slowdown**.

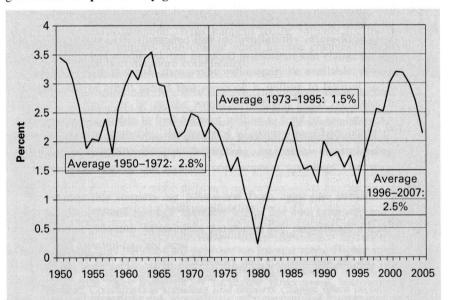

Figure 5.2 Labor Productivity Growth.

The U.S. labor productivity growth rate averaged 2.8% between 1950 and 1972. Labor productivity growth then slowed down to an average of 1.5% between 1973 and 1995. A resurgence in labor productivity growth began in the mid-1990s. Labor productivity grew 2.5% on average between 1996 and 2007. Because year-to-year changes in labor productivity growth can be quite volatile, the figure presents a 5-year centered moving average. The value plotted for each year is the average for the 5 years centered on that year: 2 years before, the year itself, and 2 years after.

Economists never came to consensus regarding what caused the productivity growth slowdown. Many theories were offered, but no one theory was widely accepted.

Things turned around in the mid-1990s. From 1996 to 2007, labor productivity grew at an average annual rate of 2.5%. This period is called the **productivity growth resurgence**, because productivity growth surged to close to its previous level. Many economists attribute the productivity growth resurgence to information technology—both the increased use of computers in the workplace and the increased power of those computers.

What the future holds is anyone's guess. As you can see from Figure 5.2, the productivity growth resurgence peaked early in this century's first decade, the 2000s. We may be headed back to a slow growth regime, or growth may surge again. What happens matters, because growth in labor productivity translates directly to growth in the standard of living. Will your children be better off than you? The answer rests heavily on what happens to labor productivity growth.

TRY

14. During the productivity growth slowdown, was productivity falling?

15. Is there one widely accepted explanation for the productivity growth slowdown? How about for the productivity growth resurgence? If so, what is the explanation?

PART III

Keynesian Principles

Chapter 6

Keynesian Cross

Most of macroeconomics focuses on the short run—on quarter-to-quarter and year-to-year changes in output and employment. How much output the aggregate economy produces in any year depends upon how much output all of the buyers want to buy. In the language of economists: in the short run, real GDP depends upon aggregate demand.

KEY TERMS AND CONCEPTS

- Aggregate spending
- Aggregate demand
- Planned aggregate expenditure
- Aggregate expenditure
- Inventory accumulation
- Inventory depletion
- Macroeconomic equilibrium
- Circular flow diagram
- Keynesian cross diagram
- 45° line
- Net taxes
- Disposable income
- Personal saving

KEY EQUATIONS

- Macroeconomic equilibrium exists when Y and real GDP $= AD$
- $AD = C + I + G + NX$
- $T = TA - TR$
- $YD = Y + TR - TA = Y - T$

KEY GRAPHS

- Circular flow diagram
- Keynesian cross

UNEMPLOYMENT DEPENDS ON AGGREGATE SPENDING

The key question in macroeconomics is "In the short run, what determines the amount of unemployment?" Remember from Chapter 4: John Maynard Keynes said (essentially) that the amount of unemployment in an economy is determined by the amount of employment, which is determined by the amount of output that the economy is producing, which is determined by aggregate (or, total) spending. Or, in short,

> Aggregate spending determines
> output, which determines
> employment, which determines
> unemployment.

Let's look at these various relationships, starting from the bottom and working up.

Employment and Unemployment

Employment is the number of people who have jobs. Unemployment is the number of people who don't have jobs but are looking for a job. The labor force is the term used to refer to both the employed and the unemployed.

The link between employment and unemployment is usually quite strong. When employment is down, unemployment is up. People in the labor force move out of the "employment" category and into the "unemployment" category. When employment is up, unemployment is down. Employment and unemployment almost always move in opposite directions.

There are exceptions. Some people who lose their jobs retire. And other people who lose their jobs emigrate from the country. When someone loses his or her job and doesn't look for another job in the same country, that person moves from being employed to being out of the labor force. In this case, employment is down, but unemployment does not rise. However, this is the exception, not the rule. Usually, the link is strong between employment and unemployment.

TRY   *(Answers to all "TRY" questions are at the back of the book.)*

1. When employment falls, what usually happens to unemployment?

2. What is one reason that a drop in employment sometimes does *not* have the effect you predicted in your answer to question 1?

Output and Employment

Output is the total amount of goods and services produced in an economy in a year. Output is measured as real gross domestic product, or real GDP. Employment is the number of people who have jobs.

The link between real GDP and employment is usually quite strong. In order to produce more output, more people are employed. When less output is produced, fewer people are needed and so fewer people are employed. Output and employment almost always rise and fall together.

There are exceptions. Sometimes more output is produced with no change in employment, because existing workers are asked to work harder or faster or longer hours. And sometimes less output is produced with no change in employment, because firms maintain their workforce even in the face of declining production, at least for awhile. These occasions are the exception, not the rule. Usually the link is strong between output and employment.

TRY

3. When output falls, what usually happens to employment?

4. What is one reason that a drop in output sometimes does *not* have the effect you predicted in your answer to question 3?

Aggregate Spending and Output

Total demand for output in a year is called **aggregate spending**, **aggregate demand**, **planned aggregate expenditure**, or, sometimes, **aggregate expenditure**. Some textbooks use one term; some use another. Regardless of which term your textbook uses, the meaning is the total, for one year, of planned spending for goods and services by households, businesses, governments, and the rest of the world.

Aggregate spending and output rise or fall together. When aggregate spending rises, more output is produced. When aggregate spending falls, less output is produced.

There are exceptions. Sometimes firms will only change prices, rather than changing output, when aggregate spending changes. But that is the exception, not the rule. Usually the link between aggregate spending and output is very strong.

TRY

5. When aggregate spending falls, what usually happens to output?

6. What is one reason that a drop in aggregate spending sometimes does *not* have the effect you predicted in your answer to question 5?

Putting these three links together, we have the essence of the Keynesian story. When aggregate spending changes, output changes. When output changes, employment changes. When employment changes, unemployment changes. Put it all together: a change in aggregate spending ultimately changes unemployment.

AGGREGATE DEMAND AND AGGREGATE EXPENDITURES: AN IMPORTANT NOTE

Confusion alert. There are several terms that some textbooks use interchangeably but that others don't. So far we have used the term "aggregate spending." But is that the same as "aggregate demand"? As "aggregate expenditures"? As "planned aggregate expenditures"? So far we have been deliberately vague, and have just used "aggregate spending," because there is no common terminology shared by all macroeconomics textbooks.

Two terms in particular are interchangeable. Some books use one; some use another. Both have the same meaning. Those interchangeable terms are "planned aggregate expenditures" and "aggregate expenditures." We will use (planned) aggregate expenditures when we mean either "aggregate expenditures" or "planned aggregate expenditures."

The term "aggregate demand" is, in some textbooks, a synonym for planned aggregate expenditures. In other books, aggregate demand and (planned) aggregate expenditures have two different meanings.

What is the distinction—when there is one—between aggregate demand and (planned) aggregate expenditures? In those books that make a distinction, planned aggregate expenditures refers to total spending *at a specific level of prices or inflation*. When there is a change in the level of prices or inflation, then (for reasons that we explore in Chapter 14) there is a change in planned aggregate expenditures. So books that make the distinction use "aggregate demand" to refer to the entire set of combinations of prices (or inflation rates) and planned aggregate expenditure.

It is important that you know which approach your textbook uses. If you have the term "aggregate expenditures" or "planned aggregate expenditures," it is likely that your textbook is making the distinction. "Aggregate expenditures" or "planned aggregate expenditures" will refer to aggregate spending at a specific level of prices or inflation. "Aggregate demand" will refer to the combinations of prices (or inflation) and planned aggregate expenditures.

Other textbooks use the term "aggregate demand" from the beginning and do not make a distinction between planned aggregate expenditures and aggregate demand. In conversation, most economists use the term "aggregate demand" to mean aggregate spending for output in a year.

In this book, we wait until Chapter 14 to make the distinction between (planned) aggregate expenditures and aggregate demand. Until then, the phrases are used interchangeably.

Because the terminology can be confusing, we will return to this point again in subsequent chapters.

THE LINK BETWEEN OUTPUT AND AGGREGATE DEMAND

Why does output rise when aggregate demand rises? Why does output fall when aggregate demand falls? The answer is based on how businesses react to an unexpected change in their inventory holdings.

Inventory is the word for output that has been produced (that is, it exists) but that has not been sold. The value of goods in inventory is determined as of some date. For example, we could ask: what is the value of goods in inventory as of December 31, 2010?

If the total value of goods in inventory increases between two dates, economists say there has been **inventory accumulation**. Inventories build up or accumulate between two dates if more output is produced than is sold. The extra output is added to inventory.

If the total value of goods in inventory decreases between two dates, economists say there has been **inventory depletion**. Inventories are used up or depleted between two dates if less output is produced than is sold. The extra sales are made from goods that were already being held in inventory.

If total output (that is, real GDP) is more than aggregate demand, inventories accumulate. If total output is less than aggregate demand, inventories are depleted.

$$GDP > Aggregate\ Demand \rightarrow inventory\ accumulation$$
$$GDP < Aggregate\ Demand \rightarrow inventory\ depletion$$

Businesses produce output because someone wants to buy the output. If the goods they are producing are simply accumulating in inventory, then businesses are producing too much. When inventories accumulate, businesses will decrease how much they are producing. When businesses decrease how much they are producing, GDP falls.

On the other hand, if businesses are selling more goods than they are producing, their inventories are being depleted. When inventories are depleted, businesses will increase how much they are producing. When businesses increase how much they are producing, GDP rises.

$$Inventory\ accumulation \rightarrow decrease\ GDP$$
$$Inventory\ depletion \rightarrow increase\ GDP$$

When businesses produce the same amount of output as they sell, there is no inventory accumulation and no inventory depletion. The change in inventory holdings is zero. Economists call this **macroeconomic equilibrium**. Macro-economic equilibrium exists when output equals aggregate demand. That is the same thing as saying macroeconomic equilibrium exists when inventory change equals zero.

$$Macroeconomic\ equilibrium\ exists\ when\ GDP = AD$$

TIP

Notation for total planned spending varies. Some books use *AD* (aggregate demand). Others use *AE* (aggregate expenditure). Other books use *PAE* (planned aggregate expenditure).

An Example

Suppose aggregate demand in July is $1,000 billion and real GDP in July is also $1,000 billion. Then the macroeconomy is in equilibrium in July. There is no change in inventory holdings between June 30 and July 31. If businesses don't anticipate any change in aggregate demand, they have no incentive to change how much they are producing. Production of output in August will also be $1,000 billion.

What if aggregate demand in August is $800 billion? Then, in August, output of $1,000 billion will exceed aggregate demand of $800 billion. The extra output, valued at $200 billion, will accumulate in inventories. Economists say: there will be inventory accumulation equal to $200 billion.

Businesses will react to August's inventory accumulation by decreasing the amount of output they are producing. In September, output will be less than $1,000 billion. The drop in aggregate demand caused inventories to accumulate, which caused firms to reduce production. In short, the drop in aggregate demand caused a drop in GDP.

What if instead aggregate demand increases? Let's change our example. If output in August is $1,000 billion but aggregate demand is $1,100 billion (instead of $800 billion), then inventories will be depleted by $100 billion in August. Businesses will react to August's inventory depletion by increasing the amount of output they are producing. The increase in aggregate demand will cause an increase in GDP.

TRY

7. Suppose that in the first quarter of the year, real GDP is $3,000 billion and aggregate demand is $2,800 billion. Are inventories accumulating, or being depleted? What is the value of the change in inventory holdings? Will businesses produce $3 trillion worth of output in the second quarter of the year? Is $3 trillion the equilibrium level of output?

8. Suppose that in the first quarter of the year, real GDP is $3,000 billion and aggregate demand is $3,400 billion. Are inventories accumulating, or being depleted? What is the value of the change in inventory holdings? Will businesses produce $3 trillion worth of output in the second quarter of the year? Is $3 trillion the equilibrium level of output?

9. Suppose that in the first quarter of the year, real GDP is $3,000 billion and aggregate demand is $3,000 billion. Are inventories accumulating or being depleted? What is the value of the change in inventory holdings? Will businesses produce $3 trillion worth of output in the second quarter of the year? Is $3 trillion the equilibrium level of output?

CIRCULAR FLOW

Many principles textbooks contain a drawing that shows how the various parts of the macroeconomy are connected to each other. This drawing is called the **circular**

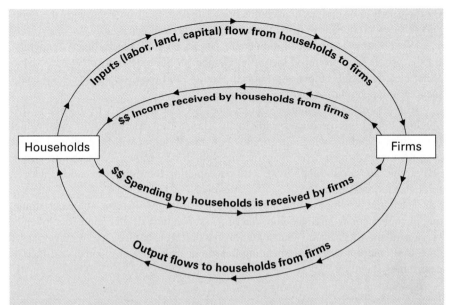

Figure 6.1 The Circular Flow Diagram.
The circular flow diagram shows the flow of economic activity and of money through the economy. Households sell inputs to firms (the top arrow) in exchange for income (the second arrow). Firms use those inputs to produce output that is sold to households (the bottom arrow) whose payments constitute the revenue received by firms (the third arrow).

flow diagram. The diagrams can be quite complicated and can vary from textbook to textbook.

No matter how complicated it looks, the circular flow diagram can be thought of as showing the connections between three concepts: output, income, and aggregate spending. Figure 6.1 shows a very simple circular flow diagram.

"Output" refers to the goods and services produced by firms. "Inputs" refers to the resources—labor, land, capital—used to produce output. "Income" refers to the money earned by those who produce output. Income consists of wages to workers, rents to landlords, interest to lenders, and profits to business owners. "Spending" refers to aggregate spending or expenditure, or total purchases of goods and services by all groups in the economy: households, businesses, government agencies, and the rest of the world.

Output is produced by firms with inputs they purchase from households. Households receive money—income—from firms in payment for the inputs. The income households receive is spent to purchase the output produced by the firms.

To decipher the diagram in Figure 6.1, start at the top. The top arrow indicates that households provide inputs to firms. The second arrow indicates that money flows from firms to households to pay for those inputs. The third arrow indicates that money also flows in the reverse direction—from households to firms—to pay for the goods and services households buy. The bottom arrow represents the goods and services produced by firms that are sold to households.

When output is produced, inputs are purchased and thus income is generated for the people who produced the output. When people receive income, they spend. When people spend, output is produced. And around the inner circle we go again: income → spending → income → spending . . .

It is a circle, rather than a straight line, because one leads to the other without end. Output is produced with inputs, input use determines income, which determines spending, which determines how much output will be produced, which requires inputs, which determines income, which determines . . . As you go around and around and around the circle, you are depicting the flow of economic activity through the macroeconomy.

The point of the circular flow diagram is simply that spending determines output and income, and income determines spending. If the more complicated version of the diagram in your textbook has left you baffled, try to stay focused on this simple but key idea: spending determines output and income, and income determines spending.

TRY

10. In the circular flow diagram, what are the roles of households? Of firms? What are the connections between households and firms?

OUTPUT EQUALS INCOME

Output refers to the goods and services produced: the textbook, the desk, the hour of tutoring, the shirt you're wearing, the pen in your hand. Income refers to the money earned when those goods and services were produced: the wages of the book seller, the earnings of the desk manufacturer, the payments received by the tutor, the profits of the stores that sold you the shirt and the pen.

In any year, the total value of output exactly equals the total value of income. Real GDP is our measure of the total value of output. Economists use the notation Y to stand for total value of income.

TIP

Why Y as the notation for income? Probably because I, N, C, O, M, and E are used for other purposes, and when you pronounce Y it sounds somewhat close to I.

It is more important to remember that output equals income than to remember why it does. But, since you asked: total income includes the profit or loss of the companies that produced the output. A company's profit or loss is equal to the value of the goods it sells (the value of output) minus its payments to its workers, landlord, lenders, and so on. Total profit or loss thus equals the difference between the value of output and the incomes of everyone other than the companies. Thus total income—the sum of profit or loss and the incomes of everyone other than the companies—must equal the total value of output.

The values are the same, but the concepts are different. When economists say, "Income equals output," they mean the *value* of income (*Y*) always equals the *value* of output (real GDP). Income is what we earn for producing goods and services. Income is money in our pocket. Output is the goods and services themselves. Output is the book, the desk, the tutoring, the shirt, the pen.

TRY

11. For each item in the list below: is it output, or income?

    a. doctor's appointment
    b. interest income earned on savings account
    c. missile
    d. a physician's annual salary
    e. rent received by the landlord
    f. restaurant meal
    g. a sales clerk's hourly wages
    h. shelter provided by an apartment
    i. soybeans
    j. textbook
    k. tip received by a waitress

MACROECONOMIC EQUILIBRIUM WITH EQUATIONS

In macroeconomic equilibrium, output equals aggregate demand. Output (real GDP) always equals income (*Y*). So economists also say: in macroeconomic equilibrium, income equals aggregate demand. As an equation:

In macroeconomic equilibrium, real GDP = AD and Y = AD

It is common to solve for macro equilibrium algebraically. Some textbooks start with a very simple relationship and gradually complicate it. We'll take that approach here.

Aggregate demand is the total demand for final goods and services by households, businesses, government agencies, and the rest of the world. When income rises, aggregate demand rises. When income falls, aggregate demand falls. One way to express this relationship is

Aggregate demand = <a constant> + <another constant> · Income

Every textbook uses different notation to refer to these constants. We will use $AD = \alpha + \beta \cdot Y$.

TIP

Notation for the constant terms α and β varies from textbook to textbook.

In macroeconomic equilibrium, real GDP $= AD$ and $Y = AD$. In general, then,

In macro equilibrium, $Y = AD = \alpha + \beta \cdot Y$.

Simplifying this equation, we have

In macro equilibrium, $Y = \alpha + \beta \cdot Y$

This is one equation, with one unknown and two constants.

Equation: $Y = \alpha + \beta \cdot Y$

Unknown: Y

Constants: α, β

Because this is one equation with one unknown, we can use algebra to solve for the value of Y.

In macro equilibrium, $Y = \alpha + \beta \cdot Y$	
subtract $\beta \cdot Y$ from both sides	$Y - \beta \cdot Y = \alpha$
remember $Y = 1 \cdot Y$	$1 \cdot Y - \beta \cdot Y = \alpha$
factor out Y	$(1 - \beta) \cdot Y = \alpha$
divide both sides by $(1 - \beta)$	$Y = \alpha/(1 - \beta)$

In macroeconomic equilibrium, the value of output and income, Y, will equal α divided by $(1 - \beta)$.

A specific example often helps. Suppose $\alpha = 100$ and $\beta = 0.75$. Then the aggregate demand equation is

$$AD = 100 + 0.75Y$$

In macroeconomic equilibrium, $Y = AD$. Again, we can use algebra to solve for the equilibrium value of Y.

In macro equilibrium, $Y = 100 + 0.75Y$	
subtract 0.75Y from both sides	$Y - 0.75Y = 100$
factor out Y (remember $Y = 1 \cdot Y$)	$(1 - 0.75)Y = 100$
divide both sides by $(1 - 0.75)$	$Y = 100/(1 - 0.75)$
simplify	$Y = 100/0.25$
simplify again	$Y = 400$

In macroeconomic equilibrium in an economy in which $AD = 100 + 0.75Y$, real GDP and Y will equal 400.

We can check the answer. When output and income equal 400, AD will equal $100 + 0.75(400) = 100 + 300 = 400$. This is equilibrium! Output and AD both equal 400.

TIP

It is common but confusing to omit the time period when computing equilibrium output. When we say "equilibrium output equals 400," we mean "in equilibrium, the amount of output produced is 400 *per some time period*." If aggregate demand is $100 + 0.75Y$ *per year*, then equilibrium output is 400 *per year*.

TRY

12. When the macroeconomy is in equilibrium, what condition is satisfied?

13. Suppose $AD = 300 + 0.8Y$.

   a. If $Y = 1,000$, what is the value of AD? Is 1,000 the equilibrium value of output?

   b. If $Y = 3,000$, what is the value of AD? Is 3,000 the equilibrium value of output?

14. Suppose $AD = 300 + 0.8Y$. What is the equilibrium value of output?

KEYNESIAN CROSS DIAGRAM

The determination of macroeconomic equilibrium is often shown with a graph. Because it is based on the work of John Maynard Keynes, the diagram is "Keynesian" (pronounced CAIN-zee-uhn). Because a key feature of the graph is two lines that cross, the diagram is called the **Keynesian cross diagram**.

The diagram in Figure 6.2 shows the determination of the equilibrium amount of output in a macroeconomy. Output and income are always equal. Output and income are measured on the horizontal axis. Aggregate demand is measured on the vertical axis. The macroeconomy is in equilibrium when output and income equal aggregate demand.

Aggregate demand usually increases as income increases. So we draw an upward-sloping line to show how aggregate demand depends on income. In Figure 6.2, that line is labeled AD.

Macroeconomic equilibrium occurs when real GDP and income equal aggregate demand. That means we are looking for the one point on the AD line that is the same distance from both the horizontal and vertical axes. How do we find that point?

A tedious method is to dig out a ruler and measure. An easier method is to draw a line that contains all the points that are the same distance from the horizontal and vertical axes. That line will have a slope of 1. Economists call it the **45° line** because a line with a slope of 1 carves out a 45° angle at the origin.

The point where the AD line crosses the 45° line is called the intersection point. The intersection point is the point of macroeconomic equilibrium. It is on the AD line, and it is the same distance from both axes. At the intersection point, output and income equal aggregate demand.

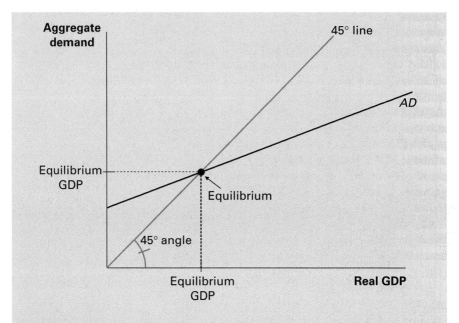

Figure 6.2 Keynesian Cross Diagram.

The Keynesian cross diagram is used to find the value of equilibrium GDP once we know aggregate demand. Aggregate demand increases as real GDP increases, which is shown with the upward-sloping line labeled AD. The 45° line shows all the points that are the same distance from both axes—all the points, that is, where aggregate demand equals real GDP. Equilibrium occurs when aggregate demand equals real GDP. So the equilibrium point on the AD line is the point where the AD line and the 45° line intersect.

Figure 6.3 draws the Keynesian Cross diagram for a specific example. As above, assume $AD = 100 + 0.75Y$. The AD line starts from 100 on the vertical axis and rises with a slope of 0.75. The 45° line starts from the origin and shows all the points where real GDP = aggregate demand. The two lines intersect when GDP and AD equal 400.

The Keynesian cross diagram is also sometimes used to show what happens when the macroeconomy is not in equilibrium. In Figure 6.4, output is less than aggregate demand, and there is inventory depletion. The amount of inventory depletion is the difference between output and aggregate demand. Businesses will react to the inventory depletion by increasing the amount of output they are producing, moving the economy toward macroeconomic equilibrium.

In Figure 6.5, output is more than aggregate demand, and there is inventory accumulation. The amount of inventory accumulation is the difference between output and aggregate demand. Businesses will react to the inventory accumulation by decreasing the amount of output they are producing, moving the economy toward macroeconomic equilibrium.

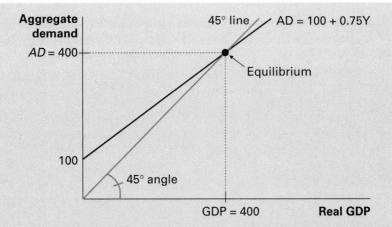

Figure 6.3 Finding Macroeconomic Equilibrium.

This graph shows a specific example. Suppose aggregate demand (AD) equals $100 + 0.75Y$. The relationship between AD and Y is depicted with a straight line that intersects the vertical axis at 100 and rises with a slope of 0.75. The equilibrium value of output and income occurs when the AD line crosses the $45°$ line. Here, equilibrium equals 400. In an economy with $AD = 100 + 0.75Y$ per year, equilibrium output is 400 per year.

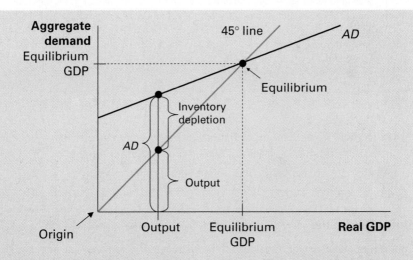

Figure 6.4 Inventory Depletion When Output Is Too Low.

When output is below equilibrium, aggregate demand exceeds output, so inventories are depleted. The amount of aggregate demand is determined by the height of the AD line at the level of output. The amount of output is the horizontal distance from the origin to "Output," which is equal to the distance from the horizontal axis to the $45°$ line at the level of output. The difference between the $45°$ line and the AD line is the amount of inventory depletion at the level of output.

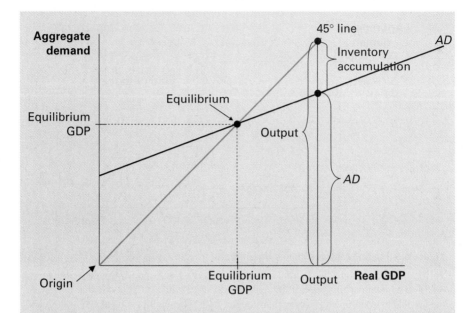

Figure 6.5 Inventory Accumulation When Output Is Too High.

When output is above equilibrium, output exceeds aggregate demand, so inventories accumulate. The amount of aggregate demand is determined by the height of the *AD* line at the level of output. The amount of output is the horizontal distance from the origin to "Output," which is equal to the distance from the horizontal axis to the 45° line at the level of output. The difference between the 45° line and the *AD* line is the amount of inventory accumulation at the level of output.

TRY

15. Draw a Keynesian cross diagram using the aggregate demand equation $AD = 300 + 0.8Y$. Mark the value of equilibrium output.

16. Why do we use a 45° line to find equilibrium output?

Shift of *AD* Line

Equilibrium GDP is the level of GDP where GDP $= AD$. What happens to the equilibrium level of GDP if *AD* changes? Then equilibrium GDP changes, too.

When *AD* increases, at every level of real GDP there is a higher level of aggregate demand. We show an increase in *AD* as an upward shift of the *AD* line. The old *AD* line in a sense ceases to exist. The old *AD* line tells us about the relationship between aggregate demand and real GDP that existed before. But it no longer tells us about the relationship between aggregate demand and real GDP that exists now.

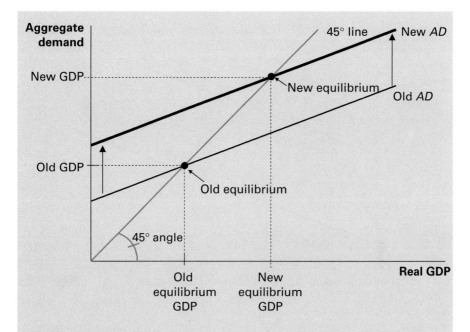

Figure 6.6 GDP Increases when *AD* Increases.

An increase in aggregate demand is shown as a shift up of the *AD* line. When *AD* increases, equilibrium real output increases as well.

When the *AD* line shifts up—that is, when aggregate demand increases—the previous equilibrium level of GDP is no longer equilibrium. The new higher value of *AD* is greater than the old values of *AD* and equilibrium GDP. At the old equilibrium GDP, there is now inventory depletion. Firms will increase the amount of output they are producing. Equilibrium GDP will rise until once again GDP equals *AD*. An increase in GDP is shown in Figure 6.6.

Algebraically, an increase in aggregate demand is shown as an increase in the constant term α. The old value of *AD* was $AD = 100 + 0.75Y$. An increase in *AD* would raise *AD* to something like $AD = 120 + 0.75Y$. The constant term—the vertical intercept—increases, but the slope remains the same. The equilibrium output rises in this example from 400 to 480 per year.

In Figure 6.7, we see a decrease in *AD*. When *AD* decreases, at every level of real GDP there is a lower level of aggregate demand. The *AD* line shifts down. When *AD* decreases, the previous equilibrium level of GDP is no longer equilibrium. The new lower value of *AD* is less than the old values of *AD* and equilibrium GDP. At the old equilibrium GDP, there is now inventory accumulation. Firms will decrease the amount of output they are producing. Equilibrium GDP will fall until once again GDP equals *AD*.

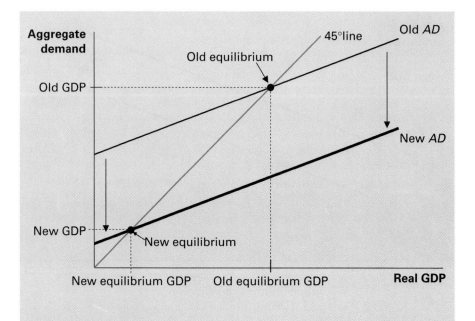

Figure 6.7 GDP Decreases when *AD* Decreases.
A decrease in aggregate demand is shown as a shift down of the *AD* line. When *AD* decreases, equilibrium real output decreases as well.

A BIT OF ACCOUNTING

The Bureau of Economic Analysis (www.bea.gov) of the U.S. Department of Commerce is responsible for estimating the value of GDP. There are many more concepts than just output and income, related in very specific ways. In fact, there is an entire system of accounts, called the National Income and Product Accounts, that is maintained by the Bureau of Economic Analysis. Some instructors require students to learn some of the detail of the NIPA.

But for understanding the essence of macroeconomics, only a few of the accounting identities are important.

- GDP = Y
    Output (GDP) equals income (Y).

- *AD* (or *AE* or *PAE*) = $C + I + G + NX$
    Aggregate demand (or aggregate expenditure, or planned aggregate expenditure) equals the sum of consumption spending by households (C), investment spending by businesses (I), government purchases by federal, state, and local government agencies (G), and net exports (NX). Chapter 7

explores the determinants of each of these four components of aggregate demand.

- $T = TA - TR$

    Net taxes (T) equals taxes paid to the government (TA) minus transfer payments received from the government (TR). Taxes include any payment to the government: income, sales, property, excise taxes, as well as government charges given different names such as "user fee" or "vehicle license fee." Transfer payments include payments we receive from the government for which no good or service is provided to the government in exchange. Examples include Social Security, unemployment benefits, Temporary Assistance to Needy Families (TANF), Pell Grants, and more.

- $YD = Y - T = Y + TR - TA$

    Disposable income (YD) equals income (Y) minus net taxes (T). Our disposable income—the income that is available to us to spend—is the money we receive from producing goods and services (Y) plus any transfer payments we receive (TR) minus any taxes we pay (TA) to the government.

TIP

Notation varies. For disposable income, your book may use YD or Yd or Y_D or Y_d or DPI or DI. There is no standard notation.

- $YD - C = S$

    Disposable income (YD) minus consumption (C) equals **personal saving** (S).

TIP

Yet again, notation varies. The usual notation for personal saving is S, but some books use PS.

TRY

17. Suppose $Y = 10,000$, $TR = 3,000$, and $TA = 4,000$. What is the value of net taxes, T? What is the value of disposable income, YD?

18. Suppose that in an economy in 2008, $Y = \$5,000$ billion per year, $T = \$2,000$ billion per year, and $C = \$2,500$ billion per year. What was the annual value of disposable income, YD? What was the annual value of personal saving, S?

Chapter 7

Aggregate Demand

$\mathbf{T}$he macroeconomy is in equilibrium when output equals aggregate demand. That was the message of Chapter 6. Aggregate demand is the total (aggregate) of spending (demand) for final goods and services. Four types of spending make up aggregate demand: consumption spending by households, investment spending by businesses, government spending by government agencies, and net spending for our exports by the rest of the world. This chapter provides an overview of the U.S. economy and then sets out the determinants of each of these four components of aggregate demand.

KEY TERMS AND CONCEPTS

- Aggregate demand
- (Planned) aggregate expenditures
- Consumption spending
- Investment spending
- Fixed investment
- Producer durable goods
- Construction
- Government spending
- Government purchases of goods and services
- Government consumption expenditures and gross investment
- Net exports
- Exports
- Imports
- Final goods
- Intermediate goods
- Wealth
- Assets
- Liabilities
- Stock variable
- Flow variable
- Interest rates
- Availability of credit
- Consumer expectations

- Consumption function
- Saving function
- Marginal propensity to consume (MPC)
- Marginal propensity to save (MPS)
- Average propensity to consume (APC)
- Average propensity to save (APS)
- Saving rate
- Lump-sum taxes
- Proportional tax
- Capital
- Expected rate of return on capital
- Investment decision rule
- External finance
- Internal finance
- Investment demand curve
- Exchange rates
- Appreciation
- Rise of the dollar
- Depreciation
- Fall of the dollar

KEY EQUATIONS

- $AD = C + I + G + NX$
- $C = a + b \cdot YD$
- $YD = Y + TR - TA = Y - T$

KEY GRAPHS

- Consumption function
- Saving function
- Investment demand curve

AN OVERVIEW OF THE FOUR TYPES OF SPENDING

Output equals aggregate spending in short-run macroeconomic equilibrium. Aggregate spending is the sum of four types of spending in the macroeconomy: consumption, investment, government, and net export spending. In this section, we look at the composition of each type of spending and its contribution to total, or **aggregate demand**.

Aggregate Demand and Aggregate Expenditures: An Important Note, Again

It's time to review the confusion alert first offered in Chapter 6. Different textbooks use different terms for total spending. In all textbooks, total spending is the sum of consumption, investment, government, and net export spending. But in some textbooks, a distinction is made between "**(planned) aggregate expenditures**" and "aggregate demand," and in other textbooks, the distinction is not made.

For those textbooks that make a distinction, (planned) aggregate expenditures refers to the sum of consumption, investment, government, and net export spending *at a specific level of prices or inflation*. When prices or inflation change, aggregate expenditures change, too. And thus in some textbooks, aggregate demand then refers to the entire set of combinations of prices or inflation and (planned) aggregate expenditure. In this book, we don't introduce a distinction between aggregate demand and aggregate expenditures until Chapter 14.

Other textbooks do not make this distinction between (planned) aggregate expenditures and aggregate demand. In these other textbooks, the terms "(planned) aggregate expenditures" and "aggregate demand" are used interchangeably.

No matter what, aggregate spending—or aggregate demand, or (planned) aggregate expenditures—is the sum of consumption, investment, government, and net export spending. Because all three phrases refer to the same sum, we use the term "aggregate demand" in this chapter.

Consumption Spending

Consumption spending is spending by households for final goods and services. Goods are tangible things you can touch and include both durable goods and nondurable goods. Durable goods are goods that last, on average, 3 years or more: automobiles, furniture, household appliances, and so on. Nondurable goods are those that last, on average, less than 3 years: food, restaurant meals, clothing, shoes, gasoline, and so on. Services are intangibles—things that exist but can't be touched: housing, household operation, transportation, medical care, and so on.

Today, about 10% of consumption spending is for durable goods, about 30% is for nondurable goods, and about 60% is for services. That's quite a change from the mid-20th century. In 1950, about 16% of consumption spending was for durable goods, about 50% was for nondurable goods, and about 33% was for services. This change occurred steadily, decade-to-decade.

Investment Spending

Investment spending is spending by businesses—both corporations and unincorporated businesses—for three things: new equipment, construction, and changes in the value of inventory holding. Economists use the term **fixed investment** to refer to spending for equipment and on construction.

TIP

What year is a building included in GDP? What matters is when someone was employed building it. Construction of a structure built in the past was included in investment in the year it was constructed.

Equipment is also sometimes called **producer durable goods** and includes computers, industrial equipment, transportation equipment, and so on. **Construction** includes construction of both residential and nonresidential structures. Realtor fees from selling an existing building are also included in construction spending.

Today, about 45% of investment spending is for equipment, about 20% for nonresidential structures, and about 35% for residential structures. Change in inventory holding is typically less than 1% of total investment spending. This distribution of investment spending has not changed much over the last 60 years.

TIP

Confusion alert! The economist's definition of "investment spending" *does not* include purchases of stocks, bonds, or other financial assets. Investment spending is business spending for three things: new equipment, construction, and changes in the value of inventory holding. Period.

Government Spending

Government spending is purchases of goods and services by government agencies: federal, state, and local. Economists also sometimes use the phrase **government purchases of goods and services**. In one of the most confusing moves ever, the U.S. Bureau of Economic Analysis now officially calls government spending **government consumption expenditures and gross investment**, which seems to combine everything we've talked about in this chapter but actually doesn't. All three terms refer to the same thing: purchases of goods and services by government agencies.

Government spending combines purchases by federal agencies and by state and local agencies. Federal agencies represent between 35 and 40% of government spending. State and local agencies are the remaining 60–65%.

Government spending is divided into two categories: government consumption expenditures and government gross investment. Government consumption expenditures are purchases of goods and services that are not subsequently used to produce other goods and services: education, national defense, jurisprudence, and so on. Government gross investment refers to purchases of goods that are subsequently used by either the public or the private sector to produce other goods and services. Examples include structures, equipment and software, and military hardware.

Government spending does *not* include government expenditures for transfer payments. Transfer payments are spending by government for which the government receives no good or service in exchange. Common examples of transfer payments are Social Security benefits, TANF (Temporary Assistance to Needy Families), and Pell Grants.

Because there is no job directly created with the transfer payment, it is excluded from government spending. When your grandmother receives her Social Security check—a transfer payment from the government—she is not currently working for the government.

Net Exports

Net exports are the difference between **exports** and **imports**. Export spending is spending by people, businesses, and government agencies *outside* the United States for goods and services produced *within* the United States. Import spending is spending by people, businesses, and government agencies *inside* the United States for goods and services produced *outside* the United States.

Exports may be goods or services. Exports may be sold to consumers, businesses, or government agencies. The purchase can take place outside the United States or inside the United States. The key is that the goods and services are produced *inside* the United States but are purchased by a nonresident. Exports include a Ford car manufactured in the United States and sold in Mexico, as well as a restaurant meal purchased in New York City by a family visiting from Brazil.

Imports may also be goods or services. Imports may be sold to consumers, businesses, or government agencies within the United States. The purchase can take place inside the United States or outside the United States. The key is that the goods and services are produced *outside* the United States but are purchased by a U.S. resident. Imports include an Italian wine sold in New York City as well as a bus ticket sold in Rome to a family visiting from Illinois.

Export and import spending include spending for both **final goods** and **intermediate goods**. Economists use the phrase "final goods" to refer to goods that are being sold to the final consumer. "Intermediate goods" are goods that a business will use to produce a final good. Some final goods are assembled in the United States with parts manufactured abroad. The parts are intermediate goods. The purchase of those foreign-manufactured intermediate goods by an American manufacturer is recorded as an import of a good.

Today, about 50% of exports and 50% of imports are durable goods. About 20% of exports and 35% of imports are nondurable goods. And about 30% of exports and 15% of imports are services. The mix has changed since the mid-20th century; in 1950, about 40% of exports and 25% of imports were durable goods. About 40% of exports and over 50% of imports were nondurable goods. And about 20% of both exports and imports were services. We import far more cars than we did sixty years ago.

TRY   *(Answers to all "TRY" questions are at the back of the book.)*

1. For each of the four types of spending, what group does the spending?

2. What is a common error made when defining the word "investment"?

3. For each activity listed below, is it consumption, investment, government, export, or import spending? (In some cases, the activity is simultaneously two of these types of spending.)

    a. You pay for a doctor's appointment
    b. The government pays the salary of a doctor who works at a Veterans Administration hospital in Texas
    c. The U.S. Army buys a missile manufactured in Michigan
    d. The U.S. Army buys fruit grown in Chile

 e. You pay your monthly rent on your apartment
 f. Chase Bank buys new desks for its branch banks in New York
 g. You buy a shirt manufactured in India
 h. Canadian companies purchase fruit grown in the United States
 i. Your town's public library buys new books
 j. You buy a new book
 k. A law office buys new books for the company's corporate library

The Distribution of Total Spending

Aggregate demand is the sum of four types of spending: consumption spending, investment spending, government spending, and net exports. The usual notation is

$$AD = C + I + G + NX$$

The U.S. distribution of aggregate demand among these four components is shown in Figures 7.1 and 7.2. The charts begin in 1930, during the Great Depression, because earlier data are not available.

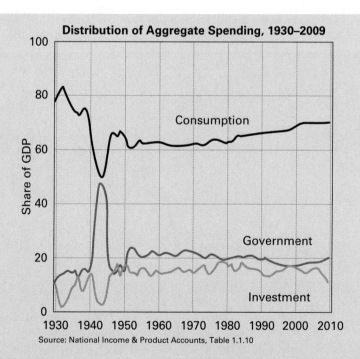

Figure 7.1 Consumption, Investment, and Government Spending as a Share of GDP, 1930–2009.

Consumption, investment, and government spending are shown as shares of total spending, which equals GDP. The volatility of the Great Depression and World War II were followed by 60 years of relative stability. The most notable feature of the last half-century is the rise in consumption spending as a share of total spending.

Remember from Figure 4.1 that GDP was generally growing after World War II. In Figures 7.1 and 7.2, we look at the mix of output. As output grew, did any component grow faster than the total, thus increasing its share? Did any component grow slower than the total, thus decreasing its share?

Consumption spending was a steady 62% of total spending for about three decades after World War II. Beginning in the early 1980s, consumption grew faster than total GDP. As a share of total spending, consumption began rising toward its current level of 70% of GDP.

Investment spending is the most volatile component of total spending. Its value fluctuates quite a bit over the course of a business cycle. Investment spending is typically about 15–18% of total spending, though its share falls in recessions.

Government spending for goods and services accounts for about 20% of total spending. Government spending is a relatively steady share of total spending after World War II.

A couple of historical notes: First, notice that government's share of spending does not rise much between 1933 (the beginning of the New Deal) and 1940. That's

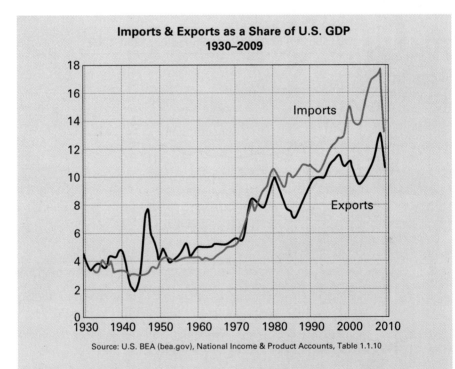

Imports & Exports as a Share of U.S. GDP 1930–2009

Source: U.S. BEA (bea.gov), National Income & Product Accounts, Table 1.1.10

Figure 7.2 Imports and Exports as a Share of GDP, 1930–2009.

Imports and exports are shown as a share of GDP. From 1950 until about 1980, exports and imports were roughly balanced. Starting in the early 1980s, imports as a share of GDP rose much more rapidly than exports. Net exports were thus negative beginning in the early 1980s.

because the New Deal was a largely legislative reform effort and did not involve a large amount of spending. Second, look at the 1940s. The enormous military effort, combined with mandatory rationing, shifted the nation's output mix from consumption to military goods.

Perhaps you've noticed that consumption, investment, and government spending together account for more than 100% of total spending. The solution to this apparent puzzle is in Figure 7.2.

Net export spending equals exports minus imports. When exports exceed imports, net exports are positive. But when imports exceed exports, net exports are negative. Figure 7.2 illustrates that the gap between imports and exports increased markedly after the mid-1970s. The post-1980 rise in consumption spending as a share of total spending goes roughly hand-in-hand with the fall in net exports. The worldwide nature of the Great Recession of 2007–2009 was reflected in a sharp drop in both exports and imports in 2009.

TRY

4. Consumption plus investment plus government spending as a share of total spending is more than 100%. But consumption, investment, and government are just three of the four components of total spending. How could their sum be more than 100% of the total?

5. Many people say the United States is a more open economy now than it was in the 1950s and 1960s. What data support this statement?

DETERMINANTS OF CONSUMPTION SPENDING

What determines consumption spending? Remember that we are thinking about total spending by all households, not just about how any one household behaves. What makes total consumption spending increase or decrease?

Consumption spending is believed to depend upon each of the following factors:

- *Disposable Income*: More disposable income, more consumption spending
- *Wealth*: More wealth, more consumption spending
- *Interest Rates (perhaps)*: Higher interest rates, less consumption spending (perhaps)
- *Availability of Credit*: Less availability of credit, less consumption spending
- *Expectations of the Future*: More optimistic expectations, more consumption spending

Let's examine each of these five determinants of consumption spending in turn.

Disposable Income

Disposable income *YD* is the sum of income we receive from producing goods and services *Y*, plus transfer payments we receive from the government *TR*, minus taxes and user fees that we pay to the government *TA*. Equivalently, *YD* is the difference between income *Y* and net taxes *T*, the taxes we pay *TA* minus the transfer payments we receive *TR*. So disposable income is

$$YD = Y + TR - TA = Y - T$$

TIP

There is no common notation for disposable income. Your textbook may use *YD*, *DI*, Y_d, *DPI*, Y_D, or some other notation.

When disposable income rises, people tend to spend more on goods and services. When disposable income falls, people tend to spend less on goods and services. One way to capture this idea is to write

$$\uparrow YD \ \rightarrow \ \uparrow C$$
$$\downarrow YD \ \rightarrow \ \downarrow C$$

Economists also say: disposable income and consumption are directly related, which means that they rise together and fall together.

TIP

If you are having a hard time understanding the concept "disposable income," then thinking "take-home pay" can be helpful. This is not strictly correct, because disposable income includes transfer payments and take-home pay does not. But it is more intuitive.

Wealth

Wealth is the difference between the value of what we own—our **assets**—and the value of what we owe—our **liabilities**.

Wealth = Assets − Liabilities

If you own a house that could sell for $240,000 and you owe $180,000 on the mortgage, the wealth you have in your home is $240,000 − $180,000 = $60,000. If your assets are worth $30,000 and you owe $40,000 on credit cards and student loans, then your wealth is negative: −$10,000.

For most Americans, their home is their largest single asset. Other assets owned by households include financial assets such as checking accounts, savings accounts, stocks, bonds, mutual funds, and retirement accounts, and real assets, which in addition to the house include items such as cars, furniture, and jewelry.

Wealth is not the same thing as income. Wealth is the value of what we own, and its value is determined as of a moment in time. Economists say wealth is a **stock variable** because its value is something that exists as of a moment in time—wealth as of January 1, 2010. Income is what we earn for producing goods and services, and its value is determined over time. Economists say income is a **flow variable** because its value exists over time—income per month—and does not exist as of a moment in time. When we save some of our income, our wealth increases. But the two concepts are very different: income is what we're paid for working; wealth is the total net value of the assets that we own.

The value of our wealth can go up because the assets we own increase in value, because we obtain more assets, or because we reduce our liabilities. If nearby houses just like yours start selling for $400,000 rather than $240,000, your house has increased in value, and you have more wealth. Or if you use part of your disposable income to buy shares of stock, you own more assets and have more wealth. Or, if you pay off an outstanding car loan, you have fewer liabilities and more wealth.

Conversely, the value of our wealth can go down because the assets we own decline in value, because we own fewer assets, or because our liabilities increase. If nearby houses just like yours start selling for $200,000 rather than $240,000, your house has declined in value, and you have less wealth. Or if you sell your house and spend the proceeds on college tuition, you own fewer assets and have less wealth. Or, if you charge a $3,000 trip to Europe to your credit card, you have less wealth.

When wealth rises, people tend to spend more buying goods and services. When wealth falls, people tend to spend less on goods and services. One way to capture this idea is to write

$$\uparrow Wealth \;\rightarrow\; \uparrow C$$

$$\downarrow Wealth \;\rightarrow\; \downarrow C$$

Economists also say: wealth and consumption are directly related, which means they rise together and fall together.

TRY

6. What is the difference between the concepts of "wealth" and "income"?

7. When disposable income falls, what happens to consumption spending? When wealth falls, what happens to consumption spending?

Interest Rates

Interest rates have a mixed effect on total consumption. That's because for some people, higher interest rates make them spend less. But for other people, higher interest rates lead them to spend more.

For borrowers, higher interest rates dissuade borrowing and spending. So for people who are borrowing in order to consume—car buyers, for instance—consumption spending declines when interest rates rise.

For savers, higher interest rates can lead to more spending. If you are saving in order to accumulate a certain nest egg—"I want to have $20,000 saved by my birthday 3 years from now so I can buy a condo"—then earning higher interest rates on your savings means you can save less each month (and spend more each month) and still accumulate $20,000 in three years.

The net effect of an increase in interest rates on total consumption spending depends on the mix of borrowers and savers in the economy. In recent years, the borrowers have dominated. So in recent years, interest rates and consumption spending have moved in opposite directions. Economists say: in recent years, interest rates and consumption have been inversely related.

Availability of Credit

The 2007–2009 episode illustrated that the **availability of credit** matters as well. If someone is a bad credit risk but financial institutions can charge an interest rate commensurate with that risk, then credit will usually be available. A restriction in the availability of credit means that someone is willing to borrow and is willing to pay the interest rate he or she would be charged based on his or her credit worthiness, but is unable to find a lender willing to lend *at any interest rate*.

A decrease in availability of credit, at prevailing interest rates, will decrease borrowing and decrease consumption spending. An increase in availability of credit will increase borrowing and increase consumption spending. One way to write this is

$$\downarrow Credit\ Availability\ \rightarrow\ \downarrow C$$

$$\uparrow Credit\ Availability\ \rightarrow\ \uparrow C$$

Economists also say: credit availability and consumption are directly related, which means that they rise together and fall together.

Expectations of the Future

How consumers feel about the future direction of the economy—in particular, how they feel about their own jobs and economic fortunes—impacts decisions made today about spending. When people start to worry that they are at risk of unemployment or a wage cut, economists say **consumer expectations** have worsened. When people start to feel optimistic about the future, expecting raises or better jobs, economists say consumer expectations have improved.

When consumer expectations worsen, consumers tend to cut back on spending. When consumer expectations improve, consumers tend to increase their spending. One way to capture this idea is to write

$$\downarrow Expectations \;\rightarrow\; \downarrow C$$

$$\uparrow Expectations \;\rightarrow\; \uparrow C$$

Economists also say: consumer expectations and consumption are directly related, which means that they rise together and fall together.

TRY

8. List the five factors that commonly affect consumption spending. For each, what change in that factor (increase or decrease) would cause consumption to rise?

9. If consumers each receive a $1,000 tax cut today, but are told that next year their taxes will rise by $1,000, what effect would this have on consumption spending? Why?

THE CONSUMPTION FUNCTION AND RELATED CONCEPTS

Macroeconomics is most often expressed with equations. Algebra is a key tool. So the next step in learning macroeconomics is to take this rich discussion of the determinants of consumption and condense it down into an equation that can be easily manipulated algebraically.

Some students think that what we are about to do makes macroeconomics unrealistic. The retort—not always useful—is "It's a model." A model airplane may be a helpful analogy here. No one would expect a 12-inch model airplane made of balsa wood to include all of the details found on a Boeing 757 airplane. Engineers who want the Boeing plane to take off, stay in the sky, and land safely have to think about details associated with the overhead bins and the bathrooms. But to get some of the basic ideas about planes and flight, the 12-inch model is a good place to start.

What we're about to do is similar. Consumption spending depends upon those five factors just discussed (and probably more). But to highlight some basic ideas about how the various parts of the macroeconomy work together, a stripped-down model is a good place to start.

The Consumption Function

Most changes in consumption spending over time are associated with changes in disposable income. Not all—just most. For this reason, and to make the math easier, principles textbooks focus on the relationship between consumption spending and disposable income. Economists say: the primary determinant of consumption spending is disposable income.

We capture this relationship between consumption spending C and disposable income YD with equations. The general form of the **consumption function**, in math language, is

$$C = f(YD)$$

The notation $f(\cdot)$ is read "is a function of," which is math language for "depends upon." So an economist reads $C = f(YD)$ as either "consumption is a function of disposable income" or "consumption depends upon disposable income."

TIP

If your textbook says $C = f(Y)$, keep reading. By the end of this section, we'll explain why some books talk about "disposable income" but others mention just "income" in connection with consumption spending.

The specific form of a consumption function that is easiest to work with mathematically is a linear consumption function. When graphed, a linear consumption function is a straight line. In general, a linear consumption function is an equation that looks like

$$C = \textit{<a constant>} + \textit{<another constant>} \cdot YD$$

or

$$C = a + b \cdot YD$$

For example,

$$C = 50 + 0.8 \cdot YD$$

is a consumption function. It says: for the economy as a whole, consumption spending (during some time period, like a month or a year) equals a constant amount 50 (in your mind, put a $ sign in front and some units on the back, such as $50 billion) plus eight-tenths times disposable income.

Table 7.1 uses this consumption function to calculate consumption spending in each period. The numbers are all made up. Economists say: it's a hypothetical example. In January, disposable income is $1,000 billion. So consumption spending in January is $50 + 0.8 \cdot (1,000) = 850$. Put a $ sign in front and units on the back: Consumption spending in January is $850 billion.

Table 7.1 Calculating Consumption Using a Consumption Function

	Disposable Income	Calculation	Consumption
January	$1,000 billion	$50 + 0.8 \cdot (1,000)$	$850 billion
February	$1,200 billion	$50 + 0.8 \cdot (1,200)$	$1,010 billion
March	$500 billion	$50 + 0.8 \cdot (500)$	$450 billion

When disposable income rises from \$1,000 to \$1,200 billion in February, consumption spending rises. When disposable income falls from \$1,200 to \$500 billion in March, consumption spending falls. Economists say: consumption spending and income move together

Figure 7.3 shows this consumption function. We graph consumption on the vertical axis and disposable income on the horizontal axis. The first constant, which is 50 in our example, is the vertical intercept. The second constant, 0.8 in our example, is the slope.

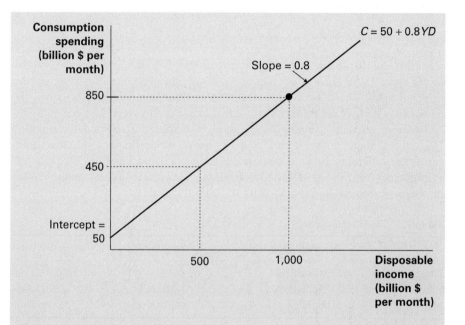

Figure 7.3 Consumption Function.

The consumption function shows the relationship between consumption spending by households and disposable income. The consumption function here is $C = 50 + 0.8YD$. The vertical intercept is \$50 billion. The slope is 0.8. When disposable income is \$1,000 billion per month, consumption spending is \$850 billion per month. When disposable income is \$500 billion per month, consumption spending is \$450 billion per month.

TRY

10. Suppose the consumption function is $C = 1000 + 0.75YD$. Assume the units are billions of \$ per quarter.

    a. If $YD = 2,000$ (that is, \$2 trillion per quarter), what is C?
    b. If instead $YD = 3,000$, what is C?

c. When disposable income increased by $1,000 billion per quarter, how much did consumption spending per quarter change?

d. Graph this consumption function. What is the value of the vertical intercept? What is the slope of the consumption function?

Saving

Personal saving is the amount of our disposable income that we *don't* spend on currently produced goods and services.

$$S = YD - C$$

We save whenever we spend less on *currently produced* goods and services than we receive in disposable income. One way to save is to accumulate assets—more in the checking or savings account, or in a retirement account, or in some other financial asset. The other way to save is to reduce our liabilities or debt—pay down what we owe on credit cards, student loans, car loans, and so on.

We can calculate saving once we know disposable income and consumption. Using the example above, with $C = 50 + 0.8YD$, we see in Table 7.2 that saving equals the difference between disposable income and consumption. When disposable income rises from $1,000 to $1,200 billion in February, saving increases. When disposable income falls from $1,200 to $500 billion in March, saving decreases.

Table 7.2   Calculating Saving

	Disposable Income	Consumption	Saving
January	$1,000 billion	$850 billion	$150 billion
February	$1,200 billion	$1,010 billion	$190 billion
March	$500 billion	$450 billion	$50 billion

We can determine the **saving function** and graph it. We know that saving equals disposable income minus consumption spending.

$$S = YD - C$$

In this case, our consumption function is $C = 50 + 0.8YD$. Substitute the consumption function into the saving function, and simplify.

$$S = YD - C = YD - (50 + 0.8YD)$$
$$S = YD - 50 - 0.8YD$$
$$S = -50 + 1YD - 0.8YD$$
$$S = -50 + (1 - 0.8)YD = -50 + 0.2YD$$

Figure 7.4 shows the saving function. We put saving on the vertical axis and disposable income on the horizontal axis. The first constant, -50 in our example, is the vertical intercept. The second constant, 0.2 in our example, is the slope. The values of saving given in Table 7.2 are shown in Figure 7.4.

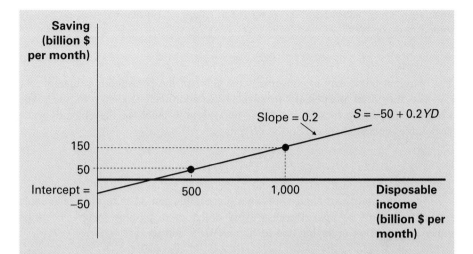

Figure 7.4 Saving Function.

The saving function shows the relationship between saving by households and disposable income. The saving function shown is $S = -50 + 0.2YD$. The vertical intercept is $-\$50$ billion. The slope is 0.2. When disposable income is $1,000 billion per month, saving is $150 billion per month. When disposable income is $500 billion per month, saving is $50 billion per month.

TRY

11. Suppose the consumption function is $C = 1,000 + 0.75YD$. Assume the units are billions of $ per quarter.
    a. If $YD = 2,000$ (that is, $2 trillion per quarter), what is S?
    b. If instead $YD = 3,000$, what is S?
    c. When disposable income increased by $1,000 billion per quarter, how much did saving per quarter change?

12. Graph this saving function. What is the value of the vertical intercept? What is the slope of the saving function?

13. Why is paying off debt considered "saving"?

Marginal and Average Propensities to Consume and Save

One important concept in thinking about consumption is what economists call the **marginal propensity to consume**. Marginal means additional. Propensity means tendency. So the marginal propensity to consume is the additional tendency to consume.

Specifically, the marginal propensity to consume tells us how much consumption changes when disposable income changes. Remember that economists use the uppercase Greek letter delta, Δ, to stand for "change." So the marginal propensity to consume, or MPC, is

$$MPC = \frac{\Delta C}{\Delta YD}$$

The marginal propensity to consume is the slope of the consumption function.

The **marginal propensity to save** is the additional tendency to save. The marginal propensity to save, or MPS, tells us how much saving changes when disposable income changes. So the MPS is

$$MPS = \frac{\Delta S}{\Delta YD}$$

The marginal propensity to save is the slope of the saving function.

There are only two choices of what households can do with their disposable income: consume or save. Because every dollar of disposable income becomes either consumption or saving, the MPC and MPS add up to 1.

$$MPC + MPS = \frac{\Delta C}{\Delta YD} + \frac{\Delta S}{\Delta YD} = \frac{\Delta C + \Delta S}{\Delta YD} = 1$$

The marginal propensities to consume and save tell us what consumers do with an *additional dollar* of disposable income. If the MPC is 0.8, or 80%, that means that 80% of each additional dollar of disposable income is consumed, and the remaining 20% saved. An MPC of 0.8 also tells us that for every dollar drop in disposable income, consumption spending will fall by 80 cents and saving will fall by 20 cents.

Sometimes we are interested instead in what *share* of disposable income is spent and what share is saved. This is the **average propensity to consume** and the **average propensity to save**. The average propensity to consume, or APC, tells us on average, what share or percent of disposable income is spent on consumer goods and services.

$$APC = \frac{C}{YD}$$

The average propensity to save, or *aps*, tells us on average, what share or percent of disposable income is saved. Economists refer to the *aps* as the personal saving rate, or simply the **saving rate**.

$$APS = saving\ rate = \frac{S}{YD}$$

TRY

14. Suppose the consumption function is $C = 1000 + 0.75YD$. (Assume the units are billions of $ per quarter.)

   a. What is the value of the MPC? Of the MPS?

   b. If $YD = 2000$ (that is, $2 trillion per quarter), what is the APC? The APS?

c. If instead $YD = 3000$, what is the *apc*? The *aps*?

d. As disposable income increases, the average propensity to consume decreases. Why?

Taxes or No Taxes, Disposable Income or Income

Disposable income equals income plus transfer payments minus taxes.

$$YD = Y + TR - TA$$

Most textbooks simplify by defining net taxes as the difference between taxes and transfer payments. Then disposable income is just income minus net taxes.

$$YD = Y - T$$

TIP

The two equations for YD say the same thing. Some books never mention transfer payments and simply state $YD = Y - T$.

Confusion alert! Some textbooks immediately allow for the existence of taxes. Other textbooks initially assume there is no government sector and no taxes, but then introduce the government sector and taxes a few chapters later.

Most principles books assume taxes are **lump-sum taxes**. A lump-sum tax is a constant amount that doesn't automatically change as income changes. Most real-world taxes are *not* lump-sum taxes. Another type of tax is a **proportional tax**, which is a proportion or percent of the tax base.

TIP

The algebra we do is easier with lump-sum taxes than with proportional taxes. Most introductory textbooks use lump-sum taxes. Most intermediate macro textbooks use proportional taxes.

What type of taxes we use impacts a number of things at this point. Table 7.3 summarizes.

Because most principles textbooks do not use proportional taxes, we will not look at proportional taxes again in this chapter. Those textbooks that assume that there are no taxes drop that assumption within a chapter or two, so we also won't look at a world with no taxes again. Going forward, then, we'll assume that taxes are lump-sum taxes, taxes of a constant amount that doesn't vary as income varies but that can be changed as a result of policy decisions.

Table 7.3   Effect of Assumption about Taxes

	No taxes	Lump-sum tax	Proportional tax
Tax equation	$T = 0$	$T = $ constant	$T = $ tax rate $\cdot Y = tY$
Example	$T = 0$	$T = 100$	$T = 0.2Y$
In words	There are no taxes	Taxes are a constant amount	Taxes are a constant proportion of income
Simplifying $YD = Y - T$	$YD = Y - 0 = Y$	$YD = Y - T$ Example: $YD = Y - 100$	$YD = Y - tY$ $= (1 - t)Y$ Example: $YD = Y - 0.2\,Y$ $= 0.8\,Y$
$MPC = \Delta C/\Delta YD$ $APC = C/YD$	$MPC = \Delta C/\Delta Y$ $APC = C/Y$	$MPC = \Delta C/\Delta YD$ $APC = C/YD$	$MPC = \Delta C/\Delta YD$ $APC = C/YD$
Graphing consumption function	C on vertical axis, Y on horizontal axis	C on vertical axis, YD on horizontal axis	C on vertical axis; YD on horizontal axis
Simplifying $C = a + bYD$	$C = a + bY$	$C = a + b(Y - T)$ $= a + bY - bT$ $= (a - bT) + bY$	$C = a + b(Y - tY)$ $= a + b(1 - t)Y$
Vertical intercept when graphing C versus Y	a	$a - bT$	a
Slope when graphing C versus Y	b	b	$b(1 - t)$

Shifts of the Consumption Function

In the beginning of this section, we set out five factors that are believed to affect consumption spending:

- Disposable Income
- Wealth
- Interest Rates (perhaps)
- Availability of Credit
- Expectations of the Future

The consumption function we use is:

$$C = a + b \cdot YD$$

A change in disposable income YD produces a change in consumption spending C that equals $b \cdot \Delta YD$.

When YD changes, $\Delta C = b \cdot \Delta YD$

It doesn't matter why disposable income changes. If income Y rises by 100, disposable income rises by 100, and so consumption rises by $b \cdot 100$. If net taxes fall by 100, disposable income rises by 100, and so consumption rises by $b \cdot 100$.

When any other factor changes—wealth, interest rates, availability of credit, expectations of the future, or, for that matter, anything else that affects consumption—its effect is captured by a change in the constant a. If wealth increases, interest rates fall, availability of credit increases, or expectations of the future improve, then the value of a increases. If wealth decreases, interest rates rise, availability of credit decreases, or expectations of the future worsen, then the value of a decreases.

We can show these effects graphically. When we are graphing consumption versus disposable income as in Figure 7.5a, a change in consumption due to a change in disposable income is shown as a *movement along* the consumption function. A change in consumption due to any other factor is shown as a *shift* of the consumption function.

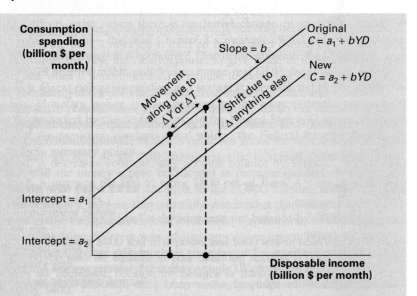

Figure 7.5a Shifts of the Consumption Function.

When consumption is graphed as a function of disposable income, the effect on consumption of a change in disposable income is shown by a movement along the consumption function. The effect on consumption of a change in any other factor is shown as a shift of the consumption function.

TIP

Remember the universal graphing rule. Is the independent variable on one of the axes? If the independent variable *is* measured on one of the axes and it changes, you *move along* an existing curve. If the independent variable is *not* measured on one of the axes and it changes, you *shift* a curve.

When we are graphing consumption versus income (not disposable income, just income), a change in consumption due to a change in disposable income that is itself due to a change in *income* is shown as a *movement along* the consumption function. A change in consumption due to a change in disposable income that is itself due to a change in *taxes* is shown as a *shift* of the consumption function. And, as before, a change in consumption due to any other factor is shown as a shift of the consumption function. Figure 7.5b illustrates.

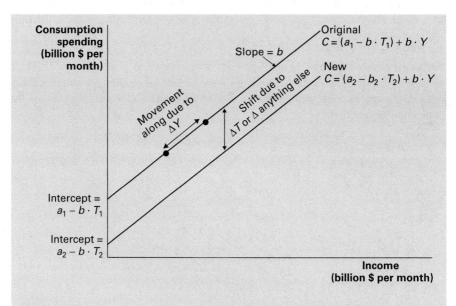

Figure 7.5b Shifts of the Consumption Function.

When consumption is graphed as a function of income, the effect on consumption of a change in disposable income *due to a change in income* is shown by a movement along the consumption function. The effect on consumption of a change in disposable income *due to a change in taxes* is shown by a shift of the consumption function. The effect on consumption of a change in any other factor is shown as a shift of the consumption function.

TRY

15. For each event below, consider how it would affect a graph of consumption as a function of income. Would the event be shown as a shift of the consumption function, or a movement along it? If it's a shift, does the consumption function shift up, or down? If it's a movement along, does the economy move along the consumption function to the left, or to the right?

   a. Consumers experience pay cuts
   b. Taxes are cut
   c. Stock prices fall

d. Interest rates rise
e. Credit availability is restricted
f. Consumer expectations turn optimistic
g. Consumers expect their pay to be cut next year, but so far there have been no pay cuts

DETERMINANTS OF INVESTMENT SPENDING

Investment spending is businesses' purchases of **capital**—new equipment and construction of structures. Remember that we are thinking about total spending by all businesses. What makes investment spending increase or decrease?

Investment spending is believed to depend upon the following factors:

- *Interest Rates*: Higher interest rates, less investment spending
- *Expected Revenue from Selling the Product Made with the Capital*: More expected revenue, more investment spending
- *Price of Capital*: Higher price of capital, less investment spending
- *Costs of Using the Capital*: More costly to use capital, less investment spending

That list of factors condenses down to just two. Investment spending depends upon interest rates and the **expected rate of return on capital**.

TIP

Remember: "capital" is buildings and machines. Do not think money when you hear "capital." Think of the physical assets that businesses use to produce goods and services.

Expected Rate of Return on Capital

The expected rate of return on capital is a number that compares the cost of buying the capital with the net gain in revenue from using the capital. It is expressed in percentage terms. The calculation of expected rate of return—when done correctly—is quite complicated. We leave that to the finance experts. We can think of it, though, in simple terms.

Mary's Clothing Shop is looking at a new display rack that costs $500. It is not well made, so at the end of one year it will need to be thrown away. The increase in revenue from buying and using the new rack is $575. The display rack is paid for out of that $575, leaving a gain of $75 for Mary's Clothing Shop. The expected rate of return from buying and using the display rack is $75/$500 = 15%.

Anything that changes the expected rate of return affects investment spending. Three factors affect the expected rate of return:

- *Expected Revenue from Selling the Product Made with the Capital*: More expected revenue, higher expected rate of return

- *Price of Capital*: Higher price of capital, lower expected rate of return
- *Costs of Using the Capital*: More costly to use capital, lower expected rate of return

Not coincidentally, those are the same factors we listed as affecting investment spending.

A profit-maximizing business compares its gain with its cost. Will buying the display rack increase profit? The answer comes from comparing the expected rate of return and interest rates. The gain is the increase in revenue from buying and using the capital. Its cost is the cost of borrowing money to buy the capital. If the gain is greater than the cost, buy the capital. If the gain is less than the cost, don't buy the capital.

The profit-maximizing business follows this rule:

> *If the expected rate of return > interest rate, buy the capital*
>
> *If the expected rate of return < interest rate, do not buy the capital*

Economists sometimes call this the **investment decision rule**.

Which Interest Rate?

When a business borrows money in order to purchase capital, economists say it is using **external finance**. The cost of using external finance is the interest rate the business pays to borrow money.

If Mary's Clothing Shop buys the display rack, it expects to earn $75, which is 15% of the $500 cost of the display rack. But if Mary's Clothing Shop must borrow at an interest rate of 18%, its cost is $90, which is 18% of $500. If Mary's Clothing Shop must borrow, it should not buy the display rack. The expected gain of 15% is less than the interest costs of 18%.

What if the business can just pay for the capital by writing a check? Economists say that a business using its own money has used **internal finance**. The cost of using internal finance is an opportunity cost. It is the forgone interest income the business could have earned.

Mary's Clothing Shop expects to earn 15% if it buys a $500 display rack. Mary's Clothing Shop can write a check to pay for the rack. The bank pays Mary's Clothing Shop interest of 3% on the checking account balance. The cost of using the $500 to buy the display rack is 3%, the forgone interest income. If Mary's Clothing Shop can write a check for the display rack, it should buy the rack. The expected gain of 15% is more than the forgone interest income of 3%.

TRY

16. What is the definition of "capital"?

17. Suppose the expected rate of return from buying and using a piece of equipment is 10%. Under what circumstances should a profit-maximizing business buy the equipment?

18. Suppose the interest rate charged on loans and received on savings is 4%. Which investment projects are profitable and should be undertaken?

Investment Demand Curve

At higher interest rates, fewer investment projects—construction or purchases of machinery—will have expected rates of return in excess of the higher interest rate. So at higher interest rates, businesses spend less on purchasing capital. Investment spending falls.

At lower interest rates, more investment projects—construction or purchases of machinery—will have expected rates of return in excess of the lower interest rate. So at lower interest rates, businesses spend more on purchasing capital. Investment spending rises.

TIP

Economists use the term "investment" to refer to purchases of physical capital. Do not get confused. "Investment" has nothing to do with stocks, bonds, or other financial assets.

The **investment demand curve** captures the relationship between interest rates and investment spending. Figure 7.6 is an investment demand curve. A change in interest rates *moves us along* an existing investment demand curve. As interest rates fall along the vertical axis, the amount of investment spending rises along the horizontal axis.

The investment demand curve *shifts* if there is a change in the expected rate of return on physical capital. When businesses become more optimistic about the future, they think their revenue will rise, which raises their expected rates of return. Lower cost of using the physical capital also raises the expected rate of return. And the lower cost of acquiring the capital raises the expected rate of return. Any increase in the expected rate of return shifts the entire investment demand curve to the right.

When businesses become pessimistic about the future, they think their revenue will fall, which lowers their expected rates of return. The higher cost of using the physical capital also lowers the expected rate of return. And the higher cost of acquiring the capital lowers the expected rate of return. Any decrease in the expected rate of return shifts the entire investment demand curve to the left.

TRY

19. For each event below, consider how it would affect a graph of investment demand. Would the event be shown as a shift along the investment

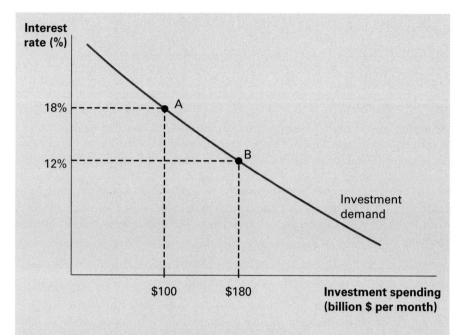

Figure 7.6 An Investment Demand Curve.

An investment demand curve shows how much money businesses will spend on physical capital—machines and buildings—at each interest rate. When interest rates change, we move along an existing investment demand curve. A rise in interest rates from 12 to 18% lowers investment spending from $180 billion to $100 billion per month. When expected rates of return on investment projects change, the entire investment demand curve shifts.

demand curve, or as a movement of it? If a shift, does the investment demand curve shift left, or right? If it's a movement along, does the economy move along the investment demand curve up and to the left, or down and to the right?

a. Interest rates rise
b. Businesses' expectations for future sales improve
c. The price of producer durable equipment falls

DETERMINANTS OF GOVERNMENT SPENDING

Government spending for goods and services can and does change. But the determinants of government spending are not something we focus on in macroeconomics. Instead, we say that government spending is exogenous, which means that its determinants are unrelated to the rest of macroeconomics.

The implication is that government spending G is a constant. It does not change systematically as income or interest rates or wealth change.

TIP

Some textbooks use the phrase "government purchases" rather than "government spending." The two terms are interchangeable.

DETERMINANTS OF NET EXPORT SPENDING

Net exports NX are the difference between exports EX and imports IM. Export spending EX depends primarily upon two factors: income abroad and exchange rates.

When income abroad rises, foreigners' spending rises, too. Some of the goods and services they purchase will be produced in the United States. So an increase in income abroad leads to an increase in U.S. exports. A decrease in income abroad leads to a decrease in U.S. exports. We can write this as

$$\uparrow Income\ abroad\ \rightarrow\ \uparrow EX$$

$$\downarrow Income\ abroad\ \rightarrow\ \downarrow EX$$

Exchange rates are the rate at which one currency exchanges for another. For instance, the exchange rate between the dollar and the euro tells us how many dollars it costs to buy 1 euro, and how many euros it costs to buy 1 dollar.

When the exchange rate changes so that it takes more foreign currency to buy dollars, then U.S. exports have become more expensive. Foreigners buy fewer U.S. goods and services, decreasing U.S. exports.

When the exchange rate changes so that it is less expensive to buy dollars, then U.S. exports are less expensive and foreigners buy more U.S. goods and services. U.S. exports rise. We can write this as

$$\uparrow Foreign\ price\ of\ \$1 \rightarrow\ \downarrow U.S.\ exports\ (EX)$$

$$\downarrow Foreign\ price\ of\ \$1 \rightarrow\ \uparrow U.S.\ exports\ (EX)$$

Import spending IM depends primarily upon two factors: income in the United States, and exchange rates. When income in the United States rises, U.S. spending rises, too. Some of the goods and services we purchase will be produced outside the United States. So an increase in income in the United States leads to an increase in U.S. imports. A decrease in income in the United States leads to a decrease in U.S. imports. We can write this as

$$\uparrow Income\ in\ the\ United\ States\ \rightarrow\ \uparrow IM$$

$$\downarrow Income\ in\ the\ United\ States\ \rightarrow\ \downarrow IM$$

When the exchange rate changes so that it takes more dollars to buy foreign currency, then imports are more expensive. We will buy fewer foreign goods and services, decreasing imports into the United States. When the exchange rate changes so that it is less expensive to buy foreign currency, then imports are less expensive and we buy more foreign goods and services. Imports into the United States rise.

$\uparrow$ *Dollar price of 1 unit of foreign currency* $\rightarrow$ $\downarrow$ *U.S. imports (IM)*

$\downarrow$ *Dollar price of 1 unit of foreign currency* $\rightarrow$ $\uparrow$ *U.S. imports (IM)*

Exchange rates impact both exports and imports. It is important to realize that the foreign price of $1 and the dollar price of 1 unit of foreign currency are the same ratio, just flipped over. An example clarifies.

If it costs 0.80 euros to buy 1 dollar, the euro price of $1 is €0.8. We could write that as a ratio:

$$euro \ for \ dollar \ exchange \ rate = \frac{0.80 \ euro}{1 \ dollar}$$

Flip that ratio over and then simplify so that the denominator—the bottom of the fraction—equals 1.

$$dollar \ for \ euro \ exchange \ rate = \frac{1 \ dollar}{0.80 \ euro} \times \frac{1.25}{1.25} = \frac{1.25 \ dollars}{1 \ euro}$$

It costs $1/0.8 = 1.25$ dollars to buy 1 euro.

Because the dollar for euro exchange rate is just the reciprocal of the euro for dollar exchange rate, a decrease in the dollar price of 1 euro is simultaneously an increase in the euro price of 1 dollar. More generally

$\downarrow$ *Dollar price of 1 unit of foreign currency* $\rightarrow$ $\uparrow$ *Foreign price of* $1

$\uparrow$ *Dollar price of 1 unit of foreign currency* $\rightarrow$ $\downarrow$ *Foreign price of* $1

Economists call a decrease in the dollar price of 1 unit of foreign currency an **appreciation** of the dollar, or a **rise of the dollar** relative to the foreign currency. An increase in the dollar price of 1 unit of foreign currency is called a **depreciation** of the dollar, or a **fall of the dollar** relative to the foreign currency.

Now let's bring together our discussion of the determinants of exports and of imports.

Exports EX depend upon
- Income abroad
- Foreign price of $1

Imports IM depend upon
- Income in the U.S.
- $ price of foreign currency

Net exports *NX* equals exports minus imports. So we have

$\uparrow$ *Income abroad* $\rightarrow$ $\uparrow$ *EX* $\rightarrow$ $\uparrow$ *NX*

$\downarrow$ *Income abroad* $\rightarrow$ $\downarrow$ *EX* $\rightarrow$ $\downarrow$ *NX*

$\uparrow$ *Income in the U.S.* $\rightarrow$ $\uparrow$ *IM* $\rightarrow$ $\downarrow$ *NX*

$\downarrow$ *Income in the U.S.* $\rightarrow$ $\downarrow$ *IM* $\rightarrow$ $\uparrow$ *NX*

$\uparrow$ *Foreign price of* $1 = \downarrow$ $ *price of foreign currency* $\rightarrow$ $\downarrow$ *EX and* $\uparrow$ *IM* $\rightarrow$ $\downarrow$ *NX*

$\downarrow$ *Foreign price of* $1 = \uparrow$ $ *price of foreign currency* $\rightarrow$ $\uparrow$ *EX and* $\downarrow$ *IM* $\rightarrow$ $\uparrow$ *NX*

When the dollar appreciates or rises relative to foreign currency, our exports go down and our imports go up, lowering net exports. When the dollar depreciates or falls relative to foreign currency, our imports go up and our exports go down, raising net exports.

TRY

20. For each event below, what (if anything) is its effect on exports? On imports? On net exports?

a. European incomes fall
b. U.S. incomes fall
c. The dollar depreciates relative to the euro

SUMMARY

We have covered a lot of ground in this chapter. Most principles textbooks spread this material out over several chapters. This summary table may be helpful.

	Rises when	Falls when
Consumption	YD rises	YD falls
	Wealth rises	Wealth falls
	Interest rates fall	Interest rates rise
	Credit availability rises	Credit availability falls
	Expectations rise	Expectations fall
Investment	Interest rates fall	Interest rates rise
	Expected rates of return rise	Expected rates of return fall
Government	<exogenously determined>	
Net exports =	Income abroad rises	Income abroad falls
exports – imports	Income in the United States falls	Income in the United States rises
	Dollar falls relative to foreign currency	Dollar rises relative to foreign currency

Chapter **8**

The Spending Multiplier

Output or real GDP equals aggregate demand in short-run macroeconomic equilibrium (Chapter 6's message). Aggregate demand or aggregate spending equals the sum of consumption, investment, government, and net export spending (Chapter 7's message). But what happens to output when there is an initial change in spending? That answer—that output changes by more than the initial change in spending—is the message of Chapter 8.

One person's spending is another person's income. When our income changes, we tend to change how much we spend. So an initial burst of spending generates income for someone, who spends part or all of that income, generating income for someone else. The cycle continues. This chain of events is called the multiplier process. The multiplier is a number that tells the total change in spending that results from an initial change in spending. The size or value of the multiplier depends on how much we change our spending on domestically produced goods when our income changes.

KEY TERMS AND CONCEPTS

- Multiplier process
- Multiplier effect
- Keynesian cross diagram
- Multiplier
- Size of the multiplier
- Lump-sum taxes
- Proportional taxes
- Proportional tax rate
- Leakage
- Marginal propensity to import
- Open economy multiplier
- Closed economy multiplier

KEY EQUATIONS

- Definition of multiplier $= \dfrac{total \ \Delta Y}{initial \ \Delta spending}$

- Simplest spending multiplier $= \dfrac{1}{1 \ - \ mpc}$

- Proportional tax multiplier $= \dfrac{1}{1 \ - \ (1 \ - \ t) \cdot mpc}$

- Open economy multiplier $= \dfrac{1}{1 \ - \ mpc \ + \ mpm}$

THE MULTIPLIER PROCESS

An initial change in spending causes output to change. The total change in output is greater than the initial change in spending. Because the change in output is some multiple greater than 1 of the initial change in spending, economists say that a **multiplier process** kicks in when there is an initial change in spending.

The multiplier process is really very intuitive. There are just two ideas that form its basis:

- One person's spending is another person's income.

- When income changes, spending changes.

Spending changes income, which changes spending, which changes income, which changes spending... and round and round and round we go. That's the essence of the multiplier process.

The multiplier process works in either direction: with spending going up, or going down. When spending increases, income rises. Those who have received more income will spend more. Someone else's income rises, and their spending rises. That spending generates more income for someone else, who spends more. The total change in income for the aggregate economy is the sum of the increases in income in each of these rounds. An initial burst of spending generates a much larger total increase in income.

What looks pretty on the upside is ugly on the downside. When someone spends less, someone else's income goes down. (Remember: one person's spending is another person's income.) When someone's income falls, his or her spending falls. That cutback in spending means less income for someone else, who in turn spends less. The total change in income for the aggregate economy is the sum of the decreases in income in each of these rounds. An initial reduction in spending generates a much larger total drop in income.

TIP

We're about to complicate matters. But if you understand those last two paragraphs, you understand the multiplier.

Economists dress up the multiplier in more formal language and with mathematics. Let's start with the language. This is how economists describe the multiplier process: An initial increase in aggregate spending causes income to rise. When income rises, aggregate spending rises again. Each increase in aggregate spending causes income to rise further. Each increase in income causes aggregate spending to increase again. The total change in income is the sum of the changes in income in each round of the multiplier process.

The multiplier process also works in reverse. An initial decrease in aggregate spending causes income to fall. When income falls, aggregate spending falls again. Each decrease in aggregate spending causes income to fall further. Each decrease in income causes aggregate spending to decrease again. The total change in income is the sum of the changes in income in each round of the multiplier process.

TIP

Remember our confusion alert from Chapters 6 and 7: Some textbooks make a distinction between "aggregate demand" and "aggregate expenditures." Other textbooks don't. What we care about in this chapter is the sum of consumption, investment, government, and net export spending. "Aggregate demand," "aggregate expenditures," and "aggregate spending" all refer to that sum.

The initial change in aggregate spending can come from any of the four components of aggregate demand: consumption, investment, government spending, or

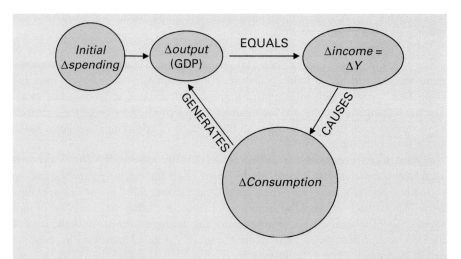

Figure 8.1 The Multiplier Process.

The multiplier process begins with an initial change in aggregate spending, which triggers a change in how much output is produced, and thus a change in income. A change in income causes a change in consumption spending, triggering a change in output and in income. Again, there is a change in consumption spending. And round and round we go.

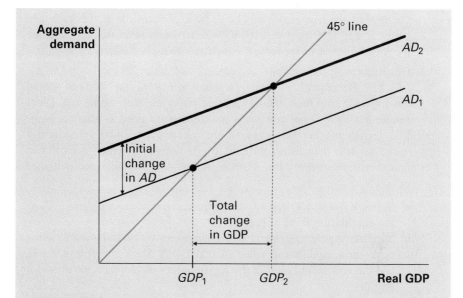

Figure 8.2 The Multiplier Effect in the Keynesian Cross Diagram.

The effect of the multiplier process can be seen with a Keynesian cross diagram. The initial change in aggregate demand is measured by the vertical distance between the two lines. The total change in GDP is measured by the horizontal distance between the two equilibrium values of GDP. Due to the multiplier process, the change in GDP is greater than the initial change in aggregate demand.

net exports. The subsequent changes in aggregate spending are in the components of aggregate demand that change when income changes. Usually, it is just consumption spending that changes in response to a change in income. (Though this is not always true—see the last two sections of this chapter.) One way to capture the multiplier process is shown in Figure 8.1.

The **multiplier effect** can also be seen in the **Keynesian cross diagram**. When aggregate demand increases, as seen in Figure 8.2, equilibrium income changes by more than the initial change in aggregate demand, due to the multiplier effect.

The total change in GDP equals the initial change in aggregate spending plus the changes in spending from all the subsequent rounds of the multiplier process. How *much* does GDP change—that is, what is the size or value of the multiplier? As we'll see in the next section, the answer depends upon how much spending changes when income changes.

TRY   *(Answers to all "TRY" questions are at the back of the book.)*

1. Government spending rises as local communities pay paving companies to fill potholes and repave roads. The paving companies purchase tar and gravel from suppliers, and hire new employees to do the paving work.

On payday, the new employees buy new appliances for their homes, and enjoy dinner at a local restaurant. Which activities in this scenario are the initial change in spending? Which are multiplier effects?

2. Government spending falls as teachers and aides at local schools are laid off. Because they have just lost their jobs, the laid-off school employees cancel their annual vacation plans and stop eating out. Local restaurants have fewer customers and thus don't need as many servers. The restaurants lay off some of their employees, who subsequently spend far less than usual on holiday gift shopping. Which activities in this scenario are the initial change in spending? Which are multiplier effects?

3. a. Suppose $AD = 100 + 0.8Y$. Draw the Keynesian cross diagram. Show the equilibrium level of real GDP.

   b. Suppose aggregate demand now changes to $AD = 250 + 0.8Y$. What is the new equilibrium value of real GDP? Show the new AD line and the new equilibrium in the Keynesian cross diagram you drew for part (a).

   c. When aggregate demand changed from $AD = 100 + 0.8Y$ to $AD = 250 + 0.8Y$, what is the initial change in spending? What is the total change in GDP?

   d. Finish this sentence: The total change in GDP is greater than the initial change in spending because of the _____.

THE SIZE OF THE MULTIPLIER

The **multiplier** tells us how much GDP changes when there is some initial change in aggregate spending. It is the ratio of the total change in GDP to the initial change in aggregate spending. Because GDP and income Y are always equal, the multiplier is equivalently the ratio of the total change in Y to the initial change in aggregate spending.

$$Multiplier = \frac{Total\ \Delta GDP}{Initial\ \Delta spending} = \frac{Total\ \Delta Y}{Initial\ \Delta spending}$$

Looking at Figure 8.2, the multiplier is the ratio of the horizontal distance between the two equilibrium values of GDP (total change in GDP) to the vertical distance between the two AD lines (initial change in AD).

TRY

4. If the total change in GDP is $400 billion per year and the initial change in spending is $100 billion per year, what is the value of the multiplier?

5. If the total change in GDP is a decrease of $500 billion per year and the initial change in spending is a drop of $200 billion per year, what is the value of the multiplier?

The multiplier exists because spending changes when income changes. If no one changed how much they spent when their income rose or fell, there would be no multiplier process. In that case, the total change in GDP would simply equal the initial change in aggregate spending. End of story.

But spending *does* change when income changes. And for this reason, the size or value of the multiplier is greater than 1.

What is the value or **size of the multiplier**? The answer depends upon how much spending changes when income changes. Now things get mathematical.

TIP

Don't lose sight of the essence. The multiplier exists because one person's spending is another person's income, and people tend to change their spending when their income changes.

Most textbooks begin with the simplest example. So will we. Let's make some assumptions.

- Assume: Taxes do not change when income changes.

    Any change in income Y is also a change in disposable income YD. $\Delta Y = \Delta YD$.

- Assume: Consumption spending is the only part of $C + I + G + NX$ that changes when income changes.

    After an initial change in aggregate spending, all subsequent changes in spending will be due to consumption spending.

The **marginal propensity to consume**, or *mpc*, was introduced in Chapter 7.

$$mpc = \frac{\Delta C}{\Delta YD}$$

Multiply both sides of that equation by ΔYD. You now have an equation that tells you how much consumption changes when disposable income changes.

$$\Delta C = mpc \times \Delta YD$$

We are ready to show how the multiplier works. To make the example easier to follow, let's use numbers. Let's assume the following:

- Initial change in aggregate spending, $\Delta spending$, is +$1,000 billion.
- Marginal propensity to consume, *mpc*, is 0.8.
- Only consumption changes when income changes.

An initial change in aggregate spending of $1,000 billion leads to additional output and income of $1,000 billion. Because we are assuming no change in taxes, disposable income also changes by $1,000 billion.

When disposable income rises by $1,000 billion, households spend more. The change in consumption equals the change in disposable income times the marginal propensity to consume, $1,000 billion · 0.8 = $800 billion. The increase in consumption spending of $800 billion leads to additional output and income of $800 billion. Assuming no change in taxes, disposable income also changes by $800 billion.

The process continues. When disposable income rises by $800 billion, the households that received this additional income spend more. Their change in consumption equals the change in disposable income times the marginal propensity to consume, $800 billion · 0.8 = $640 billion. The increase in consumption spending of $640 billion leads to additional output and income of $640 billion. Assuming no change in taxes, disposable income also changes by $640 billion.

Again and again and again, more spending by one group of households will generate additional income for other households, who will in turn increase their spending as well. Table 8.1 shows how the multiplier process unfolds.

Table 8.1   The Multiplier Process (Initial Δspending = $1,000 billion; mpc = 0.8)

Round #	ΔSpending (billions of $)	$\Delta Y = \Delta YD$ (billions of $)
1	Initial Δspending = 1,000	1,000
2	$\Delta C = \Delta YD \cdot mpc = 1,000 \cdot 0.8 = 800$	800
3	$\Delta C = 800 \cdot 0.8 = 640$	640
4	$\Delta C = 640 \cdot 0.8 = 512$	512

TRY

6. Create a table similar to Table 8.1. Assume that the initial change in spending is a drop of $1,000 billion and that the mpc is 0.75. Complete the rows representing the first three rounds of the multiplier process.

The total change in income and output is the sum of the changes in each round of the multiplier process.

$$Total \ \Delta Y = 1,000 + 800 + 640 + 512 + \cdots$$

To determine what that adds up to requires a bit of math. Let's walk through the math (because most of your textbooks do so as well). Then take a deep breath and focus just on the quick trick for determining the total effect.

$$Total \ \Delta Y = 1,000 + 800 + 640 + 512 + \cdots$$

Remember we used the mpc of 0.8 to find each round of spending:

$$Total \ \Delta Y = 1,000 + 1,000 \cdot 0.8 + 800 \cdot 0.8 + 640 \cdot 0.8 + \cdots$$

And each round's change in disposable income was itself the product of the previous round's change in spending and the *mpc*, so we have

$$Total \ \Delta Y = 1,000 + 1,000 \cdot 0.8 + (1,000 \cdot 0.8) \cdot 0.8$$
$$+ [(1,000 \cdot 0.8) \cdot 0.8] \cdot 0.8 + \cdots$$

Now let's simplify

$$Total \ \Delta Y = 1,000 + 1,000 \cdot 0.8 + 1,000 \cdot 0.8^2 + 1,000 \cdot 0.8^3 + \cdots$$

And factor out the 1,000

$$Total \ \Delta Y = 1,000 \cdot [1 + 0.8 + 0.8^2 + 0.8^3 + \cdots]$$

Perhaps you've learned elsewhere about the sum of an infinite series. If not, just accept this:

$$1 + 0.8 + 0.8^2 + 0.8^3 + \cdots = \frac{1}{1 - 0.8}$$

So therefore

$$Total \ \Delta Y = 1,000 \cdot \left(\frac{1}{1 - 0.8} \right) = 1,000 \cdot \left(\frac{1}{0.2} \right) = 1,000 \cdot 5 = 5,000$$

In general, the total change in income due to an initial change in aggregate spending, *assuming that taxes do not change when income changes, and assuming that consumption is the only type of spending that changes when income changes*, is

$$Total \ \Delta Y = Initial \ \Delta spending \cdot \left(\frac{1}{1 - mpc} \right)$$

The size or value of the multiplier—*assuming that taxes do not change when income changes, and that consumption is the only type of spending that changes when income changes*—is

$$Multiplier = \frac{1}{1 - mpc}$$

The formula for the value of the multiplier contains the marginal propensity to consume, the *mpc*, because the *mpc* tells us how much spending changes in response to a change in disposable income.

The value of the multiplier gets larger as the *mpc* gets larger. Table 8.2 shows different values of the multiplier associated with different values of the *mpc*. As the *mpc* gets larger, there is more spending in each round of the multiplier process, so the total change in income from any initial change in aggregate spending will be larger.

If the *mpc* equals 0, the multiplier equals 1. After the first round, there are no subsequent rounds of changes in spending and income. The change in income equals the initial change in aggregate spending.

If the *mpc* equals 1, the multiplier is infinitely large. When the *mpc* equals 1, each round of the multiplier process is the same as the previous round. Using the example in Table 8.1, in each round there would be another $1,000 billion in additional spending. Because the spending amounts do not get smaller with each

Table 8.2   The Value of the Multiplier
(Assuming taxes do not change when income
changes, and only consumption spending
changes when income changes)

mpc	Multiplier
0	1
0.5	2
0.6	2.5
0.7	3.33
0.8	5
0.9	10
1	∞

round, the total of all the rounds never converges to some finite number. The total change in output and income is instead infinite.

The multiplier applies to any initial change in aggregate spending. The definition of the multiplier is

$$Multiplier = \frac{Total\ \Delta Y}{Initial\ \Delta spending}$$

It doesn't matter if the initial change in aggregate spending is a change in investment spending, government spending, exports, or the autonomous part of consumption spending. Some textbooks use different names for each of those multipliers. So you may see

$$Investment\ Spending\ Multiplier = \frac{Total\ \Delta Y}{Initial\ \Delta I} = \frac{1}{1 - mpc}$$

$$Government\ Spending\ Multiplier = \frac{Total\ \Delta Y}{Initial\ \Delta G} = \frac{1}{1 - mpc}$$

$$Export\ Spending\ Multiplier = \frac{Total\ \Delta Y}{Initial\ \Delta EX} = \frac{1}{1 - mpc}$$

It's all the same thing. When we assume that taxes do not change when income changes and that consumption is the only type of spending that changes when income changes, the value of the multiplier is determined by the formula

$$Multiplier = \frac{1}{1 - mpc}$$

The Multiplier Effect When Spending Falls

What happens when aggregate spending decreases? The same multiplier process kicks in. A drop in spending causes a drop in income through layoffs or wage cuts. When families lose their jobs or have their income reduced, they reduce their spending. When they spend less, the work of people in other households is not needed, so there are more layoffs or wage cuts, or both. Those families whose income has fallen reduce their spending. And round and round and round we go.

When aggregate spending decreases, the multiplier process consists of cycles in which spending is falling, output is falling, people are being laid off, and income is falling. The total drop in output and income will be greater than the initial drop in spending. How much larger? The answer depends upon the size of the multiplier.

The formula for the multiplier is unchanged. When we assume that taxes do not change when income changes, and that consumption is the only type of spending that changes when income changes, the value of the multiplier is determined by the formula

$$Multiplier = \frac{1}{1 - mpc}$$

Investment spending drops by $300 billion per year. The *mpc* equals 0.75 and taxes do not change when income changes. The total drop in output and income will equal ($300 billion) $\cdot$ [$1/(1 - 0.75)$] = $1,200 billion per year.

TRY

7. If the initial Δspending $= -1,000$ and the *mpc* $= 0.75$, what is the total change in output and income?

8. If the initial Δspending $= +200$ and the *mpc* $= 0.4$, what is the total change in output and income?

9. If the *mpc* equals 0, what is the value of the multiplier? Why?

10. If the *mpc* equals 1, what is the value of the multiplier? Why?

11. When the *mpc* increases, does the value of the multiplier increase or decrease? Why?

The key to determining the value or size of the multiplier is knowing the change in spending for domestically produced goods and services when there is a change in income. In the simplest multiplier—*assuming that taxes do not change when income changes, and that consumption is the only type of spending that changes when income changes*—the value of the multiplier depends on just the marginal propensity to consume, the *mpc*. But what if we make different assumptions about how taxes or spending change when income changes? Then the formula for the multiplier changes.

TIP

You may be able to stop here. Many principles textbooks never move beyond the simple multiplier of $1/(1 - mpc)$. But in an intermediate macro class, you will see the more complicated multipliers we are about to cover.

MORE COMPLICATED MULTIPLIERS: TAXES

When we assume that taxes are **lump-sum taxes**, then there is no change in taxes when income changes. Lump-sum taxes are a constant dollar amount regardless of income. Economists often express lump-sum taxes as

Lump-sum tax $T = \overline{T}$. (For example, $T = \$100$ billion.)

When taxes are lump-sum taxes, then the simple formula for the multiplier, $1/(1-mpc)$, is correct.

If instead we assume taxes are **proportional taxes**, then taxes *do* change when income changes. Proportional taxes are a constant share or proportion of income. The **proportional tax rate** t is the share of income that is paid in taxes. Economists often express proportional taxes as

Proportional tax $T = t \cdot Y$. (For example, $T = 0.2Y$.)

The simple formula for the multiplier, $1/(1-mpc)$, is not correct when we assume taxes are proportional taxes.

When taxes are proportional taxes, the change in disposable income will be different from the change in income. With proportional taxes, the change in taxes will be the proportional tax rate t times the change in income Y.

$$\Delta YD = \Delta Y - \Delta T = \Delta Y - t \cdot \Delta Y = (1 - t) \cdot \Delta Y$$

TRY

12. If income increases by $1,000 billion per year and the proportional tax rate is 20%, what is the annual change in taxes? What is the change in disposable income?

13. If income decreases by $500 billion per year and the proportional tax rate is 30%, what is the annual change in taxes? What is the change in disposable income?

The multiplier process unfolds slightly differently now. The basic ideas are unchanged:

- One person's spending is another person's income.
- When someone's income changes, their spending changes, too.

But now we add one more piece:

- When someone's income changes, the taxes they pay change, too.

Figure 8.3 illustrates the multiplier process when there are proportional taxes.

The total change in income will be smaller when there are proportional taxes than when there are lump-sum taxes. In each round of the multiplier process, the change in consumption spending is smaller than it would be if taxes were lump-sum. With proportional taxes, some proportion of the change in income goes to

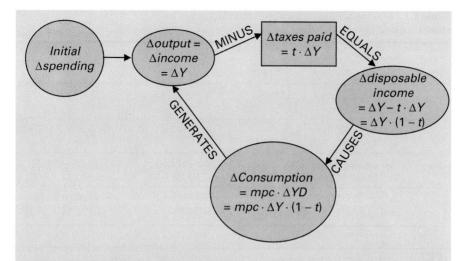

Figure 8.3 Multiplier Process with Proportional Taxes.

As always, an initial change in aggregate spending leads to a change in output and in income for the households that produced the output. When taxes are proportional to income, taxes change in response to the change in income. The change in income minus the change in taxes equals the change in disposable income. Those households that have received the change in disposable income adjust their consumption spending. Output is increased or decreased to meet this change in consumption, starting us around the multiplier process again.

pay taxes, making the change in disposable income smaller with proportional taxes than with lump-sum taxes.

Economists use the word **leakage** to describe the effect of proportional taxes on the multiplier process. Part of the potential for spending is "leaking out" of the economy when taxes are paid.

A numerical example is in Table 8.3. We start with the same assumptions as before but now include proportional taxes.

- Initial change in aggregate spending = +$1,000 billion.

- Marginal propensity to consume $mpc = 0.8$.

- Proportional tax rate $t = 0.3$.

The total change in output and income is $2,273 billion. This is again the sum of an infinite series.

$Total\ \Delta Y = 1,000 + 560 + 314 + 176 + \cdots$

$Total\ \Delta Y = 1,000 + 1,000 \cdot (1 - 0.3) \cdot 0.8$
$\qquad\qquad + [1,000 \cdot (1 - 0.3) \cdot 0.8] \cdot (1 - 0.3) \cdot 0.8 + \cdots$

$Total\ \Delta Y = 1,000 + 1,000 \cdot (1 - 0.3) \cdot 0.8 + 1,000 \cdot [(1 - 0.3) \cdot 0.8]^2 + \cdots$

$Total\ \Delta Y = 1,000 \cdot \left[1 + [(1 - 0.3) \cdot 0.8] + [(1 - 0.3) \cdot 0.8]^2 + \cdots \right]$

Table 8.3 Multiplier Process with Proportional Taxes
(Initial Δspending $= \$1,000$ billion; $mpc = 0.8$; $t = 0.3$)

Round #	ΔSpending (billions of $)	ΔY (billions of $)	ΔT (billions of $)	ΔYD (billions of $)
1	Initial Δspending $= 1,000$	1,000	$0.3 \cdot 1,000 = 300$	$1,000 - 300 = 700$
2	$\Delta C = \Delta YD \cdot mpc$ $= 700 \cdot 0.8 = 560$	560	$0.3 \cdot 560 = 168$	$560 - 168 = 392$
3	$\Delta C = 392 \cdot 0.8$ $= 313.60$	313.60	$0.3 \cdot 313.60$ $= 94.08$	$313.60 - 94.08$ $= 219.52$
4	$\Delta C = 219.52 \cdot 0.8$ $= 175.62$	175.62	$0.3 \cdot 175.62$ $= 52.68$	$175.62 - 52.68$ $= 122.94$

TRY

14. Create a table similar to Table 8.3. Assume that the initial change in spending is a drop of $1,000 billion, that the *mpc* is 0.75, and that the proportional tax rate is 20%. Complete the rows representing the first three rounds of the multiplier process.

This is an infinite series. In this example, we have the term $(1-0.3) \cdot 0.8$. The sum of this series is

$$1 + [(1 - 0.3) \cdot 0.8] + [(1 - 0.3) \cdot 0.8]^2 + [(1 - 0.3) \cdot 0.8]^3 + \cdots$$

$$= \frac{1}{1 - (1 - 0.3) \cdot 0.8}$$

And so the total change in output and income is

$$\text{Total } \Delta Y = 1,000 \cdot \left(\frac{1}{1 - (1 - 0.3) \cdot 0.8} \right)$$

$$= 1,000 \cdot \left(\frac{1}{1 - 0.7(0.8)} \right) = 1,000 \cdot \left(\frac{1}{1 - 0.56} \right)$$

$$= 1,000 \cdot \left(\frac{1}{0.44} \right) = 1,000 \cdot 2.273 = 2,273$$

When there are proportional taxes, the total change in income is smaller than when there are lump-sum taxes. With an initial change in spending of $1,000 billion and an *mpc* of 0.8, the total change in GDP and Y was $5,000 billion with lump-sum taxes but is just $2,273 billion with a 30% proportional tax.

The value of the multiplier can always be found by using the definition of the multiplier:

$$\text{Multiplier} = \frac{\text{Total } \Delta GDP}{\text{Initial } \Delta spending} = \frac{\text{Total } \Delta Y}{\text{Initial } \Delta spending}$$

In this case, the multiplier = $2,273 billion/$1,000 billion = 2.27.

The formula for the multiplier, *assuming that taxes are proportional to income, and that consumption is the only type of spending that changes when income changes*, is

$$Multiplier = \frac{1}{1 - (1 - t) \cdot mpc}$$

TIP

Look carefully at the denominator. You want to multiply the *mpc* by (1 – tax rate). *Then* subtract that product from 1. If you enter the terms of the denominator into your calculator in the order in which they're written, with no parentheses, you'll get the wrong answer.

As with the simple multiplier, the larger the *mpc*, the larger the multiplier. A larger *mpc* means that consumers are spending a greater share of any increase in disposable income than they would be with a smaller *mpc*. When the changes in consumption spending are larger, the total change in output and income will be larger, so the multiplier is larger, too.

We've now included the proportional tax rate, *t*. The larger the tax rate, the smaller the multiplier. A larger tax rate means that for any given change in income, the change in disposable income is smaller. Consumption spending depends on disposable income. In every round of spending, the smaller change in disposable income (due to a higher tax rate) results in a smaller change in consumption spending. Because the changes in consumption spending in each round are smaller, the total change in output and income will also be smaller. The spending multiplier is therefore smaller with a higher proportional tax rate.

Table 8.4 shows the value of the multiplier for a variety of combinations of *mpc* and tax rates. Notice that as the *mpc* increases (holding constant the tax rate), the multiplier increases. As the tax rate increases (holding constant the *mpc*), the multiplier decreases.

Table 8.4 The Value of the Proportional Tax Multiplier (Assuming proportional taxes, and only consumption spending changes when income changes)

mpc	Tax rate	Calculation of multiplier	Value of multiplier
0.5	0.1	$1/[1 - (1 - 0.1) \cdot 0.5] = 1/0.55$	1.82
0.6	0.1	$1/[1 - (1 - 0.1) \cdot 0.6] = 1/0.46$	2.17
0.7	0.1	$1/[1 - (1 - 0.1) \cdot 0.7] = 1/0.37$	2.70
0.8	0.1	$1/[1 - (1 - 0.1) \cdot 0.8] = 1/0.28$	3.57
0.8	0.2	$1/[1 - (1 - 0.2) \cdot 0.8] = 1/0.36$	2.78
0.8	0.3	$1/[1 - (1 - 0.3) \cdot 0.8] = 1/0.44$	2.27
0.8	0.4	$1/[1 - (1 - 0.4) \cdot 0.8] = 1/0.52$	1.92

15. If the initial Δspending $= -1,000$, $mpc = 0.75$, and tax rate $= 0.2$, what is the total change in output and income?
16. If the initial Δspending $= +200$, $mpc = 0.4$, and tax rate $= 0.1$, what is the total change in output and income?
17. If the tax rate equals 1, what is the value of the multiplier? Why?
18. When the tax rate increases, does the value of the multiplier increase, or decrease? Why?

MORE COMPLICATED MULTIPLIERS: IMPORTS

When we derived the simplest of multipliers, $1/(1 - mpc)$, we invoked two assumptions: (1) taxes do not change when income changes, and (2) consumption spending is the only part of aggregate spending that changes when income changes. With those two assumptions, the simple multiplier formula is correct. The total change in output and income will equal $1/(1 - mpc)$ times the initial change in aggregate spending. In the previous section we changed the first assumption. Now let's instead change the second assumption. What happens to the formula for the multiplier if consumption *and* imports both change when income changes? The multiplier formula will again become more complicated.

TIP

In most principles textbooks, this material is covered in a later chapter, typically entitled "Open Economy Macroeconomics."

Remember that imports are *subtracted* from aggregate demand. When we import more goods and services, spending leaves our own economy and generates jobs in another economy. Economists sometimes say: imports are a leakage.

Our two assumptions are now

- Assume: Taxes do not change when income changes.
- Assume: Consumption spending *and imports* change when income changes.

How does the multiplier process unfold now?

An initial change in aggregate spending generates a change in output and income. Assuming taxes are lump-sum, the change in income ΔY is also the change in disposable income ΔYD.

Now two things happen. As usual, consumption changes because households change their spending when their disposable income changes. And—here's the new piece—imports change because some percentage of everything we buy is produced abroad.

The net effect on aggregate spending for domestically produced goods and services is the difference between the change in consumption ΔC and the change in imports ΔIM.

$$\Delta\text{spending} = \Delta C - \Delta IM$$

Output changes to meet this new net demand for domestically produced goods and services, generating a change in income for the households that produce and sell those items. Back around we go again: ΔC and ΔIM, which changes output and income and disposable income. And again and again and again, the multiplier process continues. Figure 8.4 illustrates.

The total change in income will be smaller when there are imports than when there are no imports. In each round of the multiplier process, the net change in demand for domestically-produced goods and services is smaller than the change in consumption spending.

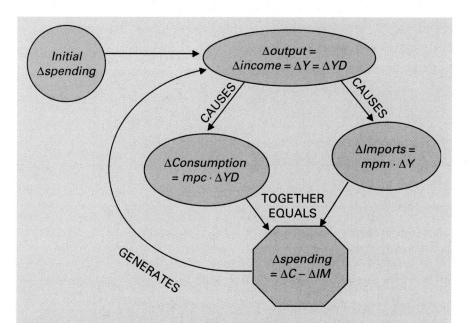

Figure 8.4 Multiplier Process with Imports and Lump-Sum Taxes.

As always, an initial change in aggregate spending leads to a change in output and in income for the households that produced the output. Because taxes are lump-sum, the change in income equals the change in disposable income. Households whose income has changed adjust their consumption spending. At the same time, the change in income causes a change in imports. The net change in aggregate spending for domestically produced goods and services is the change in consumption spending minus the change in imports. Output changes to meet this change in aggregate spending, starting us around the multiplier process again.

A Numerical Example

To build a numerical example, we need the concept **marginal propensity to import**. The marginal propensity to import *mpm* is equal to the change in imports divided by the change in income.

$$mpm = \frac{\Delta IM}{\Delta Y}$$

Multiply both sides of that equation by ΔY. Now you have an equation that tells you how much imports change when there is a change in income.

$$\Delta IM = mpm \cdot \Delta Y$$

TIP

Notation varies. Most books use either *mpm* or *mpi*. We will use *mpm* to stand for the *M*arginal *P*ropensity to i*M*port.

Table 8.5 shows how the multiplier works when there are imports. We start with the same assumptions as before. Now we will also include imports.

- Initial change in aggregate spending = +$1,000 billion.
- Marginal propensity to consume *mpc* = 0.8.
- Marginal propensity to import *mpm* = 0.3.
- Lump-sum taxes, so $\Delta Y = \Delta YD$.

Table 8.5   Multiplier Process with Imports and Lump-Sum Taxes
(Initial Δspending = $1,000 billion; *mpc* = 0.8; *mpm* = 0.3)

Round #	ΔSpending (billions of $)	$\Delta Y = \Delta YD$ (billions of $)	ΔC (billions of $) = $mpc \cdot \Delta YD$	ΔIM (billions of $) = $mpm \cdot \Delta Y$
1	Initial Δspending = 1,000	1,000	$0.8 \cdot 1{,}000 = 800$	$0.3 \cdot 1{,}000 = 300$
2	$\Delta C - \Delta IM$ = 800 − 300 = 500	500	$0.8 \cdot 500 = 400$	$0.3 \cdot 500 = 150$
3	$\Delta C - \Delta IM$ = 400 − 150 = 250	250	$0.8 \cdot 250 = 200$	$0.3 \cdot 250 = 75$
4	$\Delta C - \Delta IM$ = 200 − 75 = 125	125	$0.8 \cdot 125 = 100$	$0.3 \cdot 125 = 37.5$

TRY

19. If income increases by $1,000 billion per year and the marginal propensity to import is 15%, what is the annual change in imports?

20. If income decreases by $500 billion per year and the marginal propensity to import is 20%, what is the annual change in imports?

21. Create a table similar to Table 8.5. Assume that the initial change in spending is a drop of $1,000 billion, that the *mpc* is 0.75, and that the marginal propensity to import is 25%. Complete the rows representing the first three rounds of the multiplier process.

The total change in output and income is once again the sum of an infinite series. This time we have

$$Total\ \Delta Y = 1,000 + 500 + 250 + 125 + \cdots$$

$$Total\ \Delta Y = 1,000 + 1,000 \cdot (0.8 - 0.3) + [1,000 \cdot (0.8 - 0.3)] \cdot (0.8 - 0.3) + \cdots$$

$$Total\ \Delta Y = 1,000 + 1,000 \cdot (0.8 - 0.3) + 1,000 \cdot (0.8 - 0.3)^2 + \cdots$$

$$Total\ \Delta Y = 1,000 \cdot [1 + (0.8 - 0.3) + (0.8 - 0.3)^2 + \cdots]$$

The sum of this infinite series is

$$1 + (0.8 - 0.3) + (0.8 - 0.3)^2 + \cdots = \frac{1}{1 - (0.8 - 0.3)}$$

So the total change in output and income is

$$Total\ \Delta Y = 1,000 \cdot \left(\frac{1}{[1 - (0.8 - 0.3)]} \right)$$

$$= 1,000 \cdot \left(\frac{1}{[1 - 0.5]} \right)$$

$$= 1,000 \cdot \left(\frac{1}{0.5} \right)$$

$$= 1,000 \cdot 2 = 2,000$$

Remember: when we had lump-sum taxes and no imports, an initial change in spending of $1,000 billion and an *mpc* of 0.8 produced a total change in output and income of $5,000 billion. What happens when there are also imports and an *mpm* of 0.3? The total change in output and income is just $2,000 billion.

So many things are still the same! The definition of the multiplier is still

$$Multiplier = \frac{Total\ \Delta Y}{Initial\ \Delta spending}$$

The multiplier process is still the same: an initial change in aggregate spending generates round after round after round of changes in output, changes in income, and changes in spending.

What has changed is the formula for the value of the multiplier. *When taxes do not change as income changes, and both consumption and imports do change when income changes*, the formula for the multiplier is

$$Multiplier = \frac{1}{1 - mpc + mpm}$$

Economists call this multiplier the **open economy multiplier**.

Again, the larger the *mpc*, the larger the multiplier. This conclusion has not changed, and will not change as we complicate the multiplier. The more goods and services that households consume in each round of the multiplier, the larger the total change in output and income emanating from an initial change in aggregate spending.

The new term is the marginal propensity to import, *mpm*. The larger the *mpm*, the smaller the multiplier. A larger *mpm* means that for any given change in income, the change in imports will be larger. Every dollar of imports is a leakage from our economy. Import spending generates employment and income—but in another economy, not in ours. So the more we spend on imports, all else constant, the smaller the change in demand for domestically produced goods and services. And the smaller the change in demand for domestically produced goods and services, the smaller the change in output and income in each round of the multiplier process. Because the changes in output and income in each round are smaller, the total change in output and income will also be smaller. The spending multiplier is therefore smaller with a larger marginal propensity to import.

Fluctuations in GDP and in income are smaller when imports change with domestic income. This conclusion holds whether aggregate spending, output, and income are increasing or decreasing. When aggregate spending initially increases, our propensity to import means that not all of the increase in spending stays in the domestic economy generating output and jobs and income here. The multiplier process will be smaller than it would have been in the absence of imports.

When aggregate spending initially decreases, our propensity to import again means that some of the goods and services we are no longer buying would have been produced abroad—imports fall. The rest of the goods and services we are no longer buying would have been produced here—domestic production falls. But because some of our spending would have been for imports, when we cut back on how much we are spending, some of the resulting layoffs occur in other economies. The impact on our domestic economy is smaller than it would have been in the absence of imports.

Table 8.6 shows the value of the multiplier for a variety of combinations of *mpc* and *mpm*. As the marginal propensity to consume *mpc* increases (holding

Table 8.6   The Value of the Open Economy Multiplier.
(Assuming lump-sum taxes, and both consumption and import spending change when income changes)

mpc	*mpm*	Calculation of multiplier	Value of multiplier
0.5	0.1	$1/[1 - (0.5 - 0.1)] = 1/0.6$	1.67
0.6	0.1	$1/[1 - (0.6 - 0.1)] = 1/0.5$	2.00
0.7	0.1	$1/[1 - (0.7 - 0.1)] = 1/0.4$	2.50
0.8	0.1	$1/[1 - (0.8 - 0.1)] = 1/0.3$	3.33
0.8	0.2	$1/[1 - (0.8 - 0.2)] = 1/0.4$	2.50
0.8	0.3	$1/[1 - (0.8 - 0.3)] = 1/0.5$	2.00
0.8	0.4	$1/[1 - (0.8 - 0.4)] = 1/0.6$	1.67

constant the *mpm*), the multiplier increases. As the marginal propensity to import *mpm* increases (holding constant the *mpc*), the multiplier decreases.

The change in output and income is much smaller in the presence of imports. Economists say: the open economy multiplier is smaller than the **closed economy multiplier**. Fluctuations in output and income—whether increasing or decreasing—are smaller when part of our income is spent on imports.

TRY

22. If the initial Δspending $= -1{,}000$, $mpc = 0.75$, and $mpm = 0.25$, what is the total change in output and income?
23. If the initial Δspending $= +200$, $mpc = 0.4$, and $mpm = 0.1$, what is the total change in output and income?
24. If the marginal propensity to import equals the marginal propensity to consume, what is the value of the multiplier? Why?
25. When the marginal propensity to import increases, does the value of the multiplier increase, or decrease? Why?

SUMMARY

Remember the distinction between the definition of the multiplier and the formula for the value of the multiplier. The definition of the multiplier is always the same:

$$Multiplier = \frac{Total\ \Delta Y}{Initial\ \Delta spending}$$

The definition of the multiplier does not depend upon the assumptions we make about what changes when income changes.

But the formula for the value of the multiplier does depend upon the assumptions we make about what changes when income changes. The simplest multiplier assumes only consumption changes when income changes. The proportional tax multiplier assumes both consumption and taxes change when income changes. The open-economy multiplier assumes that both consumption and imports change when income changes.

We could complicate things further. What if consumption, taxes, and imports all changed when income changed? We'd have another formula for the value of the multiplier. What if investment changed when income changed? We'd have yet another formula for the value of the multiplier.

Rather than simply memorizing each of those formulas, remember what matters. The multiplier process is always the same: an initial change in aggregate spending generates round after round after round of changes in output, changes in income, and changes in spending. The size of the multiplier depends upon how much aggregate spending changes in response to a change in income. The more aggregate spending changes, the larger the multiplier. The less aggregate spending changes, the smaller the multiplier.

PART IV

Policy

Chapter 9

Macroeconomic Policy: The Overview

Real GDP depends upon aggregate demand—that was Chapter 6's message. Aggregate demand or (planned) aggregate expenditure is the sum of consumption, investment, government and net export spending—that was Chapter 7's message. Multiplier effects exist: when there is an initial change in spending, real GDP changes by even more—that was Chapter 8's message. What policy actions can trigger those initial changes in spending? That is the question for Chapter 9.

Two types of government policy can change real GDP: fiscal policy and monetary policy. Fiscal policy is spending and taxing; it is conducted by the legislative authorities. Monetary policy is manipulation of the money supply and interest rates; it is conducted by the central bank. In the United States, Congress, with the approval of the president, conducts fiscal policy; the Federal Reserve Board (the Fed) conducts monetary policy.

KEY TERMS AND CONCEPTS

- Full-employment output
- Output gap
- Recessionary gap
- Inflationary gap
- Insufficient aggregate demand
- Fiscal policy
- Monetary policy
- Direct fiscal policy
- Indirect fiscal policy
- Money supply
- Financial assets
- Interest rate
- Price of money
- Central bank
- European Central Bank
- Federal Reserve System
- Expansionary fiscal policy

- Expansionary monetary policy
- Easy money
- Contractionary fiscal policy
- Contractionary monetary policy
- Tight money
- Recognition lag
- Implementation lag
- Response lag
- Financial crisis
- Worldwide recession
- Federal funds rate
- Zero lower bound
- Troubled Asset Relief Program (TARP)
- American Recovery and Reinvestment Act (ARRA)
- Counterfactual
- Outlier

WHEN EQUILIBRIUM OUTPUT DOESN'T EQUAL FULL EMPLOYMENT OUTPUT

In equilibrium, real GDP equals aggregate demand. That was the message of Chapter 6. But nothing about the determination of equilibrium output mentioned full employment.

Remember from Chapter 4 that "full employment" does not mean 0% unemployment. The labor force is said to be fully employed when there is no cyclical or structural unemployment. In the United States, "full employment" means that the unemployment rate is between 4 and 6%.

The amount of output that would generate full employment of the labor force is what economists call **full-employment output**. Equilibrium output does not depend upon whether or not the labor force is fully employed. Equilibrium output depends upon aggregate demand. It is possible for equilibrium output to be less than full-employment output.

TIP

Remember our "confusion alert" from previous chapters: some textbooks use the phrase "(planned) aggregate expenditures" and reserve the phrase "aggregate demand" for later chapters. In those textbooks, they would say "equilibrium output depends upon aggregate demand and aggregate supply." The distinction matters in Chapter 14.

The full-employment level of output is a hypothetical amount. It is how much output would be produced in the economy in a year *if* the labor force was fully employed. When the economy is at full employment, then the amount of output equals full-employment output.

When equilibrium output is less than full-employment output, economists say that there is an **output gap** or **recessionary gap**. The difference between equilibrium GDP and full-employment GDP equals the size of the output gap. If full-employment output equals $15 trillion per year and equilibrium output equals $13 trillion per year, then the output gap is $15 − $13 = $2 trillion per year. The economy would need to produce $2 trillion more in goods and services per year to fully employ the labor force. Figure 9.1 illustrates an output gap.

When equilibrium output is greater than full-employment output, economists say there is an **inflationary gap**. If full-employment output equals $15 trillion per year and equilibrium output equals $16 trillion per year, then the inflationary gap is $16 − $15 = $1 trillion per year.

Inflationary gaps occur when the economy is operating beyond full employment. Factories are operating additional hours. Workers are working overtime. Inflationary gaps most often occur during periods of war, when all the economy's resources are being used, sometimes beyond their normal capacity, to produce goods and services. In an inflationary gap, the unemployment rate is unusually low. There are pressures on prices to rise rapidly.

Output gaps are more common than inflationary gaps. Output gaps occur when there is an unemployment problem. Some workers are unemployed due to **insufficient aggregate demand**. Output gaps emerge in a recession, and shrink in a recovery.

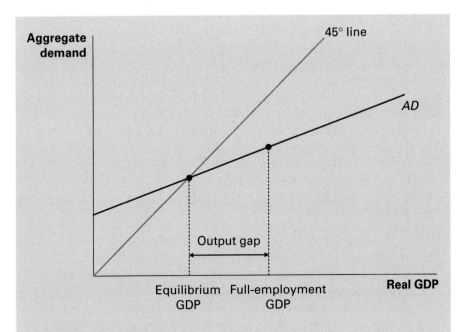

Figure 9.1 An Output Gap.
The difference between full-employment GDP and equilibrium GDP, when equilibrium is less than full employment, is called an output gap.

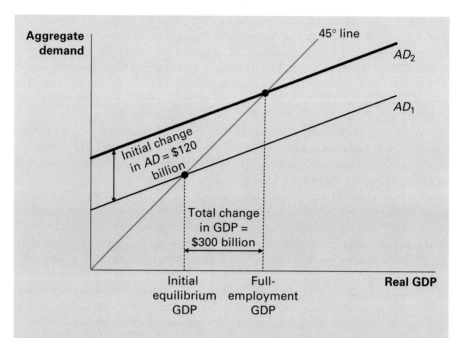

Figure 9.2 Policy Can Close an Output Gap.

When the spending multiplier equals 2.5, an initial change in aggregate demand of $120 billion will kick off multiplier effects that close a $300 billion output gap.

Output gaps are a key concern of policy makers. Closing an output gap requires an increase in aggregate demand. But the initial increase in aggregate demand can be smaller than the output gap. That's because multiplier effects will kick in. Output will increase by the initial increase in aggregate demand *times* the spending multiplier.

Figure 9.2 illustrates. Suppose the output gap is $300 billion and the spending multiplier is 2.5. The aggregate demand curve shifts up by the amount of the initial change in aggregate demand. An initial increase in aggregate demand of $120 billion will result in a total change in GDP equal to $120 billion *times* the multiplier of 2.5, or $300 billion.

TRY   *(Answers to all "TRY" questions are at the back of the book.)*

1. Draw a graph similar to Figure 9.1 that depicts an inflationary gap.

2. Suppose that real GDP equals $9 trillion per year and that the full employment level of output is $10 trillion per year. Is there an output gap, or an inflationary gap? Is the unemployment rate above, below, or equal to the full-employment rate of unemployment?

FISCAL AND MONETARY POLICY

Fiscal policy and monetary policy are the two types of policies that can be used to close an output gap. **Fiscal policy** refers to changes in government spending, transfer payments, or taxes, and is conducted by the legislative authorities. **Monetary policy** refers to changes in the money supply and interest rates, and is conducted by the central bank.

Fiscal Policy

Fiscal policy refers to changes in

- Government spending (G)
- Transfer payments (TR)
- Taxes (TA)

undertaken with the goal of changing GDP and unemployment.

TIP

Some textbooks call *any* change in G, TR, or TA "fiscal policy." Other books use the phrase "fiscal policy" only for changes in G, TR, and TA made *with the goal* of changing GDP.

Government spending (G) is purchases of goods and services by government agencies. Examples include hiring teachers and professors for public schools, building schools, paying military salaries, purchasing munitions, building bridges, paving roads, and much more.

Transfer payments (TR) are payments by a government agency for which no good or service is expected by the government in exchange. Examples include Social Security, unemployment insurance benefits, temporary assistance to needy families (TANF), Pell Grants, and more.

Taxes (TA) are payments to a government agency. Some taxes are called "taxes"; others are not. Examples include property taxes, sales taxes, income taxes, excise taxes, as well as national and state park entrance fees, public boat launch fees, car registration fees, and much more.

In the United States, fiscal policy is conducted on a federal level by the U.S. Congress with the approval of the president. Economists often refer to eras of fiscal policy with reference to the president: Bush administration fiscal policy, Obama administration fiscal policy, and so on. Linking fiscal policy with the president's name can—incorrectly—make it seem that the president alone conducts fiscal policy. But the American political system requires that legislation itself be introduced and passed by members of Congress, and only then signed into law by the president.

Fiscal policy can have a direct or indirect effect on aggregate demand. Changes in government spending (G) are **direct fiscal policy** because G is part of $C + I + G + NX$. Changes in transfer payments (TR) and taxes (TA) are **indirect fiscal policy** because TR and TA are not in $C + I + G + NX$. Changes in transfer payments and taxes change disposable income, which in turn changes consumption spending (C).

TRY

3. What is the difference between direct fiscal policy and indirect fiscal policy?

Monetary Policy

Monetary policy refers to changes in

- Money supply (MS)
- Interest rates (i)

undertaken by the central bank with the goal of changing GDP, employment, or inflation.

TIP

Notation varies. Money supply can be indicated by MS, M^S, M_S, or M. Interest rates can be indicated by i or r.

The **money supply** is the total value of **financial assets** that can be used to pay for goods and services. A financial asset is an asset (something you own) that represents a claim. Stocks, bonds, savings accounts, and bank accounts are all examples of financial assets. The financial assets that are part of the money supply are those assets that can most easily be used to pay for goods and services: coins, currency, and balances in checking accounts. More detail about the money supply is in Chapter 11.

An **interest rate** is the price of borrowed money. Interest rates are expressed in percentage terms rather than dollar terms, because not every loan is the same size. The amount borrowed is called the principal of a loan. An interest rate of 10% assessed on $1,000 borrowed for 1 year equals interest cost of $1,000 \cdot 0.10 = \$100$. The same interest rate of 10% assessed on $85,000 borrowed for 1 year equals interest cost of $8,500. So the interest rate is the price—expressed as a percentage of the principal—of borrowed money. Many economists simply say: an interest rate is the **price of money**.

Monetary policy is conducted by a nation's central bank. A **central bank** is a financial institution created by a nation's government. A central bank can

- Provide banking services to banks
- Regulate financial institutions
- Create money

The central bank may be a branch of the government, or it may be independent of the government. The central bank of the euro-zone is the **European Central Bank**. The central bank of the United States is the **Federal Reserve System**. Both of these central banks are largely independent of the government.

The Federal Reserve System was established by Congress in 1913 and was restructured in the 1930s. It consists of

- Federal Reserve Board of Governors
- 12 regional Federal Reserve Banks

The seven governors of the Federal Reserve Board—the chairman and six members—are appointed to 14-year terms by the president and are confirmed by the U.S. Senate. The current chairman of the Federal Reserve is Ben Bernanke. The 12 Federal Reserve Banks spread across the country, together with the board of governors headquartered in Washington, D.C., make up the Federal Reserve. The nickname for the Federal Reserve is the Fed.

Monetary policy is an indirect policy. Monetary policy changes the money supply and interest rates, which in turn causes aggregate demand to change. So monetary policy is an indirect policy, because the money supply and interest rates are not themselves part of aggregate demand.

TRY

4. What is the Fed? Where is it located?
5. You borrow $10,000 from ABC Loans at an interest rate of 5%. To whom is that interest rate a cost? To whom is it the rate of return?

CONTRACTIONARY AND EXPANSIONARY POLICY

Actions that increase aggregate demand are called expansionary. **Expansionary fiscal policy** refers to fiscal policy actions that increase aggregate demand: increases in G, increases in TR, and decreases in TA. **Expansionary monetary policy** refers to monetary policy actions that increase aggregate demand: increasing money supply and decreasing interest rates. Expansionary monetary policy is sometimes called **easy money**.

Actions that decrease aggregate demand are called contractionary. **Contractionary fiscal policy** refers to fiscal policy actions that decrease aggregate demand: decreases in G, decreases in TR, and increases in TA. **Contractionary monetary policy** refers to monetary policy actions that decrease aggregate demand: decreasing money supply and increasing interest rates. Contractionary monetary policy is sometimes called **tight money**.

To summarize,

Expansionary fiscal policy: $\uparrow G, \uparrow TR, or \downarrow TA \rightarrow \uparrow AD$

Expansionary monetary policy: $\uparrow money\ supply\ or \downarrow interest\ rates \rightarrow \uparrow AD$

Contractionary fiscal policy: $\downarrow G, \downarrow TR, or \uparrow TA \rightarrow \downarrow AD$

Contractionary monetary policy: $\downarrow money\ supply\ or \uparrow interest\ rates \rightarrow \downarrow AD$

> ### TRY
>
> **6.** The government simultaneously increases taxes by $10 billion and increases transfer payments by $30 billion. Is this expansionary fiscal policy, or contractionary fiscal policy?
>
> **7.** What is expansionary monetary policy? What is contractionary monetary policy?

POLICY LAGS

Using policy to close an output or inflationary gap can be challenging because of the time lags involved. Economists identify three different types of policy lags:

- *Recognition Lag:* The amount of time it takes to recognize the existence of a problem
- *Implementation Lag:* The amount of time it takes to design and implement a policy
- *Response Lag:* The amount of time it takes for the economy to change in response to the policy

There is a **recognition lag** because it takes time to know what is happening in the economy. Government agencies or the Fed must gather information about the entire economy. Economists and other analysts need time to interpret the many pieces of data gathered.

The **implementation lag** is usually longer for fiscal policy than for monetary policy. Fiscal policy requires time for legislation to move through Congress. A bill must be drafted. Committee hearings are held. The bill is voted out of committee. It is presented to the full House and voted on. A similar—but often different—bill went through the same process on the Senate side. Once both the House and the Senate have passed their bills, a conference committee of members from both the House and the Senate write a third bill that is a compromise between the House and Senate versions. That conference bill is then passed by both the House and the Senate, and sent to the president to be signed. But that's not all! Now the policy in the bill must be implemented. If the bill calls for tax cuts, the IRS must prepare new tax tables for all the employers in the country. If the bill calls for additional spending, the agencies that will do the spending—the departments of transportation or energy or defense, and so on—must receive authorization to spend, design projects, solicit bids, award contracts. And then, finally, the spending can begin.

By contrast, monetary policy simply requires that the central bank decide to change interest rates or the money supply, a decision that a committee can make in one brief meeting. Actually making the change in interest rates can take minutes, or at most, hours. The implementation lag for monetary policy is measured in hours, or at most, days.

There is a **response lag** because it takes time for additional spending to impact the economy. Direct fiscal policy begins increasing equilibrium output when the government spending begins. Indirect fiscal policy first changes disposable income; only then does consumption and thus aggregate demand begin increasing. Monetary policy changes interest rates, which affect aggregate demand. Multiplier effects then kick in, but even those take time.

A disadvantage to using fiscal policy is the long implementation lag. An advantage to using fiscal policy is that it can focus on weak sectors or weak regions. For example, policy encouraging purchases of U.S.-built cars benefits the auto sector (a relatively weak sector in recent years) and benefits Michigan and surrounding areas (a relatively high unemployment region).

An advantage to monetary policy is the short implementation lag. A disadvantage is that the same policy applies in all regions of the country and all sectors. If the West is booming but the Midwest is in recession, monetary policy can't be used to help just the Midwest.

TRY

8. Define each of the three types of lags.

9. What type of expansionary policy do you think has a longer response lag: increase in government purchases (ΔG) or decrease in taxes (ΔT)? Why?

FISCAL AND MONETARY POLICY IN THE GREAT RECESSION OF 2007–2009

Even though much more detail about fiscal and monetary policy follows in Chapters 10–13, you now have enough background to appreciate the outlines of the Great Recession of 2007–2009. Your textbook may or may not include a section on the use of policy during the Great Recession that began in December 2007. And what you read here or in your textbook may already be out of date.

The Great Recession of 2007–2009 is characterized by a **financial crisis**, a drop in aggregate demand, a steep rise in unemployment, and temporary deflation in consumer prices. In many regards, it is the worst economic crisis since the Great Depression of the 1930s. The Great Recession—like the 1930s episode—was experienced globally. Indeed, 2009 was the first time since the 1930s that global output declined, creating what economists term a **worldwide recession**.

"Financial crisis" is a term that does not have one specific definition. It refers to a period when an economy's financial assets and financial institutions lose a great deal of value, quickly. Different scholars have different criteria by which they judge whether a crisis has occurred. What share of banks has failed? How far have stock prices fallen and how quickly? What has happened to interest rates? By nearly all criteria, fall 2008 was a period of financial crisis in the United States and abroad.

The decline in GDP began earlier, in December 2007. Economic historians are still debating the causes of the Great Depression of the 1930s. No doubt they will be debating the exact causes of the Great Recession for the next 70 years as well. But the contours of the decline are clear: there was a drop in investment spending—first for housing construction, then for producer durable goods—followed by drops in consumption, export, and import spending. The unemployment rate rose from about 5% in 2007 to 10% in 2009. Measures of unemployment that include discouraged workers and people who are part-time but want full-time work neared 20%, the highest rates since the 1930s.

The Great Recession of 2007–2009 came on the heels of two decades of unparalleled success in the conduct of monetary policy. Alan Greenspan had chaired the Federal Reserve from 1987 to 2006. Greenspan was perceived, as one author termed it, as a maestro in full command of the economy. It was not uncommon by the end of the twentieth century to hear pundits and even some economists claim that the Fed had successfully tamed the business cycle, that recessions were part of our past but not our future.

Many economists believed that monetary policy was all we needed to manage the economy. Fiscal policy was seen as unnecessary at best and fraught with economic danger at worst. Its political and cumbersome nature, and the long lags associated with fiscal policy, left many convinced that fiscal policy could not and should not be used to actively manage the economy.

In September 2007, following a few weeks of turmoil in financial markets that, in retrospect, marked the beginning of the financial crisis, the Federal Reserve began lowering interest rates. Its target interest rate is the **federal funds rate**, which is the interest rate that banks charge each other on overnight loans brokered to cover a Federal Reserve requirement. (More details about the federal funds rate are in Chapter 12.) The federal funds rate had been 5.25% since mid-2006. The Fed lowered the rate in $1/4$, $1/2$, and $3/4$ percentage point steps until by mid-December 2008, the target value of the federal funds rate was "between 0 and 0.25%." The Fed had hit the **zero lower bound** for the federal funds rate. The rate can not go any lower than 0.

The Federal Reserve had relied on the federal funds rate as its tool of monetary policy for over twenty years. But by the end of 2008, when the economy was still in dire straits, its traditional tool was essentially used up. They couldn't push that interest rate any lower than 0, its lower bound.

Creativity became the name of the game. The Fed, at times working with the U.S. Treasury, came up with new ways of aiding the economy. The Fed's goal was to stabilize financial markets. They believed the way to do this was by increasing liquidity—cash—in the financial system. And so the Fed expanded the usual list of assets it was willing to purchase from banks. Traditionally the Fed had been willing to purchase short-term U.S. government bills and notes from banks. Now the Fed stood ready to purchase a much larger array of securities. In 2008 and 2009, the Fed bought long-term government bonds, mortgage backed securities, and other debt from financial institutions.

In addition to the Fed's creative monetary policy actions, the federal government engaged in fiscal policy. Despite the long lags, despite the political nature, despite the objections from some economists, Congress approved two large fiscal policy measures. In October 2008, with world financial markets on the reputed brink of collapse, Congress passed and President Bush signed into law the $700 billion **Troubled Asset Relief Program**, or TARP. This program authorized the U.S. Treasury to purchase "troubled assets" from banks and other financial institutions. The goal was to inject liquidity into the financial system and get credit flowing again. In this sense, TARP is not traditional fiscal policy; it was not designed to directly affect aggregate demand. But a widely held fear was that if financial markets did collapse—stop working—then businesses would not be able to obtain the short-term operating credit that allowed them to order supplies and pay workers, shutting down much of the economy. Many variations on the terms "Wall Street" and "Main Street" were used to describe the interplay between financial institutions (Wall Street) and business activity (Main Street). Congress and President Bush believed TARP could save both Wall Street and Main Street from imminent collapse.

A second discretionary fiscal policy action was taken in February 2009. Congress passed and President Obama signed into law the $787 billion **American Recovery and Reinvestment Act (ARRA)**. This program was classic fiscal policy. It combined temporary tax cuts and government spending increases over three years, together totaling $787 billion. The goal was to stimulate aggregate demand and prevent GDP from falling.

The effects of any policy are difficult to judge by looking at published data. The difficulty is that the policy's effects are not seen by comparing the economy today with the economy yesterday. The policy's effects are seen by comparing the economy today with something hypothetical: what the economy would have been today had the policy not been implemented. Economists call that hypothetical the **counterfactual**. A counterfactual is by definition unobservable. It is "what would have happened if different—counter—facts had prevailed." What would the unemployment rate have been in December 2009 had ARRA not passed? That is the counterfactual value of the unemployment rate.

ARRA was signed into law in February 2009. Its first effects were a cut in personal income tax withholding starting in April 2009. The additional government spending authorized by ARRA started in mid-2009, peaked in 2010, and ends in 2011. Has ARRA helped the economy? Looking at the actual pattern of unemployment or GDP growth doesn't answer the question (though any number of pundits and even a few economists offer that answer nonetheless). To determine whether ARRA has helped the economy, we compare measures of the economy *with* ARRA and measures of the economy *without* ARRA.

But, you ask, how can we get values for GDP for an economy that never existed—a U.S. economy without a fiscal policy action that clearly does exist? Economists use computer simulations to estimate the counterfactual value of GDP. Their computer models are much more complicated than the simple equations presented in this book. But they start from the same principles. Aggregate spending is the sum of consumption, investment, government, and net export spending. The factors that determine C, I, G, and NX are taken into account.

A series of equations then relate aggregate spending to real GDP, employment, and unemployment.

Different groups of economists have slightly different equations. Sometimes the difference is in the values of the coefficients: what is the value of the marginal propensity to consume? Sometimes the difference is in the mathematical expression: is it income or the natural log of income or income and income squared that influences consumption? Sometimes the difference is in the underlying concepts and assumptions: how do aggregate spending and real GDP relate to each other?

Because different groups of economists have slightly different equations, you will hear different estimates for the counterfactual values of GDP, employment, and unemployment. No one estimate is best. And so, to assess the effectiveness of policy, we have to accept a range of possible answers.

For example, suppose the estimates of the counterfactual value of the unemployment rate ranged from 8 to 15%, with all but two of the estimates in the range of 11 to 13%. The estimate of 8% is outside the range of all the other estimates, so economists would call it an **outlier**. The estimate of 15% is also an outlier. The "true" counterfactual value of the unemployment rate is probably between 11 and 13%.

If the actual value of unemployment is 10%, then the unemployment rate is lower than the counterfactual rate of 11 to 13%. We can conclude that the policy appears to have lowered the unemployment rate by 1 to 3%.

If instead the actual value of unemployment is 12%, then the unemployment rate is in the range of counterfactual values. The actual rate may be lower and may be higher than the unemployment rate would have been in the absence of the policy. Was the policy successful? We would have to say: According to some models, yes. According to other models, no.

Have fiscal and monetary policy been successful in battling the Great Recession of 2007–2009? Success is measured by comparing what is with what would have been. Most (not all) economists believe that the economy, as bad as it has become, is better off than it would have been in the absence of monetary and fiscal policy.

But unfortunately, that's a far stretch from saying the economy is better than it used to be. An unemployment rate near 10% is definitely worse than one near 5%.

TRY

10. What do economists mean by "zero lower bound"? What did the Fed do once it hit the zero lower bound?

11. What do economists mean by "the counterfactual value of the unemployment rate"?

12. Suppose a jobs-creation policy is put in place when the unemployment rate is 7%. A year later, the actual unemployment rate is 10% and the counterfactual unemployment rate is 12%. Was the policy successful in lowering the unemployment rate?

Chapter 10

Fiscal Policy

$\mathbf{F}$iscal policy—changes in government spending, transfer payments, and taxes—has a multiplied effect on GDP. But the multiplier for government spending is larger than the multiplier for transfer payments or taxes. Some changes in transfer payments and taxes happen automatically as the economy moves into or out of recession, whereas other fiscal policy actions are discretionary. Changes in fiscal policy affect government deficits and debt. The consequences of increased government debt are the subject of debate.

KEY TERMS AND CONCEPTS

- Government spending multiplier
- Lump-sum taxes
- Tax multiplier
- Transfer payments multiplier
- Discretionary fiscal policy
- Proportional taxes
- Automatic (built-in) stabilizer
- Outlays
- Receipts
- Budget balance
- Fiscal year
- Deficit
- Government budget deficit
- Balanced budget
- Surplus
- Government budget surplus
- Government debt
- Structural deficit
- High-employment (cyclically-adjusted) government budget deficit
- Government securities
- Treasuries
- Treasury bill
- Treasury note
- Treasury bond

- Crowding out
- Accommodate
- Sovereign default
- Austerity plan

KEY EQUATIONS

- Government spending multiplier
- Tax multiplier

GOVERNMENT SPENDING AND TAX MULTIPLIERS

A spending multiplier tells us how big the total change in output and income is for any initial change in aggregate demand. Remember: the multiplier is the ratio of the total change in output and income to the initial change in aggregate demand or aggregate spending.

$$multiplier = \frac{total \; \Delta Y}{initial \; \Delta AD}$$

Multiplying both sides of the equation by *initial* ΔAD, we get

$$total \; \Delta Y = initial \; \Delta AD \cdot multiplier$$

The total change in output and income will equal the initial change in aggregate demand times the spending multiplier.

In Chapter 8, we saw that the spending multiplier, *if we assume taxes are lump-sum and that only consumption changes when income changes*, is

$$spending \; multiplier = \frac{1}{1 - mpc}$$

Government spending is direct fiscal policy. The initial change in aggregate demand *is* the change in government spending. That's why the **government spending multiplier** of chapter 8 simply equaled the spending multiplier.

$$government \; spending \; multiplier = \frac{1}{1 - mpc}$$

When government spending changes, the total change in income equals the initial change in government spending times the multiplier.

$$Total \; \Delta Y = \Delta G \cdot \left(\frac{1}{1 - mpc} \right)$$

What if instead the government changes taxes? A change in taxes is indirect fiscal policy. The change in taxes affects aggregate demand indirectly: taxes fall, disposable income rises, and therefore consumption spending rises. Taxes are not part of aggregate demand; consumption is. The initial change in aggregate demand is the change in consumption spending.

All principles textbooks look at the effect of a change in **lump-sum taxes**, which are taxes whose amount does not change as income changes. How much does consumption spending initially change when there is a change in lump-sum taxes? The answer depends on the marginal propensity to consume, the *mpc*. There are just two steps to determining the change in consumption.

- Remember: $YD = Y - T$. So $\Delta YD = -\Delta T$.
- Remember: $\Delta C = mpc \cdot \Delta YD$. So $\Delta C = mpc \cdot (-\Delta T) = -(mpc \cdot \Delta T)$.

The initial change in aggregate demand equals the opposite of the *mpc* times the change in taxes. If taxes go down, aggregate demand goes up. If taxes go up, aggregate demand goes down.

How much does total income change? The spending multiplier we saw in Chapter 8 is

$$spending \ multiplier = \frac{1}{1 - mpc}$$

So the total change in income following a change in lump-sum taxes is

$$total \ \Delta Y = initial \ \Delta AD \cdot \left(\frac{1}{1 - mpc}\right) = -(mpc \cdot \Delta T) \cdot \frac{1}{1 - mpc}$$

$$= -\Delta T \cdot \frac{mpc}{1 - mpc}$$

The **tax multiplier** is the total change in income divided by the initial change in taxes.

$$tax \ multiplier = \frac{total \ \Delta Y}{initial \ \Delta TA} = -\frac{mpc}{1 - mpc}$$

TIP

Some textbooks ignore the minus sign in the tax multiplier, assuming that you realize that a drop in taxes raises income and an increase in taxes lowers income.

An increase in transfer payments has the same effect on disposable income as a decrease in taxes. A decrease in transfer payments and an increase in taxes have the same effect on disposable income. So a change in transfer payments affects total income and output in the same way (but with the opposite sign) as a change in taxes. The **transfer payments multiplier** is the total change in income divided by the initial change in transfer payments.

$$transfer \ payments \ multiplier = \frac{total \ \Delta Y}{initial \ \Delta TR} = \frac{mpc}{1 - mpc}$$

Suppose the marginal propensity to consume is 0.6. Then the government spending multiplier is $1/(1 - 0.6) = 2.5$. The tax multiplier is $-0.6/(1 - 0.6) = -1.5$. The transfer payments multiplier is $+0.6/(1 - 0.6) = +1.5$. A \$700 billion increase in government spending would increase income by (\$700 billion)·(2.5) $= +\$1{,}750$ billion. A \$700 billion cut in taxes would increase income by just $-(\$700 \ billion)\cdot(-1.5) = +\$1{,}050$ billion. A \$700 billion increase in transfer payments would increase income by just (\$700 billion)·(1.5) $= +\$1{,}050$ billion.

A \$1 increase in government spending has a larger impact on the economy than does a \$1 decrease in taxes or a \$1 increase in transfer payments. The tax and transfer payments multipliers are smaller than the government spending multiplier because not every penny of a $1 drop in taxes or $1 increase in transfer payments will be spent. So long as the *mpc* is less than 1, the change in consumption spending—the initial change in aggregate demand—will be smaller than the change in taxes or transfer payments.

TRY   *(Answers to all "TRY" questions are at the back of the book.)*

1. Suppose the *mpc* is 0.8. What is the total change in income and output when government spending rises by $100 billion? What is the total change in income and output when taxes are cut by $100 billion?

2. Suppose the *mpc* is 0.8. If Congress cuts government spending by $400 billion per year, what is the effect on GDP? If instead Congress cuts transfer payments by $400 billion per year, what is the effect on GDP?

How much fiscal policy is needed to close an output gap? Because multiplier effects will kick in, the initial increase in aggregate demand can be smaller than the output gap. And because the tax and transfer payments multipliers are smaller than the government spending multiplier, to close an output gap requires a larger change in taxes or transfer payments than a change in government spending. Closing an output gap by lowering taxes or raising transfer payments thus costs the government more than does closing an output gap by raising spending.

To see why, remember that the multipliers are

$$government\ spending\ multiplier = \frac{total\ \Delta Y}{initial\ \Delta G}$$

$$tax\ multiplier = \frac{total\ \Delta Y}{initial\ \Delta TA}$$

$$transfer\ payments\ multiplier = \frac{total\ \Delta Y}{initial\ \Delta TR}$$

Rearrange those equations slightly, and you have

$$initial\ \Delta G = \frac{total\ \Delta Y}{government\ spending\ multiplier}$$

$$initial\ \Delta TA = \frac{total\ \Delta Y}{tax\ multiplier}$$

$$initial\ \Delta TR = \frac{total\ \Delta Y}{transfer\ payments\ multiplier}$$

Assume the output gap is $300 billion. Assume the marginal propensity to consume is 0.6. The three multipliers will equal

$$government\ spending\ multiplier = \frac{1}{1 - 0.6} = \frac{1}{0.4} = 2.5$$

$$tax\ multiplier = -\frac{0.6}{1-0.6} = -\frac{0.6}{0.4} = -1.5$$

$$transfer\ payments\ multiplier = \frac{0.6}{1-0.6} = \frac{0.6}{0.4} = 1.5$$

To close the output gap using government spending, the required increase in government spending would be $120 billion.

$$initial\ \Delta G = \frac{total\ \Delta Y}{government\ spending\ multiplier}$$

$$= \frac{\$300\ billion}{2.5} = \$120\ billion$$

To close the output gap using taxes, the required cut in taxes would be $200 billion.

$$initial\ \Delta TA = \frac{total\ \Delta Y}{tax\ multiplier}$$

$$= \frac{\$300\ billion}{-1.5} = -\$200\ billion$$

To close the gap using transfer payments, the required increase in transfer payments would also be $200 billion.

$$initial\ \Delta TR = \frac{total\ \Delta Y}{transfer\ payments\ multiplier}$$

$$= \frac{\$300\ billion}{1.5} = \$200\ billion$$

Notice that whether it is taxes or transfer payments or government spending that is used to close the output gap, the change in aggregate demand is the same. When government spending rises by $120 billion, aggregate demand increases initially by $120 billion. When taxes are cut by $200 billion or transfer payments are increased by $200 billion, disposable income rises by $200 billion, and so consumption spending (with an *mpc* of 0.6) rises by $0.6 \cdot 200 = \$120$ billion. Here again, aggregate demand increases initially by $120 billion. The cost to the government of direct fiscal policy in this example is $120 billion. The cost to the government of indirect fiscal policy is $200 billion.

TRY

3. Suppose the output gap is $2 trillion and the marginal propensity to consume is 0.75. How large an increase in government spending would be required to close the output gap? If instead the gap is closed by changing taxes, how large a tax cut would be required to close the gap?

4. Suppose there is an inflationary gap of $200 billion and the marginal propensity to consume is 0.5. How large a change in government spending would be required to close the inflationary gap? If instead the gap is closed by changing transfer payments, how large a transfer payments change would be required to close the gap?

DISCRETIONARY FISCAL POLICY AND AUTOMATIC STABILIZERS

Discretionary fiscal policy refers to changes in government spending, transfer payments, and taxes that do not occur automatically as a result of changes in income. When Congress increases spending to fight a recession, this is discretionary fiscal policy. When Congress increases taxes to slow the economy, this is discretionary fiscal policy as well. The $787 billion stimulus bill passed by Congress and signed by President Obama in February 2009 is an example of discretionary fiscal policy.

Other changes in government spending, transfer payments, and taxes occur automatically as output and income change. Many of the taxes we pay are **proportional taxes**, their amount calculated as a proportion or percent of income. When income rises, proportional taxes rise, too. When income falls, tax revenues fall.

Some transfer payments also change as income changes. When someone's income falls because he or she becomes unemployed, he or she may begin collecting unemployment insurance benefits. When income falls, unemployment insurance payments rise.

Economists use the phrases **automatic stabilizers** or **built-in stabilizers** to refer to changes in government spending, transfer payments, or taxes that occur automatically as output and income change. When taxes and transfer payments change as income changes, fluctuations in GDP and income will be smaller. Economists say: the economy is more stable when taxes and transfer payments act as automatic stabilizers.

An example illustrates. Suppose the tax rate is 25%. When income goes up by $1,000 million, tax payments go up by 25% of $1,000 million, which is $250 million. Disposable income is the difference between income and taxes. So disposable income goes up by $1,000 million−$250 million = $750 million. The change in disposable income, $750 million, is smaller than the change in income, $1,000 million.

To see the effect on equilibrium GDP, assume that the marginal propensity to consume equals 0.8. If taxes were lump-sum and not proportional to income, the multiplier would equal 5. An initial increase in aggregate demand and income of $1,000 million will produce a total change in real GDP that is 5 times as large: $5,000 million.

But with a proportional tax rate of 0.25 and an *mpc* of 0.8, the multiplier equals just 2.5. (See Chapter 8, multiplier with proportional taxes.) An initial increase in aggregate demand and income of $1,000 million will produce a total change in real GDP that is just 2.5 times as large: $2,500 million. Because the swings in real GDP are smaller with proportional taxes than they are without proportional taxes, economists say the economy is more stable with proportional taxes. This is the sense in which proportional taxes are automatic stabilizers.

TIP

It's easy to get confused. The example we just did compared the government spending multiplier in a world with lump-sum taxes with the government spending multiplier in a world with proportional taxes. That's different from what we did in the previous section when we looked at the tax multiplier, which examines the effect of changing *the size* of lump-sum taxes.

What happens when we start with an initial decrease in aggregate spending? Again, a proportional tax acts as an automatic stabilizer.

When there is an initial drop in aggregate spending, output and income fall. Those families whose income has fallen will see a drop in their disposable income. But—the key difference—because taxes are proportional to income, their tax bill drops when their income drops. And therefore the drop in disposable income is smaller than the drop in income.

Families experiencing a drop in disposable income will then decrease their spending, leading to another drop in output and income. Again, those whose income has fallen will experience a drop in disposable income, but the drop in disposable income will be smaller than the drop in income.

Round after round of the multiplier process ensues. In each round, due to the presence of proportional taxes, the drop in disposable income is smaller than the drop in income. And so the total drop in spending, output, and income resulting from some initial drop in aggregate spending will be smaller in the presence of proportional taxes than it would have been with lump-sum taxes.

Look back at the numerical example above. Suppose the initial change in aggregate spending is a decrease (rather than an increase) of $1,000 million. With an *mpc* of 0.8 and lump-sum taxes, the total drop in output and income would be $5,000 million. But if instead we have proportional taxes with a tax rate of 0.25, the total drop in output and income will be just $2,500 million. Whether aggregate spending is increasing or decreasing, fluctuations in GDP and income are smaller when taxes are proportional instead of lump-sum.

TRY

5. Why are proportional taxes called an "automatic stabilizer"? What is being stabilized?

6. When lump-sum taxes are decreased from $800 billion to $500 billion, is this an example of an automatic stabilizer? Explain.

DEFICIT AND DEBT

Government spending and transfer payments are the government's **outlays**—money going out of the government's coffers. Taxes, on the other hand, are the government's **receipts**—money coming into the government's coffers.

The government's **budget balance** is the difference between its receipts and its outlays.

   budget balance = receipts − outlays = TA − (G + TR) = T − G

The U.S. government measures its budget balance over a one-year period that starts on October 1 and ends on September 30. So the federal government's 2009 **fiscal year** was October 1, 2008 to September 30, 2009.

When money going out (outlays) exceeds money coming in (receipts), there is a **deficit**. This definition of deficit is true universally: for your personal finances, for your school's budget, and for a government agency's budget. When the government's budget is in deficit, the budget balance is negative.

*There is a **government budget deficit** when TA < (G + TR)*

When money going out (outlays) equals money coming in (receipts), there is a **balanced budget**. Again, this definition is true universally. When the government's budget is balanced, the budget balance is zero.

There is a balanced government budget when TA = G + TR.

When money going out (outlays) is less than money coming in (receipts), there is a **surplus**. When the government's budget is in surplus, the budget balance is positive.

*There is a **government budget surplus** when TA > (G + TR)*

TIP

Notation varies. Commonly *BB* stands for budget balance, *BD* for budget deficit, and *BS* for budget surplus.

The **government debt** is the sum, since 1789, of all the annual deficits minus the sum, since 1789, of all the annual surpluses. The debt is calculated as of a moment in time. It is the total amount that has been borrowed and not yet repaid.

In a year when the government runs a deficit, the government debt rises. In a year when the government runs a surplus, the government debt falls.

When there is expansionary fiscal policy—increases in *G*, increases in *TR*, or decreases in *TA*—the budget balance worsens: a budget deficit increases or a budget surplus decreases. When there is contractionary fiscal policy—decreases in *G*, decreases in *TR*, or increases in *TA*—the budget balance improves: a budget deficit decreases or a budget surplus increases. To summarize,

expansionary fiscal policy $\rightarrow \uparrow BD$ or $\downarrow BS$

contractionary fiscal policy $\rightarrow \downarrow BD$ or $\uparrow BS$

Automatic stabilizers—policies that make taxes and transfer payments change automatically as income changes—create automatic changes in the budget balance. When the economy moves into recession and income falls, tax revenues decline and transfer payments rise. The decrease in receipts and increase in outlays worsens the budget balance. Therefore, when the economy moves into recession and income falls, deficits automatically become larger or surpluses become smaller.

When the economy moves into recovery and income rises, tax revenues rise and transfer payments decline. The rise in receipts and fall in outlays improves the budget balance. Therefore, when the economy moves into recovery and income rises, deficits automatically become smaller or surpluses become larger.

Because the budget balance changes automatically as we move through the business cycle, economists make a distinction between the overall budget deficit and the **structural deficit**. The structural deficit (or surplus, were there one) is a hypothetical number. The structural deficit is the answer to "What would the budget deficit be if the economy were at full employment?"

To calculate the structural deficit, economists start from the current government deficit. Then they make two adjustments. What would receipts be if the economy were at full employment? What would outlays be if the economy were at full employment? The structural deficit is

Outlays at full employment − receipts at full employment

The structural deficit is also sometimes called the **high-employment government budget deficit** or the **cyclically-adjusted government budget deficit**. The structural deficit is smaller than the actual deficit that exists in the midst of a recession.

TIP

Most textbooks focus their discussion of fiscal policy on federal policy. But remember: the G, TR, and TA in macroeconomics refer to total government outlays and receipts for all levels of government: federal, state, and local.

TRY

7. Suppose government spending is $2,000 billion per year, transfer payments are $1,400 billion per year, and tax receipts are $3,000 billion per year. What's the budget balance? Is there a budget deficit, or a budget surplus?

8. Why does the budget deficit increase when a recession begins, even if there is no discretionary fiscal policy?

FINANCING A GOVERNMENT DEFICIT

When the federal government runs a deficit, it still pays its bills. The government doesn't turn to the Supreme Court justices or Army privates or your grandmother who lives on Social Security and say "Sorry, no money! You won't get your check this time." The government has fiscal obligations that it *must* meet. So where does the government get the money?

Many people say "They print it." That's not true. The Bureau of Engraving and Printing is the federal government agency that prints out new currency. But the new currency that the Bureau prints is not scooped up by the government and used to pay bills. The new currency is shipped off to banks in exchange for dirty, torn currency that is headed for the shredder. The new currency goes into ATM machines and bank teller drawers, and is given out in exchange for a lower balance in a customer's checking account. The printing press makes a nice visual on the evening news, but it is simply not the source of funds the government uses to pay its bills.

Instead, when the government runs a deficit, it borrows in order to pay its bills. The government issues IOUs, signed by the Secretary of the Treasury. Federal government IOUs are called **government securities** or **Treasuries**. When the government borrows and promises to repay in one year or less, the IOU is called a **Treasury bill**. When the government borrows and promises to repay in 2, 3, 5, or 10 years, the IOU is called a **Treasury note**. When the government borrows and promises to repay in 30 years, the IOU is called a **Treasury bond**. The total of all the outstanding bills, notes, and bonds equals the federal government's debt.

TIP

The shorthand "IOU" comes from the phrase "I owe you."

The amount of U.S. federal government deficit and debt ballooned during the Great Recession of 2007–2009. Automatic stabilizers were responsible for part of the increased deficit. Two discretionary fiscal policy actions were responsible for much of the rest: the $700 billion Troubled Asset Relief Program (TARP) initially authorized in the waning days of the Bush administration, and the $787 billion American Recovery and Reinvestment Act (ARRA) authorized in the first weeks of the Obama administration. Both of these actions are temporary policies associated with the recession and thus are not part of the structural deficit.

Figure 10.1 shows the amount of the U.S. federal government deficit and surplus since 1971. Some movements of the budget into deficit are the result of automatic stabilizers. The budget was nearly balanced in 1973, and then the economy experienced a severe recession, pushing the budget into deficit in 1974 and 1975. Some movements of the budget are due to discretionary policy. TARP and ARRA authorized nearly $1.5 trillion in additional government spending over three years, pushing the deficit in 2009 to nearly $1.7 trillion, about 12% of GDP. Assuming that ARRA is not extended, the deficit is expected to fall in 2012 back to about 4% of GDP.

Notice also in Figure 10.1 that the U.S. government budget was in surplus in the late 1990s. The move into surplus reflected in part automatic stabilizers that lowered transfer payments and raised tax revenues as the macroeconomy boomed in the late 1990s.

TIP

A good source for data on federal government deficits and debt is the federal Office of Management and Budget, http://omb.gov. Choose the "historical tables" of the budget document.

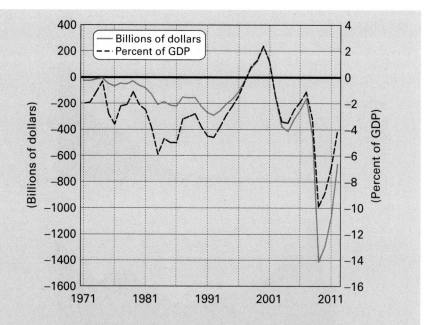

Figure 10.1 U.S. Federal Government Deficit and Surplus, 1971–2012.

The U.S. federal government deficit and surplus since 1971 is shown. The amounts for 2011–2012 are estimates provided by the federal government. The solid line shows the budget balance in billions of dollars. The dashed line shows the budget balance as a share of GDP.

Figure 10.2 shows the amount of U.S. government debt since 1939. Until 1981, total outstanding U.S. government debt was below $1 trillion. But commensurate with the series of deficits run since the late 1970s, U.S. federal government debt has risen almost nonstop. Its rise was interrupted only by the four years of budget surpluses in the late 1990s.

If there was no structural deficit, then automatic stabilizers would push the budget balance into deficit during recessions and into surplus in good times. Debt would accumulate during the bad times and be paid off in the good times. But this is not what has happened in the United States. Instead, the United States has had a nearly constant accumulation of debt since the late 1970s.

As a share of GDP, government debt remains below the levels reached during World War II. But government debt as a share of GDP has doubled in the last quarter century.

Concerns Expressed about Government Borrowing

Three concerns are sometimes expressed about government borrowing. One is about the impact on interest rates. The second is about the economic effect of paying back the debt. A third is whether there is some limit to the extent of federal borrowing.

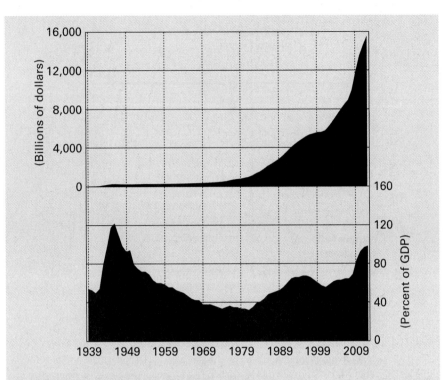

Figure 10.2 U.S. Federal Government Debt, 1939–2012.

U.S. federal government debt since 1939 is shown. The top graph shows the total out-standing government debt in billions of dollars. The bottom graph shows outstanding government debt as a share of GDP. The steady increase in government debt since 1981 reflects the large budget deficits of Figure 10.1. Since 1981, only the mid- to late 1990s, when GDP was rising faster than outstanding debt, saw a decline in the government debt-to-GDP ratio.

Interest Rates Impact?

When the government increases how much it is borrowing to pay its bills, then, *all else constant*, this puts upward pressure on interest rates. Higher interest rates lead to lower aggregate spending. A decrease in investment spending in response to higher interest rates triggered by increased government borrowing is what economists call **crowding out**. Economists say: government borrowing can crowd out investment spending.

    The phrase "all else constant" is important. Increased government borrowing does not always cause interest rates to rise. The central bank can **accommodate** fiscal policy by keeping interest rates unchanged. If the central bank keeps interest rates constant, then increased government borrowing will not crowd out investment spending.

    Even without central bank accommodation, interest rates might not rise when the government borrows more. If demand for U.S. Treasuries increases at the same time, interest rates might not change. Because the U.S. government is viewed as a reliable borrower, its debt is considered some of the safest debt in the world. As global financial markets faltered in 2008–2009, the safety of U.S. government debt attracted lenders worldwide. Big increases in U.S. borrowing did not trigger increases in interest rates.

Economic Effect?

A second concern about government borrowing is the economic effect of paying back the government debt. When the government pays off its debts, won't that lower spending in the economy?

There's both a bit of truth and a bit of exaggeration in the concern. Let's start with the exaggeration. First, about half of the government debt is owed to other government agencies. So paying back that part of the government debt doesn't drain money from the government's coffers, it just transfers it from one agency's account to another's.

Second, about one-fourth of the government debt is owed to individuals and institutions within the United States. Paying back this part of the debt does transfer money from the government to the lenders. But both the government and the domestic lenders are all part of the same macroeconomy. So paying back that part of the government debt doesn't drain money from the U.S. economy, it just transfers it from the government to U.S. individuals and institutions.

As to the bit of truth, about one-fourth of the outstanding government debt is owed to individuals and institutions outside the United States. Paying back that part of the government debt does represent a drain of money from the U.S. economy.

A quick however: those same individuals and institutions outside the United States have historically shown a strong appetite for U.S. government debt because it is seen as some of the safest debt in the world. So unless that international appetite for U.S. government debt changes, it is likely that when the government repays foreign lenders, those same foreign lenders will turn around and re-lend that same money back to the U.S. government.

Limit to Borrowing?

A third concerns arises periodically: Is there some limit to government borrowing? Can excessive government borrowing lead to the downfall of a nation? The answer is more political and psychological than economic.

So long as there are willing lenders, a government can borrow. If lenders believe the government's debt repayments are manageable, they'll lend. But if a government suggests, or if financial markets come to believe, that the government will not repay its debts—that there will be **sovereign default**—then lenders will turn away in search of a more reliable borrower.

At what point do lenders turn away? There is not one clear answer. Pundits will cite various ratios of government debt-to-GDP as the maximum. Scholars will point to history. But the real answer is simply another question: What's the debt-to-GDP ratio at which lenders *decide* that a government won't repay all of its debts?

Many factors—political, psychological, and economic—influence lenders. So that ratio might be 60% for one country, and 110% for another.

If a government cannot borrow to finance its deficit, it faces two choices. The government can implement an **austerity plan**—decreasing outlays and increasing taxes to eliminate the deficit and the need to borrow. The short-run consequence of an austerity plan is a drop in aggregate demand: recession.

Alternatively, the government can take over the central bank and force it to give money directly to the government. The consequence of a central bank directly financing a government's deficit is inflation. If deficits are large, hyperinflation can result. Because the consequences can be so dire, responsible governments—including the United States—have safeguards in place preventing a government takeover of a central bank.

TRY

9. When the federal government runs a deficit, how does it get the money to pay its bills?

10. What is the definition of "structural deficit"? Did ARRA add directly to the structural deficit? Why or why not?

11. What concerns are expressed about the possible negative effects of government borrowing?

Chapter 11

Money Creation

One of the Fed's monetary policy tactics is changing the money supply. But how is money created? Money is created when banks make loans. The Fed can influence how much money banks create because, by law, banks must keep "reserves" at the Fed. For each bank, those reserves equal a fraction of the total of the balances in all checking accounts held at the bank. When bank reserves increase, the amount of money banks can create is many times larger than the increase in reserves.

KEY TERMS AND CONCEPTS

- Money
- Medium of exchange (means of payment)
- Unit of account
- Store of value
- Commodity money
- Fiat (token) money
- Coins
- Cash
- Currency
- Federal Reserve Note
- Liquidity
- M1
- M2
- Financial institutions
- Bank
- Check
- Total deposits
- Clearinghouse
- Reserve balance at the Fed
- Banking system
- Vault cash
- In circulation
- Run on the bank
- Fractional reserve system

- Required reserves
- Required reserve ratio
- Excess reserves
- Federal funds rate
- Discount rate
- Discount window
- T-accounts
- Money multiplier

KEY EQUATIONS

- $money\ multiplier = \dfrac{1}{required\ reserve\ ratio}$

- $\Delta M = initial\ \Delta ER \cdot money\ multiplier$

WHAT IS MONEY?

Before we talk about how money is created, we need to be clear on what "money" is. The language used when discussing money can be confusing. What economists mean by the word "money" and what most people mean are often not the same.

The Definition of Money

Money is an asset that is used to pay for goods and services. An asset is something we own that has value. For an asset to be considered "money," it must serve three functions:

- Medium of exchange
- Unit of account
- Store of value

An asset is a **medium of exchange** (also sometimes called the **means of payment**) if it is accepted in exchange for goods and services. The grocer accepts checks in exchange for groceries, so checks are a medium of exchange. The grocer does not accept ice cream in exchange for groceries, so ice cream is not a medium of exchange.

An asset is a **unit of account** if it is used for expressing prices. The price of a box of cereal is expressed in dollars, so dollars are a unit of account. The price of a box of cereal is not expressed in units of ice cream, so ice cream is not a unit of account.

And an asset is a **store of value** if it does not change over time. A dollar bill placed in a drawer will still be there in the future, so it is a store of value. Ice cream placed in a drawer will be a sticky, gooey mess in the future, so it is not a store of value.

Over time and across societies, different assets have served the role of money. An oft-cited example is the use of cigarettes as money in World War II POW camps.

Cigarettes, received monthly in packages from the Red Cross, were accepted by other POWs as a medium of exchange, unit of account, and store of value. So cigarettes were money.[1]

When the asset serving as money is an item such as cigarettes that has some use other than serving as money, economists call this **commodity money**. The alternative form of money is **fiat money** or **token money**, which is an asset that has no use in and of itself. In the United States today, our money is fiat money: coins, paper currency, traveler's checks, and balances in checking accounts serve as money. **Coins** are pennies, nickels, dimes, quarters, and so on. Paper currency is paper bills. **Cash** and **currency** are terms used to refer jointly to coins and paper currency.

Currency in and of itself is not useful. You can't smoke it, as you could a cigarette. You can't make jewelry with it, as you could gold. You can't write term papers on it, as you could a blank sheet of paper. Its only use is to serve as money.

In the United States, coins are produced at the U.S. Mint. Paper currency is produced at the Bureau of Engraving and Printing, which is part of the U.S. Department of the Treasury. The bills are delivered to the Federal Reserve and then distributed to banks by the Fed. Each bill has the words **Federal Reserve Note** and the seal of the U.S. Treasury printed on it, indicating that the paper currency is an obligation of both the Fed and the federal government.

Many people incorrectly think credit cards should be counted as money. But a credit card represents a liability, not an asset. A liability is something we owe to others. When you use a credit card, you are borrowing from the credit card company. Whether you pay your bill in full each month, or carry a balance, using your credit card is incurring a liability. So your credit card is not money.

TRY   *(Answers to all "TRY" questions are at the back of the book.)*

1. Define each of the three characteristics of money. With reference to those characteristics, why are credit cards not money?
2. For each item below, is it money? If so, is it commodity money or fiat money?
   a. shells in eighteenth-century societies in western Africa
   b. bus or subway tokens in cities that use tokens
   c. euros (the currency of Europe) when used in Chicago, Illinois

---

The Measurement of Money

Liquidity describes how easily an asset can be converted to cash. Some assets are relatively liquid assets; others are relatively illiquid. A liquid asset is one that can be converted to cash easily; little time transpires and little cost is incurred in converting the asset from its current state into cash. Cash is the most liquid asset; it

---

[1]Radford, R. A. "The Economic Organisation of a P.O.W. Camp," *Economica* 12 (November 1945): 189–201.

is already cash. The balance in your checking account is a very liquid asset because you can convert it to cash simply by finding an ATM.

An illiquid asset is one that can not be easily converted to cash; much time or much cost is incurred in converting the asset from its current state into cash. A house is an illiquid asset, as is the balance in a retirement fund. In both cases, substantial fees are incurred, and some time delay is involved in converting the asset from its current state into cash.

Because assets have varying liquidity, it is not immediately clear which financial assets should be counted as money and which shouldn't. The Federal Reserve determines for the United States which assets are "money." Today it publishes two definitions of money: M1 and M2. **M1** includes only those assets that are most liquid. **M2** includes everything that is in M1 plus some additional financial assets that are a bit less liquid but that can be converted to cash at relatively low cost.

M1 consists of

- Coin and paper currency held by the nonbanking public
- Traveler's checks
- Demand deposits held by the nonbanking public at commercial banks
- Other checkable deposits held at credit unions and thrift institutions

M2 consists of

- Everything that is in M1
- Savings deposits (including money market deposit accounts)
- Time deposits in amounts of less than $100,000, not in retirement accounts
- Balances in retail money market mutual funds, not in retirement accounts

Figure 11.1 shows the amount of money in the U.S. economy since 1960. M1 rose about 5% per year over the last half-century. M2 rose by about 7% per year since 1960, reaching over $8.5 trillion by 2010.

What Money Is Not

Language matters. Money is an asset accepted as a medium of exchange, a unit of account, and a store of value. In the United States, money is generally cash and checking account balances. That's what money is. What is it not?

- Money is *not* the same as wealth.
- Money is *not* the same as income.

Wealth is the total value of our assets minus the total value of liabilities. People may say, "I want to have a lot of money before I retire." But they don't mean what they say. What they want is wealth, not just money.

They may want stocks or a big retirement fund balance or a house or jewelry. None of those things, though, are money. Money is one asset we own. But not all of our assets are money.

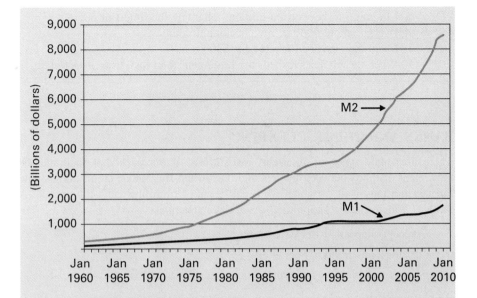

Figure 11.1 M1 and M2 for the United States, 1960–2010.

M1 includes coins, paper currency, traveler's checks, and balances in checking accounts. M1 increased from just over $100 billion in 1960 to about $1.7 trillion in 2010, an average annual increase of about 5%. M2 includes everything in M1 plus savings accounts, small certificates of deposit, and money market mutual funds. M2 increased from just under $300 billion in 1960 to about $8.5 trillion in 2010, an average annual increase of just under 7%.

Income is what we are paid in exchange for producing goods and services. People may say "I want a job that pays me more money." But they don't mean what they say. What they want is income, not just money.

Granted, many of us are paid with money—with cash or a paycheck. But are you contributing part of your income to a retirement fund, a 401(k) or 403(b)? Then part of your income is paid to you in a non-money asset, a deposit into your retirement fund. Money is one way we are paid. But not all of our income is paid to us as money.

TRY

3. What is M1? What is M2? Which measure of money—M1 or M2—has increased more rapidly in the last half-century?

4. For each of the following statements, is it describing money, income, or wealth?

a. My salary is $3,000 per month.

b. There are so many deductions from my pay that my paycheck is barely $2,000 each month.

    c. I'm going to be worth a million dollars by the time I'm 50.
    d. I've got about $900 in my checking account.
    e. I sold the artwork I created for $300.
    f. When the market crashed, my retirement fund lost 25% of its value.

BANKS AND CHECK CLEARING

There are many types of **financial institutions**—companies that facilitate the movement of funds between lenders and borrowers. But banks, credit unions, and thrift institutions—all of which we'll call "banks" from now on—are special. A **bank** is a financial institution that serves three functions:

- Accepts deposits from its customers
- Issues loans to borrowers
- Earns a profit for its shareholders

When you put money into your checking account and then want the money transferred to your landlord, how does that happen? You write a check or enter a bill payment online. The money is removed from your checking account and placed into your landlord's account. What happens behind the scenes?

    A **check** is an instruction from the check-writer to that individual's bank, instructing the bank to move a certain amount of funds out of the check-writer's account and into another individual's account. So if you write a check for $800 payable to "L. Lord, landlord," that check is simply an instruction from you to your bank to move $800 out of your account and into L. Lord's account. Paying a bill online is simply an electronic version of a check: it is an instruction to your bank to move funds out of your account and into someone else's account.

    Economists use the word "deposits" to refer to the balances in checking accounts. This can be confusing because people use "deposits" to refer to the funds they put into the account when they deposit a check. But **total deposits** refers to the total of the *balances* in everyone's account at some moment in time: the sum, determined on, say, Wednesday at 5:00 p.m., of $4,231.77 in Mary's account, $310.03 in Jay's account, $53,309.56 in L. Lord's account, and so on.

    When a check clears, the money has been transferred, as instructed, from the check-writer's account to the recipient's account. If everyone banks at the same bank—let's call it Bank A—the check-clearing process is quite simple. You instruct your bank, Bank A, to move $800 out of your account and into L. Lord's account, which is also at Bank A. The bank decreases the balance in your account by $800, increases the balance in L. Lord's account by $800. The check has cleared. There is no change in the total deposits at Bank A, just a change in who owns those total deposits.

    But what if you and L. Lord bank at different banks? Then there needs to be some way to move the money between banks. In that case, the banks use a

clearinghouse, which is an institution that transfers money between banks. In the United States, the Federal Reserve Banks serve as the clearinghouses for banks.

TIP

Remember: "Fed" is shorthand for the Federal Reserve. The Federal Reserve is not part of the federal government. It is the country's central bank, created by Congress but operated independently of it.

In the same way in which you have an account at Bank A, your bank has an account at the clearinghouse, the Federal Reserve Bank or Fed. The balance in the bank's account at the Fed is called its **reserve balance at the Fed**.

The bank's reserves at the Fed are analogous to your deposits at the bank. Your deposits are an asset—something you own—that you can draw upon. You can instruct the institution that holds your asset for you—the bank—to give some of your assets away. The bank does that when it honors checks you've written.

Similarly, the bank's reserves at the Fed are an asset owned by the bank. The bank can instruct the Fed, the clearinghouse, to give some of its assets away. The Fed does that when it honors the bank's request to move reserves to another bank.

Let's follow your $800 rent check. Your checking account is at Bank A. Your landlord, L. Lord, has a checking account at Bank B. You instruct your bank—either online or with a written check—to transfer $800 from your account to L. Lord's. What happens?

- Bank A decreases your checking account balance by $800.
- Bank A instructs the Fed to move $800 out of Bank A's reserves and into Bank B's reserves.
- Bank B increases L. Lord's checking account balance by $800.

Bank A is now holding $800 less in deposits and $800 less in reserves. Its deposits are decreased, because the balance in your checking account is decreased by $800. Its reserves are decreased, because the balance in Bank A's account at the Fed is decreased by $800.

Bank B is now holding $800 more in deposits and $800 more in reserves. Deposits increased, because L. Lord has $800 more in his checking account. Reserves increased, because the Fed moved $800 into Bank B's reserve account.

But what has happened in the banking system as a whole? The **banking system**, by which we mean all-of-the-banks in one thought, has had no change in total deposits and no change in total reserves. Total deposits have been reallocated away from you and toward L. Lord. Total reserves have been reallocated away from Bank A and toward Bank B. But overall, there's no change in total deposits or total reserves.

A similar series of events occurs when you deposit a check. Suppose that you are given a $500 paycheck by your boss, who banks at Bank B. What happens?

- You deposit your $500 paycheck at the ATM.

- Bank A increases your checking account balance by $500.
- Bank A instructs the Fed to transfer $500 *into* its reserve account from the reserve account of Bank B.
- Bank B receives notice that its reserves have been lowered by $500.
- Bank B decreases the balance in your boss's checking account by $500.

What if your boss didn't have $500 in his or her checking account? In that case, the check will bounce, which means it will not be honored. The series of events listed above will be reversed, with fees attached at each point. Bank B will return the check to Bank A, and charge your boss a fee for writing a check when there were insufficient funds in the checking account. The Fed will move the $500 back into Bank B's reserve account. Bank A will remove the $500 from your account, and charge you a fee for depositing a check that bounced. And you will be quite unhappy with your boss, to say the least.

The possibility that a check could bounce—be written against insufficient funds—is why banks sometimes place a hold on a check, waiting several days before they allow you to spend the money you have deposited into your account. In the old days, it could take a week for a bank to find out if a check was going to clear or bounce. Checks were physically transported from the bank to the Fed and then on to the originating bank. If a check was written on a bank in San Francisco and deposited in New York City, it had to be flown across the country. So there was some logic to a 10-day hold on a large or out-of-town check. Today, all of this is done electronically; not more than 24 hours elapse between the time the check is deposited at the ATM and the time the funds are withdrawn from the originating bank.

TRY

5. What is a check? Is there any difference between a check and an online bill payment?

6. You bank at Tree Bank. Your favorite charity—Help Others Now, Especially Youth, or HONEY—banks at Hive Bank. You write a $100 check payable to HONEY. How does HONEY actually get the money?

7. When you wrote a $100 check to HONEY, what was the effect on
   a. Your money holdings?
   b. HONEY's money holdings?
   c. Total deposits in the banking system?
   d. Tree Bank's reserve balance at the Fed?
   e. Hive Bank's reserve balance at the Fed?
   f. Total reserves in the banking system?

The Bank's Total Reserves

A bank's reserve balance at the Fed is one of two ways the bank holds its reserves. The second way a bank holds reserves is by having cash in its vault, tellers' drawers, and ATMs. We use the phrase **vault cash** to refer to all the cash that is inside the bank—whether or not it's literally locked up in the vault.

Banks hold only a small part of their reserves in the form of vault cash. There are two reasons banks hold so little cash: they earn no interest on vault cash, and there is the risk of theft. On average, only about 5% of reserves are held as vault cash.

TIP

Because vault cash is so small relative to the reserve balance at the Fed, most changes in reserves are changes in the reserve balance. So economists often say simply "reserves" rather than the longer phrase "reserve balance at the Fed."

Only cash that is **in circulation** is counted as money. Cash in a teller's drawer or inside the ATM or locked in the vault is not money. That same cash in your hand *is* money. The cash needs to be circulating in the economy—in the hands of the nonbanking public—for it to be considered "money."

The bank's reserves—its vault cash and its reserve balance at the Fed—are bank assets. The bank's job is to earn profit. So the bank has a financial incentive to own assets that earn a relatively high rate of return. Vault cash earns a zero rate of return. Until October 2008, the Fed paid no interest on bank reserves, so the rate of return on a bank's reserve balance was also zero. The Fed now pays a very low rate of interest, currently 0.25%, on a bank's reserve balance at the Fed. So the rate of return the bank earns on its reserve balance at the Fed is no longer zero, but it is still very low. Because of this low rate of return on assets held as reserves at the Fed, the bank has a financial incentive to hold a low level of reserves.

But while the bank has an incentive to hold a low level of reserves, you have an incentive for the bank to hold more reserves. Bank customers want banks to hold sufficient reserves to be able to honor all requests for withdrawal. Imagine if your check to L. Lord bounced because Bank A didn't have $800 in its reserve account! If the public learned that a bank could not honor a check because the bank held insufficient reserves, there would probably be a **run on the bank**. If you've seen the movies *It's a Wonderful Life* or *Mary Poppins*, you've seen illustrations of a bank run. The bank's customers run to the bank—in person, or via the bank's website—and demand the balance in their accounts.

Some people think that a bank should therefore hold reserves equal to its total deposits. But holding reserves equal to total deposits is not necessary. The bank needs to hold only enough reserves to cover a given day's withdrawals. Because not everyone will withdraw all of their money on the same day, the bank can hold reserves equal to just a fraction of its total deposits and still cover all withdrawals. Economists call a banking system in which reserves are less than deposits a **fractional reserve system**.

Federal Reserve regulations establish the minimum level of reserves that a bank must hold, which is called a bank's **required reserves**. The required reserves are not set as a dollar amount, but rather as a percent of the bank's total deposits. Except for the smallest of banks (those with total deposits under $50 million), the

Federal Reserve has set the reserve requirement at 10%. Economists call this the **required reserve ratio**. The dollar amount of required reserves is

Required reserves = required reserve ratio · total deposits

With a 10% required reserve ratio, a bank with total deposits of $500 million is required to maintain reserves of $50 million. A bank with total deposits of $750 billion must have $75 billion in reserves.

A bank may have more total reserves than are required. The gap between total reserves and required reserves is called **excess reserves**. The typical notation is

- Total reserves: *TR*
- Required reserves: *RR*
- Excess reserves: *ER*

where $ER = TR - RR$.

TIP

Remember: Total reserves are the sum of vault cash and the bank's reserve balance at the Fed.

The Fed does not compare a bank's total deposits and total reserves on the same day. Instead, the Fed compares the bank's total deposits and its total reserves 30 days later. This allows the bank time to increase its total reserves if for some reason the bank does not have sufficient reserves to meet the required reserve.

If a bank finds it has fewer reserves than are required, the bank has three options for increasing its reserves. To increase reserves, a bank can

- Call a loan, requiring a borrower to pay back a loan right away
- Borrow reserves from another bank
- Borrow reserves from the Fed

It is very unusual for banks to meet their reserve requirement by calling loans. Many loan contracts, such as home mortgages, do not allow the bank to call the loan. But some commercial loans are callable. The disruption to the bank's relationship with its borrowers is typically such a high cost that banks are very hesitant to call loans unexpectedly.

On the other hand, it is quite common for banks to borrow from other banks in order to meet their reserve requirements. The loans of reserves between banks are overnight loans, simply to cover the reserve requirement. In the United States, the interest rate that one bank charges another for these overnight loans is called the **federal funds rate**.

TIP

The phrase "federal funds rate" is misleading. The funds being borrowed are not federal money, but are bank-owned funds that the banks are holding in their reserve account at the Federal Reserve Bank.

Banks can also borrow directly from the Federal Reserve to cover a shortfall of total reserves. The interest rate that banks pay the Fed is called the **discount rate**. The borrowing is said to take place at the **discount window**. There's no longer a window; it's all done electronically. Fun fact: In some of the older Federal Reserve Bank buildings in the United States—such as the Federal Reserve Bank of Cleveland—the discount window has been maintained as a museum piece.

TRY

8. Why does the bank have an incentive to hold a relatively low level of reserves? Why does the Federal Reserve set a minimum required level of reserves?

9. The required reserve ratio is 10%. A bank has $545 million in deposits. Its total reserves are $60 million. What are the dollar amounts of the bank's required reserves and excess reserves?

10. The required reserve ratio is 10%. A bank has $545 million in deposits. Its total reserves are $50 million. What is the dollar amount of the bank's required reserves? What are the bank's options for satisfying its reserve requirement?

BANKS CREATE MONEY BY MAKING LOANS

How is money created? It's important to dispel one notion immediately: money is *not* created by printing it. The Bureau of Engraving and Printing does print paper currency and the U.S. Mint does produce coins. But their actions do not create money; that is, their actions do not increase the amount of money in the economy.

When you take $100 cash out of the ATM, there is $100 more cash in circulation but $100 less in your checking account. So there isn't any more money—the sum of coins, currency, travelers' checks, and balances in checking accounts—than there was before.

TIP

Remember: vault cash is not counted as part of the money supply. Currency in an ATM, a teller's drawer, or locked in a bank vault is not in circulation, and thus is not money.

Similarly, when more paper currency is printed or more coins are coined, there is not more money in the economy. The new paper currency replaces tired and torn paper currency that is sent to the shredder. The new coins replace lost coins. The government doesn't give the coins and currency away. The paper currency and coins are offered to banks in exchange for reserves at the Fed. The banks in turn give the paper currency and coins to customers in exchange for deposits.

So how is money created? Remember: money includes balances in checking accounts. Money is created when banks increase checking account balances in exchange for IOUs. Put another way: banks create money by making loans.

An Overview of the Money Creation Process

The process of creating money goes like this: A bank that has some excess reserves will extend a loan to one of its customers. Once the loan papers are signed, the bank will add the loan amount to the customer's checking account balance. *Money!*

TIP

The bank could also create money by lending out cash. Vault cash is not money; cash in the public's hands is. Yet nearly every loan is distributed in the form of increased deposits.

What constrains the amount of loans the bank can make? The required reserve ratio. Banks must hold reserves equal to some fraction of total deposits. The customer will use the borrowed money to buy something, instructing the bank with a check or an online payment to transfer the money to someone else. If the payment is to someone at another bank, reserves will be transferred to that other bank. The second bank will now have some excess reserves, but the first bank will not. The first bank can't make another loan if it has no excess reserves.

Let's follow one bank's excess reserves through the banking system and see when money is created. Here's what we have so far:

- Bank A has excess reserves.
- Bank A lends a customer an amount equal to its excess reserves.
- Bank A deposits the loan proceeds into the customer's checking account: *money is created.*
  - The customer spends the loan proceeds, writing a check to someone who banks at Bank B.
  - Bank A's excess reserves are transferred to Bank B, increasing Bank B's reserves.
  - The new money is transferred to the customer at Bank B.
  - Bank B must hold 10% of that new deposit as reserves, but the remaining 90% are excess reserves and can be lent out.
  - Bank B lends a customer an amount equal to its excess reserves.
  - Bank B deposits the loan proceeds into the customer's checking account: *more money is created.*
    - The customer spends the loan proceeds, writing a check to someone who banks at Bank C.
    - Bank B's excess reserves are transferred to Bank C, increasing Bank C's reserves.

- The new money is transferred to the customer at Bank C.
- Bank C must hold 10% of that new deposit as reserves, but the remaining 90% are excess reserves and can be lent out.
- Bank C lends a customer an amount equal to its excess reserves.
- Bank C deposits the loan proceeds into the customer's checking account: *more money is created.*
- And on and on we go.

Each time a bank issued a loan to one of its customers, it created money. From our starting point—Bank A recognizing it had some excess reserves—money was created at Bank A, Bank B, and Bank C. The process would continue. The banks are creating money by making loans with their excess reserves.

TRY

11. Why is printing paper currency not the same thing as creating money?

12. Tree Bank has some excess reserves. Why might it loan the excess reserves to a customer rather than simply holding on to the excess reserves? Under what circumstances might Tree Bank hold the excess reserves?

13. At what point in this story is money created? "You go to the bank to take out a student loan. After all the papers are signed, the bank loan officer hands you a check, payable to your college. You take the check to your college bursar, who will apply the amount to your tuition and fees balance. The bursar deposits the check into your college's checking account."

14. If your bank had no excess reserves, could it extend a loan to you? Explain.

Using T-Accounts

The usual way of presenting the money creation process uses what are called **T-accounts**, so named because the lines we draw form a T. There is one T-account for each institution—a bank or the Fed. The T-accounts show the assets, liabilities, and net worth of the institution. Remember: assets are the value of what we own; liabilities are the value of what we owe to others. Net worth is the difference between assets and liabilities.

$$Net\ worth\,(NW) = Assets\,(A) - Liabilities\,(L)$$

An increase in assets will increase net worth; an increase in liabilities will decrease net worth.

Standard practice is to show the assets on the left side of the T and liabilities plus net worth on the right side of the T. Rather than show the total value of assets and the total value of liabilities and net worth, we show just the changes in assets, changes in liabilities, and changes in net worth. Because net worth equals the difference between assets and liabilities, if both assets and liabilities change by the same amount, there is no change in net worth.

Your checking account balance is something you own—one of your assets. To your bank, your checking account balance is a liability. They owe the balance in your account to you. Similarly, the bank's balance in its reserve account at the Fed is one of its assets—something it owns. The reserve balance is a liability of the Fed, because they owe the reserve balance to the bank.

First, let's use the T-accounts to show a check clearing. Suppose that you write your $800 check to your landlord, L. Lord. You bank at Bank A; L. Lord banks at Bank B. Figure 11.2 shows the changes in the T-accounts. Bank A decreases the balance in your checking account by $800 and decreases the balance in its reserve account by $800. Bank B increases the balance in L. Lord's checking account by $800 and increases the balance in its reserve account by $800. The Fed transfers $800 from Bank A's reserve account to Bank B's reserve account.

Within each institution, the change in assets equals the change in liabilities. There is no change in net worth. Bank A's assets and liabilities both decreased

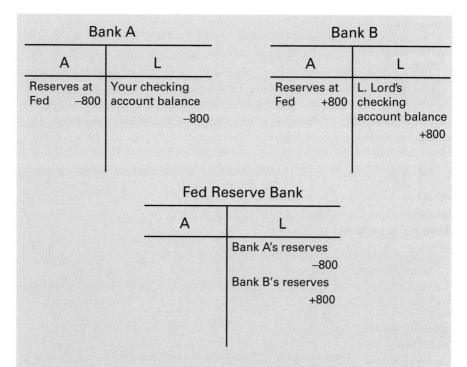

Figure 11.2 An $800 Check Moves Money from Bank A to Bank B.

T-accounts show changes in assets (on the left) and liabilities and net worth (on the right). When you give a check for $800 to L. Lord, Bank A decreases the balance in your account by $800 and Bank B increases the balance in L. Lord's account by $800. The Federal Reserve transfers reserves from Bank A to Bank B, which is recorded both by the Fed and by the individual banks.

by $800. Bank B's assets and liabilities both increased by $800. The Fed had no change in its total assets or liabilities—just a redistribution of its liabilities between the two banks.

TRY

15. To whom is each item below an asset? To whom is it a liability?
    a. The balance in your checking account at Tree Bank
    b. The balance in Tree Bank's reserve account at the Fed
    c. A $5 bill in your wallet
    d. A $5 bill in Tree Bank's vault

16. Use T-accounts to show the movement of $500 from your boss's checking account at Hive Bank into your account at Tree Bank.

17. Use T-accounts to show the movement of $100 from your checking account at Tree Bank into HONEY's checking account at Hive Bank.

Using T-Accounts to Show Money Creation

Let's use the T-accounts to show how banks create money. The process is the same as we described previously. But now we'll use a numerical example and the T-accounts to show how much money banks can create.

Suppose Bank A has $10,000 in excess reserves. (In Chapter 12 we will see how the Federal Reserve can increase or decrease the amount of excess reserves a bank has.) Figure 11.3 shows the first few steps of the money creation process. Bank A lends Mary, the owner of Mary's Clothing, $10,000 so she can buy new display racks for her store. Mary signs the loan documents, creating an IOU with the bank. This is one of the bank's financial assets. The bank has an offsetting liability: it increases the balance in Mary's checking account by $10,000. *Money is created*.

Now Mary uses the $10,000 in loan proceeds to buy display racks from Dolly's Display. Dolly banks at a different bank, so the $10,000 payment must clear through

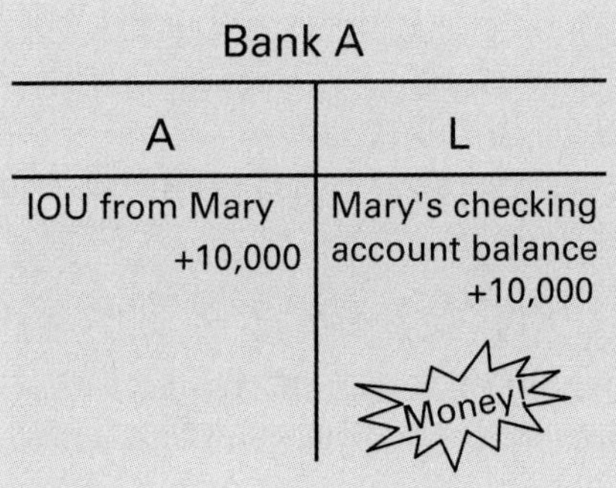

Bank A	
A	L
IOU from Mary +10,000	Mary's checking account balance +10,000

Figure 11.3 The First Loan in the Money Creation Process.

Bank A issues a $10,000 loan to Mary, the owner of Mary's Clothing. The bank now holds an IOU signed by Mary—a financial asset—and has increased the balance in Mary's checking account by $10,000. So far, $10,000 in money has been created.

Bank A		Bank B	
A	**L**	**A**	**L**
IOU from Mary +10,000	Mary's checking account balance +10,000	Reserves at Fed +10,000	Dolly Display's checking account balance
Reserves at Fed −10,000	Mary's checking account balance −10,000		+10,000

Fed Reserve Bank

A	L
	Bank A's reserves −10,000
	Bank B's reserves +10,000

Figure 11.4 The First Loan Is Spent.

Mary writes a check to Dolly's Display for $10,000, which clears through the Fed. $10,000 is deducted from Mary's account at Bank A. $10,000 is added to Dolly's account at Bank B. The Fed transfers $10,000 in reserves from Bank A to Bank B.

the clearinghouse. Figure 11.4 shows the next steps. Bank A lowers the balance in Mary's account by $10,000. The Fed transfers $10,000 in reserves from Bank A to Bank B. Bank B increases the balance in Dolly's account by $10,000. No new money is created in Figure 11.4. There is just a movement of money and reserves within the economy and the banking system.

Because of the increase in Dolly's account, Bank B now has $10,000 more in deposits. It must hold 10% of the increased deposits in reserves. So Bank B's required reserves increase by $10,000 \cdot 10\% = \$1,000$. Bank B's total reserves have increased by $10,000, and its required reserves have increased by $1,000. The difference of $9,000 is an increase in Bank B's excess reserves.

$$New\ total\ reserves\ of\ Bank\ B = 10,000$$
$$New\ required\ reserves\ of\ Bank\ B = 10,000 \cdot 0.10 = 1,000$$
$$New\ excess\ reserves\ of\ Bank\ B = 10,000 - 1,000 = 9,000$$

Bank B is a profit-maximizing institution. It earns only 0.25% on its reserve balance at the Fed, but can earn much more than that on loans. So Bank B makes a loan with its $9,000 in excess reserves.

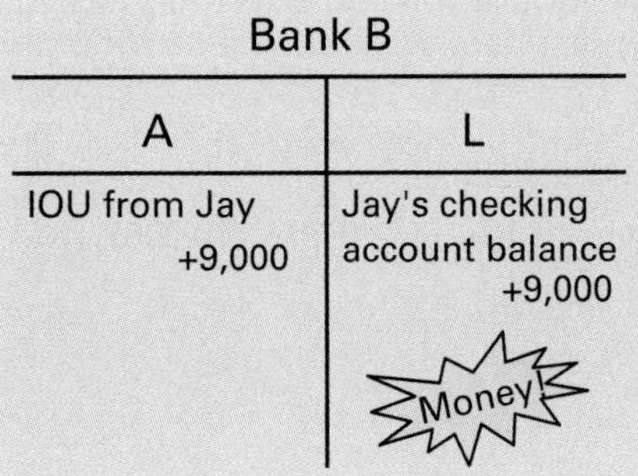

Bank B

A	L
IOU from Jay +9,000	Jay's checking account balance +9,000

Money

Figure 11.5 The Second Loan in the Money Creation Process.

Bank B has $9,000 in excess reserves. It loans $9,000 to Jay Lee, creating $9,000 in new money.

Bank B loans $9,000 to Jay Lee, a student who will use the loan proceeds to pay a quarter's tuition, fees, and housing to State College. Figure 11.5 shows the loan. Jay signs a loan document, creating an IOU for $9,000 to Bank B, which is a financial asset of Bank B. The bank creates an offsetting liability, increasing Jay's checking account balance by $9,000. *Money is created!*

Jay writes a check for $9,000 to State College, which banks at Bank C. The Fed facilitates the transfer of funds by moving $9,000 in reserves from Bank B's reserve account to Bank C's reserve account.

Bank C has acquired $9,000 in total reserves and $9,000 in new deposits. Its required reserves are 10% of deposits. So the change in its required reserves is 10% of the change in deposits: $9,000 \cdot 0.10 = $900. The rest of its new total reserves are excess reserves. Bank C can lend out those excess reserves, creating another $8,100 in money.

The money creation process goes on and on, with each bank receiving an increase in reserves that exceeds its increase in required reserves, allowing the bank to create a loan, which creates money. The $10,000 that was created when Mary took out a loan still exists. The $9,000 that was created when Jay took out a loan still exists. The total amount of money that will be created is much greater than the initial amount of excess reserves that starts the process.

TRY

18. Bank A has excess reserves of $90,000, which it loans to a customer. The customer pays the $90,000 to a contractor who will remodel her house. The contractor also banks at Bank A. Has Bank A lent out all of its excess reserves? Explain.

THE MONEY MULTIPLIER

How much money will be created? If all banks lend all of their excess reserves, and if all money is held in checking accounts rather than cash, then with a 10%

required reserve ratio, the total amount of money that will be created from an initial $10,000 increase in excess reserves will be

$$
\begin{aligned}
\text{Total } \Delta\text{money} &= 10,000 + 9,000 + 8,100 + 7,290 + \cdots \\
&= 10,000 + \big[(1 - 0.10) \cdot (10,000)\big] + \big[(1 - 0.10) \cdot (1 - 0.10) \cdot (10,000)\big] + \\
&\quad \big[(1 - 0.10) \cdot (1 - 0.10) \cdot (1 - 0.10) \cdot (10,000)\big] + \cdots \\
&= 10,000 + \big[0.9 \cdot (10,000)\big] + \big[0.9 \cdot (0.9) \cdot (10,000)\big] + \\
&\quad \big[0.9 \cdot (0.9) \cdot (0.9) \cdot (10,000)\big] + \cdots \\
&= 10,000 \cdot (1 + 0.9 + 0.9^2 + 0.9^3 + \cdots) \\
&= 10,000 \cdot \left(\frac{1}{1 - 0.9}\right) = 10,000 \cdot \left(\frac{1}{0.1}\right) = 10,000 \cdot 10 \\
&= 100,000
\end{aligned}
$$

With a 10% required reserve ratio, the total amount of money that will be created from an initial $10,000 increase in excess reserves will be $100,000.

The amount of money that is created is a multiple of the initial change in excess reserves. Economists call that multiple the **money multiplier**. The definition of the money multiplier is

$$
money\ multiplier = \frac{total\ \Delta M}{initial\ \Delta ER}
$$

In this case, the money multiplier is 10, because the amount of money that can be created is ten times as large as the initial change in excess reserves.

In general, if all banks lend all of their excess reserves, and if all money is held in checking accounts rather than cash, then the money multiplier will equal

$$
money\ multiplier = \frac{1}{required\ reserve\ ratio}
$$

The total amount of money that will be created from an initial increase in excess reserves of ΔER is

$$
\Delta M = initial\ \Delta ER \cdot money\ multiplier
$$

If the required reserve ratio is 10%, the money multiplier is 10. If the required reserve ratio is 5%, the money multiplier is $1/0.05 = 20$. If the required reserve ratio is 15%, the money multiplier is $1/0.15 = 6.67$.

TRY

19. Assume that banks lend out all of their excess reserves, and that all money is held as checking accounts. For each of the following scenarios, what is the value of the money multiplier? How much money will be created?

    a. The initial increase in excess reserves is $400,000 and the required reserve ratio is 10%.

b. The initial increase in excess reserves is $400,000 and the required reserve ratio is 12%.

c. The initial decrease in excess reserves is $200,000 and the required reserve ratio is 10%.

20. If banks decide to hold some excess reserves rather than lend out all of their excess reserves, will the total change in money equal the initial change in excess reserves times 1/(required reserve ratio)? Explain.

Chapter 12

The Money Market

The market for money illustrates the connection between money and interest rates. The central bank's actions to change interest rates also change the amount of money in the economy. Their actions to change the amount of money in the economy also change interest rates. Because of this connection, monetary policy cannot independently pursue both money supply and interest rate targets.

KEY TERMS AND CONCEPTS

- Money market
- Demand for money
- Supply of money
- Equilibrium amount of money
- Money stock
- Nonmoney assets
- Wealth portfolio
- Transactions motive
- Speculation motive (or opportunity cost, or interest rate) motive
- Real money demand
- Nominal money demand
- Price of money
- Equilibrium interest rate
- Equilibrium money stock
- Discount rate
- Lender of last resort
- Federal Open Market Operations (FOMO)
- Discount bond
- Money supply target
- Interest rate target

KEY GRAPHS

- Money market

THE MONEY MARKET

To see the connection between money and interest rates, we focus on the money market. When economists talk about the **money market**, they are referring to a market that is in many ways akin to any other market. There is a **demand for money**, which is determined by all the people and institutions who want to hold part of their wealth as money. There is a **supply of money**, which is determined by those who produce money—the banks who create money by making loans with their excess reserves. And there is an **equilibrium amount of money**, or what economists often call the **money stock**, which is the amount of money where demand equals supply.

There are two common sources of confusion. First is the phrase "money market." Economists envision demand and supply when they use the phrase "money market." But it is likely that you've heard the phrase "money market" in connection with an account at your bank or with a mutual fund. The money market account at your local bank is a type of savings account that pays interest based on the current earnings of short-term Treasury and other bills. Money market accounts are *not* what we are referring to in our discussion of the "money market."

The second source of confusion when economists talk about the money market stems from forgetting what money is . . . and isn't. In the United States, cash and checking account balances are the usual forms of money. Money is not income. Money is not wealth. Money is simply one of the ways we hold our wealth. It is a financial asset that we use to pay for goods and services. The demand for money is not about wanting more income, nor wanting more wealth. The demand for money is about how we allocate the wealth we already have between money and other assets.

To understand the money market, we look at money demand, money supply, money market equilibrium, and the shifts of money supply or money demand that change the equilibrium. Let's take each of these ideas in turn.

Money Demand

Money demand is about how we hold our wealth. Economists divide the assets we can hold into two groups: money and non-money assets. Money is cash and balances in checking accounts. **Non-money assets** are all assets other than money: stocks, bonds, houses, retirement accounts, jewelry, gold, and so on. Money demand is about how we manage our **wealth portfolio**: how much of our wealth do we want to hold as money, and how much do we want to hold as non-money assets?

In most textbooks, non-money assets are referred to collectively as "bonds." This can be confusing, because bonds are actually just one of many types of non-money assets. It is a simplification—a way of thinking about a complex idea by focusing just on what really matters. It's also frankly an easier word to say! "Money and bonds" is easier to say and easier for students to hear the distinction between than "money and non-money assets." We'll stick with the standard practice here: wealth can be held in two ways, as money or as bonds (which refers to all non-money assets).

Table 12.1 shows the advantages and disadvantages of holding money and bonds. Money can be used in transactions—to pay for goods and services—but earns no interest. Bonds earn interest income but cannot be used in transactions—cannot be used to pay for goods and services.

Table 12.1 Money versus Bonds

	Advantage	Disadvantage
Money	Can be used in transactions	Rate of return = 0
Bonds (non-money assets)	Rate of return>0	Cannot be used in transactions

---

TIP

Interest rates and rates of return are the same thing. When the bank pays you an interest rate of 3%, your rate of return is 3%.

Notice that we've made another simplifying assumption: we assume that the rate of return on money is zero, and that bonds earn some positive rate of return. Does it matter that some of us have checking accounts that pay interest? No. The idea is simply that we are dividing our wealth into two groups of assets: one group is useful for paying for goods and services (but usually pays no or low interest), and the other is not useful for paying for goods and services (but usually earns some rate of return).

Table 12.1 captures two of the factors or motives that affect money demand: transactions and rates of return. Only money—and not bonds—can be used to pay for transactions. The more transactions we undertake, the more of our wealth we thus want to hold in the form of money. So an increase in transactions leads to an increase in money demand. Economists call this the **transactions motive**.

Economists typically use income as a proxy for transactions, because we do not have a direct measure of transactions. A proxy is something that can stand in for something else, because it behaves similarly, even though it is not the same thing. Because transactions tend to rise as income rises and fall as income falls, income is a reasonable proxy for transactions.

TIP

Businesses and government agencies have wealth, too. As you think about money demand, don't think about how just you would behave. Think about businesses, too.

A rise in income (because it is associated with more transactions) leads to a rise in money demand by people and businesses. People want more money, because they are buying more things—and money is how we pay for things. Businesses want more money, because they are paying higher wages and salaries, and so they need a larger checking account balance before payday.

A fall in income leads to a fall in money demand. People have less income, and so are spending less, and so keep smaller balances in their checking accounts. Businesses have fewer employees and a smaller payroll, and thus also keep smaller balances in their checking accounts. To summarize,

$$\uparrow Income \;\rightarrow\; \uparrow Transactions \;\rightarrow\; \uparrow Money\ Demand$$
$$\downarrow Income \;\rightarrow\; \downarrow Transactions \;\rightarrow\; \downarrow Money\ Demand$$

TIP

Remember: Demanding more money is not about wanting more wealth or more income. It is about how we split our wealth between money and bonds.

Interest rates are a second factor affecting money demand. Economists have several names for the role of interest rates: some textbooks call it the **speculation motive**; others call it the *opportunity cost motive* or the *interest rate motive*. There is an opportunity cost to holding our wealth as money: every dollar of our wealth held as money is a dollar that is not earning the interest that bonds are earning. The higher the rate of return on bonds (non-money assets), the higher is the opportunity cost of holding our wealth in the form of money, and therefore the more of our wealth we want to hold in the form of bonds. As interest rates rise, we will move some of our wealth out of money and into bonds—a decrease in our money demand.

The reverse is also true. As the difference between the rate of return on bonds and the rate of return on money gets smaller, we will hold more of our wealth as money rather than as bonds—an increase in our money demand.

Is all of this realistic? Is it how we actually behave? Absolutely. Instead of "money" and "bonds," let's use phrases we're all more familiar with: "checking accounts" and "savings accounts." You can pay your rent and buy groceries with the funds in your checking account. In order to use your savings account for those transactions, you first need to swing by the ATM or go to your online banking site, and move funds from your savings to your checking account. What if you earned 1% interest on your checking account and 1.5% interest on your savings account? The extra 0.5% interest means that $1,000 left in your savings account for three weeks earns you less than 30 cents. That's simply not worth the hassle of moving funds between checking and savings.

But what if your checking account paid no interest and your savings account paid 16%—the rate savers could earn in the early 1980s? Then $1,000 left in your savings account for three weeks would earn you almost $10. In that case, you have a financial incentive to manage your money carefully. You'll deposit your monthly paycheck into your checking account, pay your first-of-the-month bills, and move the rest of the money into your savings account (after all, it takes just a click of the mouse)—and when other bills come in toward the end of the month, move those funds back to your checking account to pay your bills.

You're still spending the same amount of money each month. But when interest rates on bonds are 16% greater than what you could earn on money, you have less money demand and more bond demand; you move your wealth out of checking (money) and into savings (bonds) for part of the month. When interest rates on bonds are just 0.5% greater than what you could earn on money, you have less bond demand and more money demand; you leave your wealth in checking (money) and never move any of it into savings (bonds). Summarizing,

$$\uparrow Interest\ rate\ on\ bonds\ \rightarrow\ \downarrow Money\ Demand$$
$$\downarrow Interest\ rate\ on\ bonds\ \rightarrow\ \uparrow Money\ Demand$$

The third factor affecting money demand is prices. If you can buy a week's groceries for your family for $25, you need a smaller checking account balance—less money—than if those same groceries cost $150. The higher the average price level, such as the CPI, the greater is money demand. The lower the average price level, the smaller is money demand.

$$\uparrow Average\ Price\ Level\ \rightarrow\ \uparrow Money\ Demand$$
$$\downarrow Average\ Price\ Level\ \rightarrow\ \downarrow Money\ Demand$$

TIP

Some textbooks capture the relationship between prices and money demand by focusing on **real money demand**, MD/P. Others continue to focus on **nominal money demand**, MD, as we do here.

Economists depict the relationships between income, interest rates, prices, and money demand with a money demand curve. Figure 12.1 illustrates. The vertical axis measures interest rates. We can think of interest rates as the **price of money**, because interest rates are a measure of the opportunity cost of holding our wealth as money. The horizontal axis measures the amount of money. At higher interest rates, the amount of money demanded is lower; at lower interest rates, the amount of money demanded is higher. The money demand curve slopes down.

An increase in income or in prices shifts the money demand curve to the right. At every interest rate, we want to hold more of our wealth as money. A decrease in income or in prices shifts the money demand curve to the left. At every interest rate, we want to hold less of our wealth as money.

TRY   *(Answers to all "TRY" questions are at the back of the book.)*

1. What are the ways in which we can hold our wealth?
2. What is "money demand"? What is the "money market"?
3. What are the advantages and disadvantages of holding money? Of holding bonds?

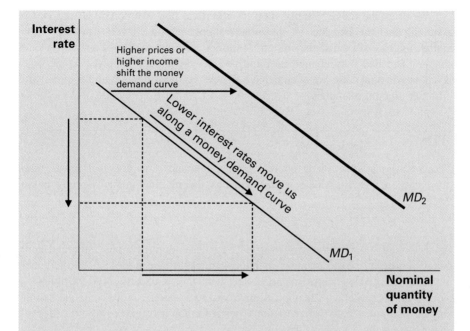

Figure 12.1 Money Demand Curve.

Because of the speculation motive, a decrease in interest rates will increase the quantity of money demanded, moving us along one money demand curve. Because of the transactions motive, an increase in income will shift the money demand curve to the right, from MD_1 to MD_2. An increase in the average price level also will shift the money demand curve to the right.

4. How does each of the following affect money demand? Is this a shift of or movement along the money demand curve?

a. Increased income
b. Increased interest rates
c. Increased prices

Money Supply

The money supply is the amount of money made available to people, businesses, and government agencies. Economists typically say "The Fed sets the money supply." This is not strictly correct. The Fed sets a goal for the money supply, but banks are the ones who create money. Banks create money by making loans with their excess reserves. And so it is banks—not the Fed—that actually determine the money supply. Nevertheless it is Fed policy that determines how many excess reserves are in the banking system. And so economists say: the Fed sets the money supply.

We draw the money supply curve as a vertical line. We do so because we are assuming that the Fed has set the money supply at some level—say, *MS*—and market forces can't cause the amount of money supplied to change as interest rates change. The Fed may change its mind and set the money supply at some other level, but in that case we would have a new vertical money supply curve at a different amount of money.

TIP

Those textbooks that focus on real money demand draw the real money supply curve, *MS/P*. Its shape is the same as the nominal money supply curve: vertical.

Is the money supply curve truly vertical? Is the amount of money supplied completely unresponsive to changes in interest rates? To be honest, no. Remember: money is created by banks making loans with their excess reserves. Only if we assume that banks *always* lend *all* of their excess reserves can we conclude that the amount of money banks create from a certain amount of excess reserves doesn't change when interest rates change.

In fact, sometimes banks do hold some excess reserves. At very low interest rates, the risk inherent in making loans is not fully compensated by the interest rate banks can charge, and banks may therefore hold some excess reserves. In that case, for a given level of excess reserves, the lower the interest rate, the less money banks would create. The money supply curve would be upward-sloping, not vertical.

Why, then, do nearly all textbooks draw the money supply curve as a vertical line? Because the general conclusions we draw about the money market are unchanged, whether the money supply curve is vertical or upward-sloping.

Money Market Equilibrium

Just like any market, the money market is in equilibrium when the quantity demanded equals the quantity supplied. In markets for goods and services, we look for the combination of equilibrium price and equilibrium quantity. With the market for money, the "price" is the interest rate on non-money assets, which measures the opportunity cost of holding wealth in the form of money. Our question is: what is the interest rate at which money demand equals money supply?

Figure 12.2 illustrates money market equilibrium. The supply of money is drawn as a vertical line at the level set by the Fed. The demand for money is downward-sloping; a lower interest rate increases the quantity of money demanded. The **equilibrium interest rate** is the interest rate at which money demand equals money supply. The equilibrium quantity of money—which economists sometimes call the **equilibrium money stock**—is the quantity of money where money demand equals money supply.

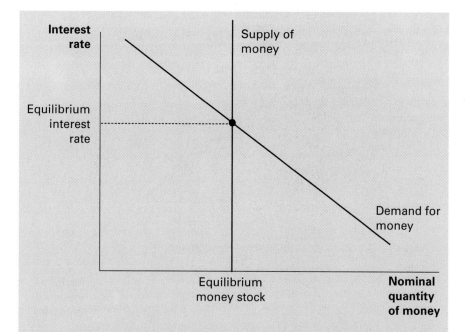

Figure 12.2 Money Market Equilibrium.

The money market is in equilibrium when the quantity of money supplied equals the quantity of money demanded. The interest rate will then equal the equilibrium interest rate. The supply of money is drawn as a vertical line, because we assume the Fed can set the money supply. The demand for money is downward-sloping, because the interest rate paid on non-money assets represents the opportunity cost of holding our wealth as money.

TIP

Because the money supply does not change when interest rates change, the equilibrium money stock and the money supply are identical. Many times the phrases are used interchangeably.

TRY

5. Why do we draw the money supply as a vertical line?
6. We say "The Fed sets the money supply." Who actually determines the amount of money in the economy?

Adjustment to Equilibrium

How does the money market move to equilibrium? Here the interactions between the money market and the bond market are key. Remember that money and bonds

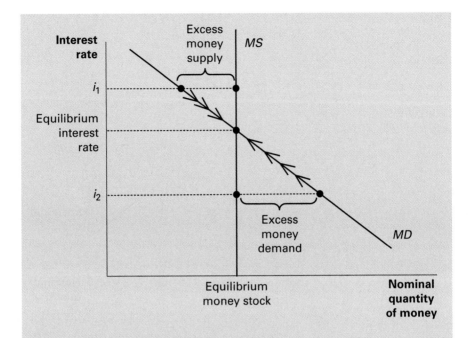

Figure 12.3 Adjustment to Money Market Equilibrium.

When interest rates are at i_1 above the equilibrium interest rate, there is excess money supply. Our actions to shift some of our wealth out of money and into bonds lower interest rates and raise the quantity of money demanded. Conversely, if interest rates are at i_2 below the equilibrium interest rate, there is excess money demand. Our actions to shift some of our wealth out of bonds and into money will drive down prices of bonds, driving up interest rates and decreasing the quantity of money demanded.

are the only two assets. (And remember: "bonds" refers to all non-money assets that can't be directly used to pay for goods and services.)

If interest rates are above equilibrium interest rates as in Figure 12.3, our demand for money is less than the supply of money. Collectively, we are holding an amount of money equal to the money stock. But we aren't happy with our current allocation of wealth. We want to hold less of our wealth in money and more of our wealth in bonds, because bonds are paying such a good interest rate.

So when interest rates are above equilibrium interest rates, we shift some of our wealth out of money and into bonds—we buy bonds (non-money assets) with some of our money. Buying more bonds pushes up the price of bonds. A bond is simply an IOU, a promise to pay the bond holder some amount of money in the future. When bond prices rise, we have to pay more now to buy the same promise-for-payments-later. Paying $1,000 today rather than $800 today for the same number of dollars paid to us later means that those later payments will constitute a smaller *rate* of return. That is, when bond prices rise, the rate of return earned on the bond falls. Our very action of trying to move our wealth out of money and into bonds has led bond prices to rise and interest rates to fall. Interest rates will continue to fall until they reach the equilibrium interest rate, at which point we are all content to be holding the amount of money we are actually holding.

What if interest rates are below equilibrium interest rates? Then our demand for money is more than the supply of money. Collectively, we want to hold more of our wealth in money and less of our wealth in bonds, because bonds are not paying a very good interest rate.

So when interest rates are below equilibrium interest rates, we shift some of our wealth out of bonds and into money—we sell bonds (non-money assets) and put the proceeds in our checking accounts. Selling bonds pushes down the price of bonds. When bond prices fall, the rate of return earned on the bond rises. Our very action of trying to move our wealth out of bonds and into money has led bond prices to fall and interest rates to rise. Higher interest rates move us along the money demand curve to a lower quantity of money demanded, making us happier with the current mix of money and bonds. Interest rates will continue to rise until they reach the equilibrium interest rate, at which point we are all content to be holding the amount of money we are actually holding.

Some textbooks describe the money market adjustment process differently. Their focus is instead on loans and the interest rate banks charge for loans. But the result is the same. When interest rates are above the equilibrium interest rate, fewer people and businesses want to take out loans. Banks are profit-maximizing businesses that earn their profit by making loans. If banks do nothing when interest rates are above their equilibrium level, they will make fewer loans. Because banks would be less profitable if they made fewer loans, banks will thus lower interest rates in an attempt to increase demand for loans. As interest rates are lowered, more people and businesses will take out loans, which they will hold in the form of money. Banks will continue to lower interest rates until the market reaches the equilibrium interest rate.

What if interest rates are below the equilibrium interest rate? In that case, people and businesses have greater demand for loans than the banks can provide. The Fed has set the money supply, which determines the maximum amount of loans the banks can make. Banks will raise interest rates on loans, lowering demand for loans, until we reach the equilibrium interest rate.

Changes of Equilibrium

A shift of the money demand curve or of the money supply curve will change the equilibrium interest rate. Money demand will shift if there is a change in income or in prices. An increase in income—the proxy for transactions—or in prices will shift the money demand curve to the right. At every interest rate, there is a greater quantity of money demanded. Interest rates will rise until the quantity of money demanded once again equals the equilibrium money stock. Figure 12.4 on page 212 illustrates. A decrease in income or in prices will shift the money demand curve to the left, lowering the equilibrium interest rate.

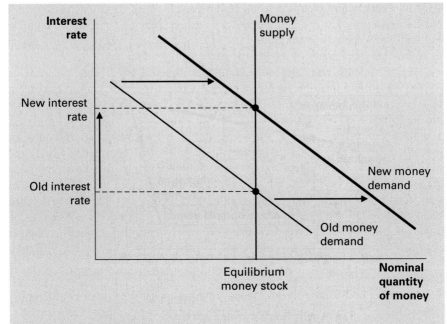

Figure 12.4 An Increase in Money Demand.

An increase in money demand causes interest rates to rise. The equilibrium money stock does not change, because it has been set by the Fed.

If the Fed increases the money supply, the money supply curve will shift to the right as in Figure 12.5. Interest rates will decline. If the Fed decreases the money supply, shifting the money supply curve to the left, interest rates will rise.

TRY

7. The money market is initially in equilibrium, but then money demand increases. Describe the process by which the market adjusts to a new equilibrium.

8. Using a graph of the money market, show the effect of a decrease in income.

How the Fed Changes the Money Supply

The Fed has traditionally had three tools at its disposal for changing the money supply:

- Changing the required reserve ratio
- Changing the discount rate
- Undertaking Federal Open Market Operations (FOMO)

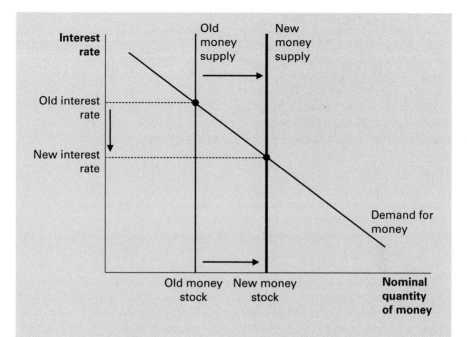

Figure 12.5 An Increase in Money Supply.

When the Fed increases the money supply, the equilibrium interest rate decreases and the equilibrium money stock increases.

Each of these three tools changes the money supply through its effect on the excess reserves held by banks. (If you need a refresher, Chapter 11 explains how banks create money with excess reserves.)

Changing the Required Reserve Ratio

When the Fed increases the required reserve ratio, excess reserves decline. When banks have a lower level of excess reserves, they can make fewer loans, creating less money. An increase in the required reserve ratio therefore decreases the money supply. Conversely, a decrease in the required reserve ratio increases the money supply.

If total deposits are $2,000 billion and the required reserve ratio is 12%, banks must have 12% of $2,000 billion, or $240 billion, in reserves. If the Fed then drops the required reserve ratio to 10%, some of those $240 billion in reserves are no longer required. The new amount of required reserves is 10% of $2,000 billion, or $200 billion. Excess reserves have increased by $40 billion. Banks can make loans with their excess reserves, increasing the money supply.

In the 1960s, the Fed changed the required reserve ratio about once a year. But since 1992, the required reserve ratio in the United States has been the same. Changing the required reserve ratio is what economists call a blunt tool: even a small change in the required reserve ratio can generate a very large change in the money supply. The required reserve ratio therefore remains one of the tools that can be used to change the money supply, but one that is rarely used.

Changing the Discount Rate

Banks that do not have enough reserves to meet the reserve requirement can borrow from other banks or from the Fed. The **discount rate** is the interest rate the Fed charges banks. An increase in the discount rate discourages banks from borrowing from the Fed. Instead banks that need reserves will borrow from other banks, thus lowering excess reserves in the banking system, and lowering the money supply. A decrease in the discount rate encourages banks to borrow from the Fed, increasing excess reserves in the banking system, and increasing the money supply.

TIP

Excess reserves can never have a negative value. Either a bank has excess reserves or it doesn't. If the bank has total reserves less than its required reserves, it is short of reserves—but we don't say the bank has a negative amount of excess reserves.

Why does borrowing from the Fed change the amount of excess reserves in the banking system? Consider two banks: Bank A has a reserve balance of $100 million, but its required reserves are $120 million; it is $20 billion short of reserves. Bank B has a reserve balance of $300 million, but its required reserves are just $250 million; Bank B has $50 million in excess reserves. If Bank A meets its reserve requirement by borrowing $20 million from Bank B, then between the two banks there will be just $30 million in excess reserves. If instead Bank A meets its reserve requirement by borrowing $20 million from the Fed, then between the two banks there will be $50 million in excess reserves. Borrowing from the Fed rather than from another bank increases the banking system's excess reserves.

The Federal Reserve—like any central bank—is considered the **lender of last resort**, the institution that will lend to a bank when no one else will. But borrowing from the Fed is usually a signal that no other banks will lend to the bank . . . a signal that can trigger extra attention from government bank regulators. As a result, the amount of borrowing at the discount window has historically been relatively small.

For many years, the Fed set the discount rate separately from other interest rates. But movements in the discount rate had little impact on the money supply. Recognizing the minor role of the discount rate as a monetary policy tool, in 2003 the Fed announced that the discount rate would simply be set by formula. From 2003 to 2008, the discount rate was "the federal funds target rate plus 100 basis points." (100 basis points equals 1 percentage point.) Effective 2008, the discount rate was the federal funds target rate plus 25 basis points. If the federal funds target rate is 0.5%, the discount rate is 0.75%.

Federal Open Market Operations

The primary tool used by the Fed to change the money supply is **Federal Open Market Operations**, or **FOMO**. Federal Open Market Operations refers to the Federal Reserve's purchases and sales ("operations") of U.S. Treasury bills, notes, and bonds ("Federal") in the market ("open market").

Many people use the word Treasuries to describe Treasury bills, notes, and bonds. Most textbooks simply use the word "bonds" to refer to Treasury bills, notes, and bonds.

There are three important keys to understanding why FOMO affects the money supply:

- The Fed has the power to increase one bank's reserve account balance without decreasing another bank's reserve balance.
- Money is cash in circulation plus balances in checking accounts.
- Banks create money by making loans with their excess reserves.

When the Fed buys bonds, the money supply increases. That's because when the Fed buys a bond from the public—be that a person, business, or government agency—the Fed gets the bond and the public gets paid with a check. The check is deposited into a bank—more money. When the check clears, reserves are added to the bank's reserve account balance at the Fed. Because the required reserve ratio is less than 1, the bank's reserves go up by more than is required. The bank has new excess reserves! The bank can make loans with the excess reserves, further increasing the amount of money in the economy.

What happens if the Fed sells bonds? Then the purchasers of the bonds adjust their wealth portfolios, increasing their bond holdings and decreasing their money holdings. The Fed owns fewer bonds and holds less reserves for banks. The purchaser's bank sees a decline in checking deposits—less money—and a corresponding decline in reserves. Banks will have fewer excess reserves, and thus will not be able to make as many loans. When the Fed sells bonds to the public, the money supply decreases.

To summarize,

When the Fed buys bonds from the public, MS increases

When the Fed sells bonds to the public, MS decreases

TRY

9. If the Fed increases the required reserve ratio from 10 to 15%, what is the effect on excess reserves? On the money supply?

10. Suppose the Fed sells a bond to you for $98,000.
    a. What is the effect of the transaction for you, your bank, and the Fed?
    b. What is the effect on excess reserves? On the money supply?

FOMO and Interest Rates

Federal open market operations not only change the money supply; FOMO also change interest rates. The Fed buys its bonds in the open market. That means the Fed's actions are part of market demand and market supply. When the Fed buys bonds from the public, that action increases demand for bonds. As with any product, price rises when demand increases. The Fed's purchase of bonds therefore raises the price of bonds.

When bond prices rise, interest rates are lower. An example illustrates why. Consider a **discount bond**, a bond that sells at a discount relative to its face value. If you pay $9,500 today for a $10,000 bond that matures in one year, you will receive the face value—$10,000—in one year. Your dollar gain, or return, will be $10,000 − $9,500 = $500. Express your return as a percentage of what you paid and you have your rate of return: $500/$9,500 = 5.26%.

What if instead you paid $9,800 for that bond? In that case your dollar return would be $10,000 − $9,800 = $200. Your rate of return will be just $200/ $9,800 = 2.04%. Your return is smaller ($200 rather than $500), and your initial outlay is larger ($9,800 rather than $9,500)—both of which decrease your rate of return.

$$\uparrow Bond\ Prices \quad \leftrightarrow \quad \downarrow Interest\ Rates$$

What happens when the Fed sells bonds? When the Fed sells bonds to the public, that action increases the supply of bonds. As with any product, price falls when supply increases. The Fed's sale of bonds therefore lowers the price of bonds. When bond prices fall, interest rates are higher.

$$\downarrow Bond\ Prices \quad \leftrightarrow \quad \uparrow Interest\ Rates$$

Notice that we now have two effects from the very same action. When the Fed buys bonds from the public, the money supply increases and interest rates fall. When the Fed sells bonds to the public, the money supply decreases and interest rates rise.

$$Fed\ buys\ bonds\ from\ the\ public \quad \rightarrow \quad \uparrow MS\ and \quad \downarrow interest\ rates$$
$$Fed\ sells\ bonds\ to\ the\ public \quad \rightarrow \quad \downarrow MS\ and \uparrow interest\ rates$$

TRY

11. Explain why the money supply increases and interest rates decrease when the Fed buys bonds from the public.

WHY THE FED MUST CHOOSE BETWEEN MONEY AND INTEREST RATES

The central bank can set a goal to have the money supply equal to some particular level. Economists call this a **money supply target**. The central bank can instead set a goal to have a key interest rate equal to some particular level. Economists call this an **interest rate target**. The connection between the money supply and interest rates means the central bank must choose which target it wants to set: money supply or interest rates. The dilemma is easiest to see with the graph in Figure 12.6.

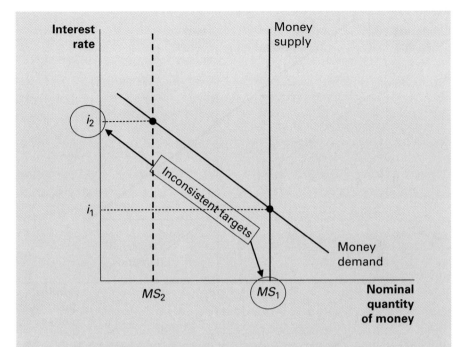

Figure 12.6 The Fed Must Choose between Money and Interest Rates.

If the Fed has set MS_1 as its money supply target, it cannot also have i_2 as its interest rate target. To achieve the money supply target of MS_1, interest rates will fall in equilibrium to i_1. If instead the Fed wants to achieve its interest rate target of i_2, the Fed must reduce the money supply to MS_2.

If the Fed independently sets a money supply target and an interest rate target, the two targets might be inconsistent with each other. A money supply target of MS_1 in Figure 12.6 would result in an equilibrium interest rate of i_1. If the Fed simultaneously wanted to achieve the goal of having interest rates equal to i_2, it could do so only by lowering the money supply to MS_2.

The consequences of having to choose between a money target and an interest rate target are felt when money demand shifts. An increase in income or in prices causes money demand to increase. In Figure 12.7, the top panel shows what happens when the Fed has set a money target and money demand subsequently increases: as money demand increases, interest rates rise if the money supply remains at MS_1. With a money supply target, the Fed must allow interest rates to rise when income or prices rise.

What if, instead, the Fed has an interest rate target? The bottom panel of Figure 12.7 demonstrates what happens when the Fed has an interest rate target. To keep interest rates fixed, the Fed must increase the money supply in response to an increase in money demand. With an interest rate target, the Fed must allow the nominal money supply to rise when income or prices rise.

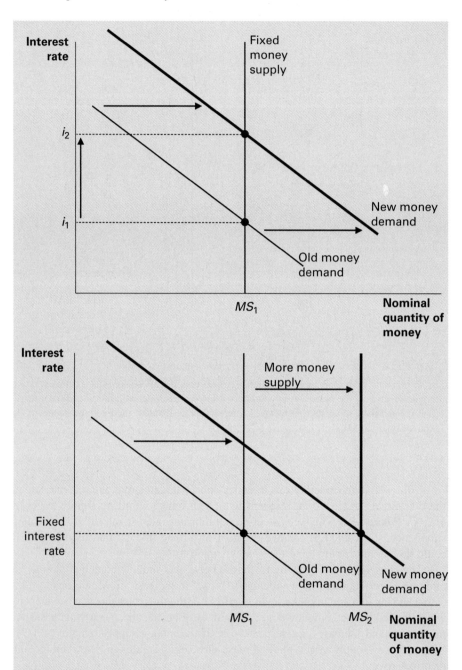

Figure 12.7 The Consequences of an Increase in Money Demand.

When money demand increases and the central bank has a money supply target as shown at the top, interest rates will rise. When money demand increases and the central bank has an interest rate target as shown at the bottom, the money supply will rise.

TRY

12. Draw a graph of the money market. Show a money supply target and an interest rate target that are consistent with each other.

13. The Fed initially has consistent money supply and interest rate targets. Then income falls. Why are those initial targets no longer consistent with each other? Supplement your answer with a graph.

14. If the Fed has a money supply target that doesn't change, what is the effect on interest rates when prices fall? If instead the Fed has an interest rate target that doesn't change, what is the effect on the money supply when prices fall?

WHAT'S AHEAD

In the next chapter, we examine the conduct of monetary policy. The Fed used a money supply target in the 1980s when it was fighting to eliminate the 1970s double-digit inflation. Since the early 1990s, the Fed has been using an interest rate target: the federal funds rate. Most modern-day central banks do the same thing: they target an interest rate and allow the money supply to change as necessary to accommodate the interest rate target.

Chapter 13

Monetary Policy and Interest Rates

$\mathbf{T}$he federal funds rate is the focus of monetary policy. But there are many other interest rates as well. Long-term rates usually (but not always) move with short-term rates. Real rates usually move with nominal rates. Economists simplify by referring to "the" interest rate, a simplification that is usually all right but that is sometimes problematic. Changes in interest rates affect aggregate demand. The quantity theory of money moves away from the focus on aggregate demand and explains inflation by simply referencing money supply growth. Whether it is best for the Fed to follow preset rules or to exercise discretion is a subject of debate.

KEY TERMS AND CONCEPTS

- Federal Open Market Committee (FOMC)
- Fed watchers
- Economic targets
- Inflation-targeting
- Interest rate target
- Money supply target
- Tools
- Short-term rates
- Long-term rates
- Risk premium
- Yield curve
- Normal yield curve
- Inverted yield curve
- Nominal interest rate
- Real interest rate
- "The" interest rate
- Equation of exchange
- Velocity
- Quantity theory of money
- Monetarism

- Rule
- Discretion
- Fed credibility
- Inflationary expectations

KEY EQUATION

- Equation of exchange: $MV = PY$

MONETARY POLICY TARGETS AND TOOLS

Monetary policy in the United States is the responsibility of the **Federal Open Market Committee** or **FOMC**. There are 12 voting members of the FOMC.

- The chairman of the Federal Reserve Board of Governors
- The six additional members of the Federal Reserve Board
- The president of the Federal Reserve Bank of New York
- The presidents of four of the other Federal Reserve Banks (each serving a one-year rotating term)

The remaining seven presidents of Federal Reserve Banks attend meetings of the FOMC, make presentations, and offer comments, but do not vote.

The FOMC meets in person every six weeks. At the end of each meeting, a public statement announces the FOMC's decisions about the direction of monetary policy for the next few weeks. Will interest rates be increased, decreased, or kept the same? Will the money supply be allowed to increase quickly, slowly, or not at all? People who pay a lot of attention to the FOMC meeting results are often called **Fed watchers**, because they carefully watch what the Fed does.

The language that is used to describe the Fed's actions can be confusing. The confusion stems from different uses of the same term: target. When we speak of the Fed's "target," are we talking about their target for economic conditions? Or their target for interest rates or the money supply? Unfortunately, it's both.

To try to clear this up, let's borrow the language of strategic planning: goal–objective–strategy–tactics. A goal is what we want to achieve in broad terms. An objective states the goal in measurable terms. A strategy is what process will be taken to achieve the objective. The tactics are the steps taken as part of the strategy.

Applying this rubric to monetary policy, we might have this:

- *Goal:* Stable prices
- *Objective:* Inflation rate between 2 and 3%
- *Strategy:* Set short-term interest rate at 4%
- *Tactic:* Purchase Treasury bills from the public

The Fed has three goals: maximum employment, stable prices, and moderate long-term interest rates. Each of these goals is a measure of the macroeconomy.

When the Fed has specific values of employment, inflation, or long-term interest rates it is trying to achieve, those are its objectives. Economists use the phrase "**economic targets**." When economists say the Fed is **inflation-targeting**, they mean that the Fed has a specific value of the inflation rate that it wants to achieve with monetary policy.

The word "target" is also used to describe the monetary policy targets: money supply and interest rates. The monetary policy target is a strategy: Will the Fed achieve its objective through setting interest rates? If so, economists say: the Fed has an **interest rate target**. Or, will the Fed achieve its goal through setting money supply growth? If so, economists say: the Fed has a **money supply target**.

As we saw in Chapter 12, the Fed has several tactics it can use in order to achieve an interest rate or money supply target. Chief among those are changes in the required reserve ratio, changes in the discount rate, and buying and selling U.S. government securities. Some economists use the term **tools** to describe the different tactics the Fed can follow.

To summarize, depending upon what book you're reading or who you're talking to, the Fed's "targets" may be economic targets (values of inflation, employment, long-term interest rates) or monetary policy targets (values of money supply growth or short-term interest rates). The Fed's "tools" are the different tactics the Fed has for achieving its monetary policy targets.

TRY   (*Answers to all "TRY" questions are at the back of the book.*)

1. What is the FOMC and what does it do?
2. For each of the following statements, is the "target" a goal, objective, strategy, or tactic?

   a. The Fed's target inflation rate is 2 to 3%.

   b. The Fed's target money supply growth rate is 4%.

   c. The Fed's target short-term interest rate is 1%.

INTEREST RATES

Like most modern central banks, the Fed currently uses an interest rate target. The Fed's target interest rate is the federal funds rate—the interest rate that banks with excess reserves charge on overnight loans to banks that can't meet their reserve requirement. The Fed hopes that increasing or decreasing the federal funds rate will cause all other interest rates to change as well.

TIP

"Federal funds" are not government money. "*Federal* funds" are loans of reserves between banks in order to meet the *Federal* Reserve's reserve requirement.

There are many interest rates in the economy. For every good or service, there is a different price. In the same sense, there is a different interest rate for every loan. We could try to list the different prices that exist in the real world, but we would soon tire of the exercise: there are prices for haircuts, books, pens, paper, chicken wings, beer, water bottles, coffee mugs, shirts, pants, and on and on. Listing each and every interest rate would generate an equally long list.

We can group the types of interest rates together into a somewhat manageable list. The most common types of interest rates include

- Treasury rates—what the federal government pays to borrow
- Corporate bond rates—what corporations pay when they borrow by issuing bonds (IOUs) to the public
- Corporate prime rate—what the best corporations pay when they borrow from the largest commercial banks
- Savings account rates—what you earn on your savings account
- Credit card rates—what you pay when you do not pay off your entire credit card balance each month
- Home mortgage rates—what you pay to borrow money to buy a house
- Home equity rates—what you pay to borrow money using your house as collateral
- Auto loan rates—what you pay to borrow money to buy a car
- Discount rate—what banks pay when they meet their reserve requirement by borrowing from the Fed
- Federal funds rate—what banks pay when they meet their reserve requirement by borrowing from other banks

Every interest rate measures both the amount paid by the borrower and the amount received by the lender. It's the same number with two different names. To the borrower, the interest rate is the cost of borrowing. To the lender, the interest rate is the earnings from lending.

Federal Funds Rate and Treasury Bill Rates

When the Fed wants the federal funds rate to decrease, the Fed cannot simply tell banks, "Decrease the rate you charge each other on overnight loans." The federal funds rate is a market rate; it responds to changes in supply and demand of federal funds, not to directives from the Fed.

Banks that have excess reserves constitute the supply of federal funds. Banks without enough reserves to meet their reserve requirement constitute the demand for federal funds. The federal funds rate is the equilibrium interest rate that clears the market for federal funds.

When the Fed increases the amount of reserves in the banking system, banks will choose to decrease the federal funds rate. With more reserves, fewer banks need to borrow to meet their reserve requirement, decreasing the demand for federal

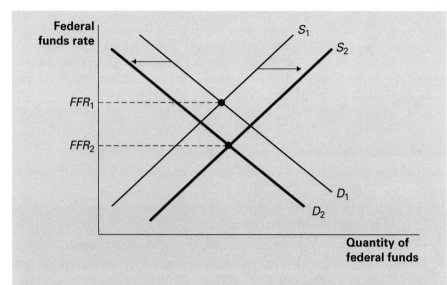

Figure 13.1 Decreasing the Federal Funds Rate.

When the Fed increases reserves in the banking system, the demand for federal funds decreases and the supply of federal funds rises. Banks decrease the federal funds rate.

funds. And with more reserves in the banking system, more banks have excess reserves to lend, increasing the supply of federal funds. Figure 13.1 illustrates. Decreased demand and increased supply have the same effect: a decrease in the federal funds rate.

How can the Fed increase the amount of reserves in the banking system? By buying Treasury bills. Moreover, buying Treasury bills increases the demand for Treasury bills, raising their price and lowering their rate of return. So two interest rates change when the Fed buys T-bills: T-bill rates and the federal funds rate both decrease.

The reverse is also true. When the Fed decreases reserves, fewer banks have excess reserves to lend, decreasing the supply of federal funds. Banks will choose to increase the federal funds rate. The Fed reduces bank reserves by selling Treasury bills. Selling T-bills increases their supply, lowering their price and raising their rate of return. So when the Fed sells T-bills, T-bill rates and the federal funds rate both increase.

TRY

3. Why can't the Fed just say to banks, "Change the federal funds rate"?

4. When the Fed sell bonds (or T-bills), what happens to the money supply and to interest rates?

All Those Rates

Each type of loan is a substitute for other types. People holding intermediate-term corporate bonds may sell some of those bonds and buy Treasury bills when the T-bill rate rises. Their sale of intermediate-term bonds will raise the supply of those bonds, lowering their price, and raising their rate of return. So when rates on one type of asset rise, substitutions out of other assets and into the asset with the higher rate will make other rates rise. Economists say: interest rates tend to move together.

But because lenders have preferences for what types of IOUs they will hold, the loans are not *perfect* substitutes and the rates are not all equal. The federal funds rate may be $1/2\%$, yet long-term government bond rates are 4% and credit card rates exceed 20%.

Interest rates are not all equal for several reasons. There is a difference in risk, the perceived likelihood that the loan will not be repaid. When a borrower does not repay the loan, the borrower is in default. The greater the risk of default, the higher the interest rate the borrower must pay.

Because risk matters, interest rates also vary by who the borrower is: government agencies, businesses, or individuals. Government agencies have the power to tax their constituents in order to repay the loan. The power to tax lowers the likelihood of default, so government agencies usually pay some of the lowest rates.

And interest rates vary by term, by the length of time the borrower has to repay the loan. Economists use the phrases **short-term rates** to refer to interest rates on short-term loans and **long-term rates** to refer to interest rates on long-term loans. Long-term rates are typically greater than short-term rates. Long-term rates reflect two factors: future expected short-term rates and a risk premium.

Imagine someone with $10,000 who faces a choice: she can lend her $10,000 to someone for 10 years; or she can lend her $10,000 to someone for 1 year today, to someone else for 1 year after the first person repays, to someone else for 1 year after the second person repays, and so on. At the end of 10 years, she would want to have the same amount of money whether she had lent to the one person for 10 years or to the series of 10 people for 1 year each. Put it another way: she would want the annual interest rate paid by the person who borrowed for 10 years to equal the average of the annual rates she charged each person in that series of 10 people. Economists express this by saying: long-term rates (the annual rate charged on the 10-year loan) should reflect the average of current and future expected short-term rates (the series of 1 year rates charged to each of the 10 people).

The second factor that determines long-term rates is that lenders want to be compensated for tying up their wealth in a loan for a long time. Over a period of many years, a lot can change. The borrower's economic situation could worsen. Short-term rates could rise unexpectedly. Economists say: lenders want to receive a **risk premium** in exchange for tying up their money long-term.

One way to capture the relationship between short-term rates and long-term rates is with a yield curve. A **yield curve** shows, for some particular day, the rate of return or yield on bonds issued by a particular borrower for a number of different terms. The most commonly seen yield curve is for U.S. Treasuries.

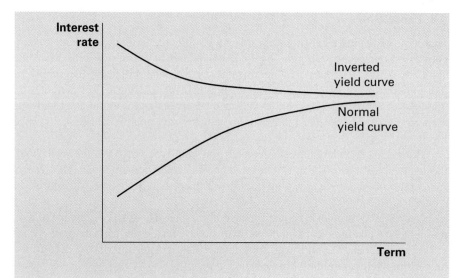

Figure 13.2 Yield Curves.

A yield curve shows how the interest rate varies with the length of the loan (the term) for a particular type of borrower on a particular day. A normal yield curve is one in which long-term rates are greater than short-term rates. An inverted yield curve is one in which long-term rates are less than short-term rates. Inverted yield curves are unusual and rarely seen.

Figure 13.2 shows two yield curves. Long-term rates are usually greater than short-term rates. A **normal yield curve** has long-term rates greater than short-term rates. In those rare times when long-term rates are less than short-term rates, the resulting yield curve is called an **inverted yield curve**.

When the Fed's change of short-term rates is widely seen as a temporary move, then short-term rates will move much more than long-term rates. For example, the federal funds rate decreased 500 basis points, from 5.25 to 0.25%, between August 2007 and December 2008. But the 10-year Treasury bill rate fell by just over 200 basis points, from 4.6 to 2.5%. Long-term rates didn't fall as much as short-term rates, because most people thought the Fed's cutting of the federal funds rate was temporary.

TRY

5. List three different types of interest rates that you personally encounter in your life.

6. Think about interest rates.

   a. Suppose today's 1-year interest rate is 4%. We expect the 1-year rate to still be 4% in one year, and we expect the 1-year rate to still be at

4% in two years. What can you say about the value of today's 3-year interest rate?
   b. Suppose today's 1-year interest rate is 4%. We expect the 1-year rate to still be 4% in one year, but now we expect the 1-year rate to rise to 8% in two years. What should happen to the 3-year interest rate? Why?
   c. Suppose today's short-term interest rate is 8% and today's yield curve is inverted. What can you say about future expected short-term rates?

The Real Interest Rate

Earning 3% on a savings account isn't bad when inflation is 1%; your wealth will increase faster than the prices of things you buy. But earning 3% when inflation is 7% is not good; prices are rising faster than the nominal value of your wealth.

Economists capture this comparison of nominal interest rates and inflation rates with the concept of the real interest rate. When you read an interest rate in the news or at the bank, that is a **nominal interest rate**—it is the rate actually charged or earned. The **real interest rate** is the nominal interest rate, adjusted for inflation. The usual way of calculating the real interest rate is

Real interest rate (r) = nominal interest rate (i) − inflation rate

TIP

The usual notation is i for the nominal interest rate and r for the real interest rate. But some textbooks use r for nominal interest rates.

Of the interest rates we've discussed, the federal funds rate and rates on bonds are nominal interest rates. But the interest rate that matters for aggregate demand is the real interest rate.

Think about investment spending. Businesses invest if the real rate of return on an investment project exceeds the real interest rate. The real rate of return assumes that prices and costs will not increase over time due to inflation. The real interest rate subtracts that same inflation rate from the nominal rate.

Note that it is equivalent to compare the nominal rate of return and nominal interest rates. Calculation of the nominal rate of return allows inflation to change future prices and costs. If the real rate of return exceeds the real interest rate, the nominal rate of return will exceed the nominal interest rate.

"The" Interest Rate

Economists often simplify the vast array of interest rates by talking about **"the" interest rate** as if there is only one interest rate. Referring to "the" interest rate implies all rates move together—that the yield curve moves up or moves down as all interest rates rise or fall together, but that it doesn't radically change its shape.

There's a good reason for making this assumption: it's often generally true. If the Fed increases short-term rates and the whole yield curve shifts up in roughly parallel fashion, then saying "the interest rate has increased" is an acceptable simplification.

Sometimes, however, the yield curve changes its shape. If the Fed raises short-term rates and long-term rates don't rise, we could have a flatter or even an inverted yield curve. Or if the Fed lowers short-term rates and long-term rates don't fall, the yield curve will be normal, but much steeper. In both cases, the Fed's action has changed short-term interest rates, but not long-term interest rates.

In these cases, talking about "the" interest rate will lead us astray. We will draw incorrect conclusions about the macroeconomic effect of monetary policy if we ignore the different behavior of long-term and short-term rates. Investment spending responds primarily to long-term rates. Monetary policy loses some of its potency if the yield curve becomes steeper or flatter when the Fed changes short-term rates.

TRY

7. The nominal interest rate is 5%. The inflation rate is 6%. What is the real interest rate?

8. When the inflation rate rises but nominal interest rates do not change, what happens to the real interest rate? All else constant, what is the effect on investment spending?

9. When is the simplification of referring to "the" interest rate problematic?

MONETARY POLICY AND THE MACROECONOMY

How does monetary policy affect the macroeconomy? Expansionary monetary policy—an increase in the money supply and decrease in interest rates—increases output. Contractionary monetary policy—a decrease in the money supply and increase in interest rates—decreases output. Two components of aggregate demand are sensitive to changes in interest rates: investment spending and net exports. Consumption spending may (or may not) be sensitive to change in interest rates.

Interest Rates and Investment Spending

We first covered the relationship between interest rates and investment spending in Chapter 7. When long-term interest rates decline, more businesses find it profitable to borrow to purchase equipment or undertake construction projects. Investment spending increases.

When long-term interest rates rise, fewer businesses find it profitable to borrow to purchase equipment or undertake construction projects. Investment spending decreases.

Did you notice that we mentioned *long-term* interest rates? What happens if the Fed lowers short-term rates by buying Treasuries, but long-term rates don't fall, making the yield curve steeper? In that case, monetary policy will be less effective.

If long-term rates don't also fall, investment spending will not rise as much as it would have had the yield curve simply shifted.

Interest Rates and Net Exports

The link between interest rates and net exports runs through exchange rates. We discuss exchange rates in a bit more detail in Chapter 16. The basic idea is this: an *exchange rate* is just a price that is determined by demand and supply. An exchange rate is the dollar price of one unit of foreign currency. The demand for foreign currency is made up of people and institutions who want to trade dollars for foreign currency. The supply of foreign currency is made up of people and institutions who want to trade foreign currency for dollars. Changes in supply and in demand have the same effect on price as they did in Chapter 3: an increase in demand or decrease in supply raises price; a decrease in demand or increase in supply lowers price.

Wealth holders around the world respond to changes in interest rates by moving their wealth into assets that earn the better rate of return. When interest rates in the United States rise, U.S. wealth holders shift some of their wealth out of foreign assets and into domestic (U.S.) assets. This decreases the demand for foreign currency, lowering the dollar price of foreign currency.

At the same time, foreign wealth holders also respond to the increase in U.S. interest rates by shifting some of their wealth out of foreign assets and into U.S. assets. This increases the supply of foreign currency, again lowering the dollar price of foreign currency. The dollar rises—strengthens—appreciates—three words that each indicate a lower dollar price for foreign currency.

As we saw in Chapter 7, a stronger dollar means it costs fewer dollars to purchase each unit of foreign currency, decreasing the cost of imported goods and services, and thus raising imports. A stronger dollar also means that it costs more units of foreign currency for each dollar, increasing how much the rest of the world pays for U.S. goods and services, and thus decreasing U.S. exports. Because imports rise and exports fall, net exports decrease.

The reverse is also true. When interest rates in the United States fall, U.S. wealth holders shift some of their wealth out of domestic (U.S.) assets and into foreign assets. The increase in demand for foreign currency raises the dollar price of foreign currency.

At the same time, foreign wealth holders respond to the decrease in U.S. interest rates by shifting some of their wealth out of U.S. assets and into foreign assets, decreasing the supply of foreign currency. This also raises the dollar price of foreign currency. The dollar falls—weakens—depreciates—three words that indicate a higher price for foreign currency.

A weaker U.S. dollar means that it costs more dollars for each unit of foreign currency, increasing the cost of imported goods and services, and thus lowering imports. A weaker U.S. dollar also means that it costs fewer units of foreign currency to purchase each dollar, decreasing how much the rest of the world pays for U.S. goods and services, and thus increasing U.S. exports. Because imports fall and exports rise, net exports increase.

Interest Rates and Consumption Spending

Interest rates have an ambiguous effect on consumption spending. We first covered this topic in Chapter 7. Borrowers and savers have opposite reactions to a change in interest rates. Whether aggregate consumption spending rises or falls depends, therefore, on the mix of borrowers and savers in a population.

Borrowers tend to borrow more when interest rates fall, and to borrow less when interest rates rise. Spending for consumer durable goods—cars, appliances, furniture—therefore tends to rise when interest rates fall. Durable goods spending tends to fall when interest rates rise.

On the other hand, savers tend to save more and spend less when interest rates fall. Lower interest rates—lower rates of return when viewed through the savers' eyes—mean that savers must save more now to achieve the same future goal. Thus, savers reduce their spending when interest rates fall, and they increase their spending when interest rates rise.

Because borrowers and savers have opposite reactions to a change in interest rates, we can't say with certainty how consumption spending changes when interest rates change.

TRY

10. Why does contractionary monetary policy decrease output?

11. Is your answer to question 10 the same if you can't assume that a change in short-term rates results in a change in long-term rates? Explain.

INFLATION AND OUTPUT: THE QUANTITY THEORY APPROACH

In Chapters 14 and 15, we will look at two approaches to understanding inflation and output, both of which start from Keynesian simplifications and assumptions: $AD = C + I + G + NX$, and output is produced in reaction to aggregate demand. An alternative approach starts from the **equation of exchange**,

$$MV = PY \text{ (or } MV = PQ)$$

M stands for the amount of money in the economy, M1 or M2. V stands for **velocity**, the number of times a dollar changes hands in a year. P is the average price level, such as the GDP deflator. Y or Q is real GDP, a proxy for transactions. Notice that PY (or, PQ) is just nominal GDP.

Velocity is not measured by marking bills and tracking them through the economy for a year. Instead, velocity is calculated by taking the ratio of nominal GDP (PY) to money (M): $V = PY/M$. Because there is no independent measure of velocity, the equation of exchange is always true.

The equation of exchange can be transformed to

$$\%\Delta M + \%\Delta V = \%\Delta P + \%\Delta Y$$

(No principles text goes through the math; it is an application of calculus.) The rate of change of money supply plus the rate of change of velocity equals the rate of change of prices plus the rate of change of real GDP. In more common terms,

Money supply growth rate + Velocity growth rate

= Inflation rate + real GDP growth rate

Rearrange that equation, and we get

Inflation rate = Money supply growth rate + Velocity growth rate

− real GDP growth rate

Still we have an equation that is always true. It is always true because velocity is not independently measured, but rather is the ratio of nominal GDP to money supply.

If we add two assumptions, we have a theory about the determinants of inflation. Assume that the velocity growth rate is constant and does not change from quarter to quarter or year to year. And assume the same thing about the real GDP growth rate—that it is constant and does not change over time. If those two assumptions are satisfied, then changes in the inflation rate will be due to changes in the money supply growth rate. This theory is called the **quantity theory of money**. The quantity theory of money is at the heart of a school of thought called **monetarism**. The economist most often associated with monetarism is Milton Friedman.

Friedman once famously said, "Inflation is always and everywhere a monetary phenomenon." He meant that faster-than-usual money growth triggers higher inflation. Slower-than-usual money growth triggers lower inflation.

The quantity theory of money is helpful when we are trying to understand hyperinflation—inflation rates of 20% or more per month. Hyperinflation is always associated with extremely rapid money supply growth.

Whether the quantity theory helps to explain short-run fluctuations in inflation and output is disputed. The quantity theory contains no explanation of how changes in the money supply cause changes in real GDP. And velocity is neither constant nor stable; its growth rate changes over time, both cyclically and structurally. That means that short-run fluctuations in money supply growth may or may not lead to short-run fluctuations in the inflation rate.

TRY

12. Suppose that velocity is growing 4% per year, that real GDP is growing 2% annually, and that the money supply growth rate is 3%. What is the inflation rate?

13. If money supply is growing 400% per year, give or take, then what is the inflation rate?

14. If the velocity growth rate falls when the growth rate of the money supply rises, does an increase in the growth rate of the money supply necessarily trigger higher inflation?

RULES VERSUS DISCRETION

One debate among scholars and Fed-watchers is about the extent to which policymaking should be left to the policymakers. Should the policymakers establish a **rule** that determines how much they change the monetary policy variables under their control, and then follow that rule? Or should the policymakers exercise **discretion**, changing the monetary policy variables by as much or as little as they decide at a particular moment?

If the FOMC followed a rule, then it might set a simple rule, such as, "Let the money supply grow by 5% each year." Or it might set a complex rule, one that said something like this:

- When inflation rises by $1/2$ percentage point, increase interest rates by 1 point. But if inflation falls by $1/2$ percentage point, decrease interest rates by 1 point.
- When GDP growth slows by $1/2$ percentage point, decrease interest rates by $1/4$ point. But if GDP growth rises by $1/2$ percentage point, increase interest rates by $1/4$ point.

Once the FOMC had agreed to its rule, its meetings would simply report on economic events and trends. Decisions about monetary policy would be predetermined by the rules.

But if the FOMC instead exercised discretion, its meetings would involve not just reporting on economic events and trends, but also then deciding what to do about monetary policy. Instead of having a rule that tells the FOMC what to do with interest rates when inflation rises by $1/2$ percentage point, a question would be addressed at the FOMC meeting: "Inflation is rising by $1/2$ percentage point. What should we do?"

TIP

Saying that the Fed exercises discretion does not mean their decisions are totally random and illogical. It simply means that the Fed is not bound to follow a hard-and-fast rule about monetary policy.

The rules-versus-discretion debate is much more complex than this discussion suggests. But at its essence, it is focused on the advantages and disadvantages to each approach.

Rules are better than discretion, some argue, because then policy decisions are more predictable. Businesses can have greater certainty about what future policy decisions will be made. More certainty about the economic future tends to encourage business investment.

But, others argue, discretion is better than rules, because then the policymakers have greater flexibility. The realities of what's happening in the economy, with all of its real-world complexity, might make a list of rules so long as to be unmanageable. Discretion in designing the right policy response—and awareness of real-time, real-world complexities—might produce a better economic outcome than mere application of a rule.

The debate over rules or discretion is also part of a discussion about **Fed credibility**. Credibility—do people believe that you will do the things you say you will?—is at the heart of the Fed's ability to influence what we think will happen in the future.

What you and I think the inflation rate will be in the future is what economists call our **inflationary expectations**. If our inflationary expectations are high, we think there will be a high rate of price inflation in the future. If our inflationary expectations are low, we think there will be a low rate of price inflation in the future.

The business world's inflationary expectations are based in part on what they think the Fed's monetary policy is and will be. If business owners believe that the Fed won't waver from a fight to keep the inflation rate low, then their inflationary expectations will be low. Economists say: if the Fed's commitment to low price inflation is credible, then inflationary expectations will be low.

But if the Fed's commitment to keeping the inflation rate low is not credible, if the business world does not believe that the Fed's monetary policy will keep prices in check, then inflationary expectations may rise. The Fed's credibility matters to our inflationary expectations.

What makes the Fed more credible: rules, or discretion? Here there is no clear answer. Some—particularly monetarists—argue that rules make the Fed more credible. If the Fed says "We will implement monetary policy rules that will keep the inflation rate at 2%," is this a credible commitment? Some say "Yes." But others say, "Not necessarily." What if keeping the inflation rate at 2% requires allowing the unemployment rate to rise to 30%? Few would see the Fed's commitment to 2% inflation as credible if it came at such a steep cost.

Others therefore argue that discretion makes the Fed more credible. If the Fed can exercise discretion in its monetary policy, then the Fed can undertake surprise policy moves that have an immediate impact on economic behavior. This might be the more effective way of achieving its price stability goal.

How does the Federal Reserve behave? It exercises discretion. At the end of each FOMC meeting, the Fed issues a press release announcing its monetary policy action and its justifications for that action. By and large, the Fed's decisions are highly predictable. But occasionally, the Fed surprises everyone. On a weekend in January 2008, as the economy began its plummet into the Great Recession of 2007–2009, the Fed announced a surprise $3/4$-point cut in interest rates. The Fed was exercising discretion.

TRY

15. What is the difference between rules and discretion? What are the advantages to each?

16. What can happen to our inflationary expectations if the Fed does not have a credible commitment to fight inflation?

CREATIVE MONETARY POLICY DURING THE GREAT RECESSION OF 2007–2009

In Chapter 9, we discussed the roles of fiscal and monetary policy in the Great Recession of 2007–2009. The Fed faced an enormous challenge in its conduct of monetary policy when both Treasury-bill rates and the federal funds rate hit the zero lower bound. If the Fed had limited itself to its usual monetary policy tactics—buying T-bills as a way of lowering both T-bill and federal funds rates—it would have had no way to help the economy.

But think more broadly about the Fed's strategy. Its goal when facing a severe recession is to expand the amount of credit in the economy, allowing businesses to invest in equipment and structures, and allowing families to purchase homes and durable goods. The Fed's usual strategy is to lower short-term rates using FOMO as their tactic. But lowering short-term rates is not the Fed's only strategy.

During the Great Recession, the Fed demonstrated its flexibility and creativity in the conduct of monetary policy. Lowering short-term rates requires increasing bank reserves. Rather than confine its open-market purchases to Treasury-bills, the Fed announced that it would buy nearly any financial asset from banks. Regardless of what the Fed buys from banks, the Fed pays by increasing the bank's balance in its reserve account. The resulting changes in the Fed's balance sheet were dramatic: the asset side surged as a variety of new assets were bought by the Fed. On the liability side, bank reserves soared.

The Fed also moved away from its usual strategy of focusing on just short-term rates, and manipulated long-term rates as well. For example, the Fed purchased $1.25 trillion in mortgage-backed securities, a long-term financial asset. These purchases directly lowered long-term mortgage interest rates.

The new tactics and strategy of the Fed during the Great Recession are new in their particulars, but are the same old thing in general. The Fed was conducting expansionary monetary policy. It did so by purchasing assets from banks, thus increasing bank reserves and lowering interest rates. Whether it's Treasury bills, mortgage-backed securities, or some other financial asset, it's still monetary policy—the same monetary policy described throughout this chapter.

TRY

17. When the Fed buys mortgage-backed securities (MBS) from a bank, what changes occur in the bank's assets and liabilities? In the Fed's assets and liabilities? In the money supply?

PART V

Inflation and Output

Chapter 14

Inflation and Output: The *AS/AD* Approach

Output depends on the sum of consumption, investment, government and net export spending. What about prices and inflation? There are two distinct approaches to modeling the macroeconomic connection between output and prices: the *AS/AD* approach covered in this chapter, and the monetary policy (Taylor Rule) approach covered in Chapter 15.

The *AS/AD* approach assumes that the Fed sets a target for the money supply and lets interest rates fluctuate. Aggregate demand is the relationship between the average price level (GDP deflator) and planned aggregate expenditure ($C + I + G + NX$). Aggregate supply is the relationship between the average price level (GDP deflator) and the economy's total production of goods and services (GDP). Changes in aggregate demand or aggregate supply affect both output and prices.

KEY TERMS AND CONCEPTS

- *AS/AD* model
- Aggregate supply (*AS*)
- Aggregate demand (*AD*)
- Planned aggregate expenditure (*AE*)
- Average price level
- Interest rate effect
- Wealth (real balance) effect
- Foreign trade (foreign purchases) effect
- Aggregate demand curve
- Supply side
- Potential output (or potential GDP, potential income, or full-employment GDP)
- Long-run aggregate supply curve (LRAS)
- Sticky wages
- Short-run aggregate supply curve (SRAS)
- Supply (cost) shock
- Demand-pull inflation

- Cost-push inflation
- Dynamic *AS/AD* model
- Static *AS/AD* model

KEY GRAPHS

- *AS/AD* model
- Dynamic *AS/AD* model

OVERVIEW OF THE *AS/AD* MODEL

The *AS/AD* **model** explains the connection between prices and output. **Aggregate supply (*AS*)** is total production of final goods and services by businesses. **Aggregate demand (*AD*)** is total demand for final goods and services by households, businesses, government agencies, and the rest of the world. There is an upward-sloping aggregate supply curve, a downward-sloping aggregate demand curve, and an equilibrium price level at which the aggregate quantity of output demanded equals the aggregate quantity of output supplied.

Sounds like the supply and demand model from Chapter 3, doesn't it? But it's not. The differences between the microeconomic model of supply and demand and the macroeconomic model of aggregate supply and aggregate demand include the following:

- In the *AS/AD* model, the "price" variable is the economy-wide average of all prices of final goods and services. In the micro supply-and-demand model, "price" is the price of just one particular product.

- In the *AS/AD* model, the "quantity" variable is the total production of all final goods and services in the economy during some time period—the gross domestic product. In the micro supply-and-demand model, "quantity" is the quantity produced of just one particular product.

- Aggregate demand is the total of all spending for final goods and services, consumption plus investment plus government plus net export spending. In the micro supply-and-demand model, demand is the quantity demanded of just one particular product.

- Aggregate demand is *not* the sum of all the demand curves for all of the particular products in the economy. Each individual demand curve in the micro supply-and-demand model is based on the assumption that all other prices are constant. But in the *AS/AD* model, all prices can be changing; there is no assumption that "all other prices" are constant.

- Aggregate supply is the amount of final goods and services produced by all firms in the economy. In the micro supply-and-demand model, supply is the amount produced by the profit-maximizing firms in one particular industry.

- Aggregate supply is *not* the sum of all the supply curves for all of the particular products in the economy. Each individual supply curve is based on the assumption that input costs are fixed. But in the *AS/AD* model, input costs can be changing.

What happens if you get the *AS/AD* model and the micro supply-and-demand model confused? Your conclusions about what happens to prices after a shift of aggregate demand or aggregate supply will be all right, but your explanations will be wrong. The reason that price rises after an increase in demand for a particular product is different from the reason that prices rise after an increase in aggregate demand.

AGGREGATE DEMAND

What is the relationship between prices and planned aggregate expenditure? That's the question answered with the idea of aggregate demand.

TIP

In previous chapters, we noted that some textbooks make a distinction between "planned aggregate expenditure" and "aggregate demand," and some don't. Now it's important to make that distinction.

Planned aggregate expenditure (*AE*) is the sum of consumption, investment, government, and net export spending *at a particular level of prices*. By "prices" we mean the **average price level** of final goods and services, the things that are counted in gross domestic product. When prices change, planned aggregate expenditure changes, too. Aggregate demand refers to the set of combinations of the average price level and planned aggregate expenditure.

Prices and Aggregate Expenditure

A higher average price level—an increase in the GDP deflator—causes planned aggregate expenditure to fall. A lower average price level causes planned aggregate expenditure to rise. There are three reasons for this inverse relationship between the average price level and planned aggregate expenditure: the interest rate effect, the wealth (or real balances) effect, and the foreign trade effect.

Interest Rate Effect

The **interest rate effect** focuses on the connection between prices, interest rates, and spending. A key assumption of the *AS/AD* model is that the Fed targets the money supply and allows interest rates to vary in response to changes in money demand. (See Chapter 12 for a discussion of why the Fed must choose between a money supply target and an interest rate target.) This assumption matters here.

When prices rise, money demand rises, too. People and businesses will want to switch some of their wealth out of bonds and into money in order to be able to pay for the same quantity of transactions. When the Fed sets a money supply target, higher money demand increases interest rates.

TIP

Some textbooks show the effect of higher prices by decreasing the real money supply (*MS/P*) rather than increasing the nominal money demand (*MD*). The result is the same: when prices rise, interest rates increase if the nominal money supply is fixed.

Higher prices thus increase interest rates, lowering investment and net export spending, and, through the multiplier, lowering planned aggregate expenditure. Lower prices have the opposite effect: when prices fall, the drop in money demand coupled with a money supply target causes interest rates to decrease, raising investment and net export spending, and through the multiplier, raising planned aggregate expenditure.

We can summarize the chain of events this way:

$\uparrow P \to \uparrow MD \to \uparrow interest\ rates \to \downarrow I\ \&\ \downarrow NX \to \downarrow C\ via\ the\ multiplier \to \downarrow AE$

$\downarrow P \to \downarrow MD \to \downarrow interest\ rates \to \uparrow I\ \&\ \uparrow NX \to \uparrow C\ via\ the\ multiplier \to \uparrow AE$

Aggregate consumption spending may also respond directly to the change in interest rates, providing a greater initial change in spending. Consumption of durable goods bought with credit, especially cars, tends to respond to changes in interest rates. On the other hand, consumers dependent upon interest income tend to spend less at lower interest rates. So the net direct effect of a change in interest rates on consumption is ambiguous. Whether or not aggregate consumption responds *directly* to interest rates, consumption will rise after a drop in interest rates, because of the spending multiplier.

Wealth Effect

The **wealth effect** (or in some textbooks, the **real balance effect**) focuses on the connections between prices, personal wealth, and consumption. A higher price level reduces the value of wealth; a lower price level raises the value of wealth. For example, suppose you have $20,000 saved for tuition and fees. If tuition and fees are $10,000 per semester, you have saved up two semesters' worth of tuition and fees. But if tuition and fees are increased to $15,000 per semester, your $20,000 only covers $1\frac{1}{3}$ semesters. Your wealth ($20,000) is worth less (only $1\frac{1}{3}$ semesters). You will need to reduce your spending and increase your saving in order to save enough to cover two semesters.

Thus, when output prices rise, the value of wealth falls. When the value of wealth falls, consumption spending falls. Multiplier effects kick in, making the drop in planned aggregate expenditure even larger.

The reverse is also true. When prices fall, the real value of wealth rises. When the value of wealth rises, consumption spending rises, too. Multiplier effects kick in, making the rise in planned aggregate expenditure even larger.

$\uparrow P \to \downarrow$ *value of wealth* $\to \downarrow C \to$ *further* $\downarrow C$ *via the multiplier* $\to \downarrow AE$

$\downarrow P \to \uparrow$ *value of wealth* $\to \uparrow C \to$ *further* $\uparrow C$ *via the multiplier* $\to \uparrow AE$

TIP

Remember: P refers to the average level of prices of output, of final goods and services. If something is not in GDP, then its price is not included in the average level of prices of final goods and services.

But there is a caveat. The wealth effect applies only to the assets whose nominal value is unchanged when output prices change. When the nominal value of an asset rises as output prices rise, the real value of the asset may stay the same. Housing prices and stock prices typically rise when output prices rise.

For U.S. households, no more than half of household wealth is subject to the wealth effect. Housing represents about 25% of U.S. household assets, and stocks (whether owned directly or through a retirement fund) represent another 25%.

Foreign Trade Effect

The **foreign trade effect** (or **foreign purchases effect**) focuses on the connections between prices and net exports. When prices rise in the United States but not in other countries, U.S. goods and services become relatively more expensive than goods and services produced abroad. Exports of goods and services from the United States to others tend to decrease; imports of goods and services into the United States from abroad tend to increase. The resulting decrease in net exports kicks off multiplier effects, further decreasing spending. Planned aggregate expenditure falls.

On the other hand, when prices fall in the United States but not in other countries, U.S. goods and services become relatively less expensive than goods and services produced abroad. Exports of goods and services from the United States to others tend to increase; imports of goods and services into the United States from abroad tend to decrease. The resulting increase in net exports kicks off multiplier effects, further increasing spending. Planned aggregate expenditure rises.

$\uparrow P$ *in the U.S.* $\to \downarrow EX$ *and* $\uparrow IM \to \downarrow C$ *via the multiplier* $\to \downarrow AE$

$\downarrow P$ *in the U.S.* $\to \uparrow EX$ *and* $\downarrow IM \to \uparrow C$ *via the multiplier* $\to \uparrow AE$

There is a caveat, of course. This chain of events assumes that prices in the rest of the world do not change when prices change in the United States. If prices rise in the rest of the world as they rise in the U.S., then there would be no change in net exports, and no foreign trade effect.

TRY (*Answers to all "TRY" questions are at the back of the book.*)

1. Why does planned aggregate expenditure decrease when interest rates increase?

2. Why does planned aggregate expenditure increase when real wealth increases?

3. Are prices of houses included in the GDP deflator? Are prices of stock included in the GDP deflator? Why, or why not?

4. Why does planned aggregate expenditure increase when output prices fall in the United States but not in the rest of the world?

5. Would planned aggregate expenditure decrease when output prices increase even if the spending multiplier equaled 1? Explain.

The Aggregate Demand Curve

Lower prices lead to increases in investment (interest rate effect), consumption (wealth effect), and net exports (interest rate and foreign trade effects), all of which kick off multiplier effects, further raising planned aggregate expenditure. Higher prices lead to decreases in investment, consumption, and net exports, all of which kick off multiplier effects, further lowering planned aggregate expenditure. We show these effects in the top half of Figure 14.1 with Chapter 6's Keynesian cross diagram.

The relationship between prices and planned aggregate expenditure is shown with the **aggregate demand curve** in the bottom half of Figure 14.1. The average price level P is on the vertical axis. The amount of output "real GDP" is on the horizontal axis. At a higher price level, planned aggregate expenditure is lower. At a lower price level, planned aggregate expenditure is higher.

TIP

There is no consensus among textbooks authors as to notation. Your textbook may use different notation than is used here.

The aggregate demand curve slopes down. If the aggregate demand curve is steep, the response to a change in prices is very small. If the aggregate demand curve is flat, the response to a change in prices is very large. Figure 14.2 on page 244 illustrates.

TRY

6. Use a Keynesian cross diagram to show how planned aggregate expenditure changes when the price level falls. Draw the associated aggregate demand curve.

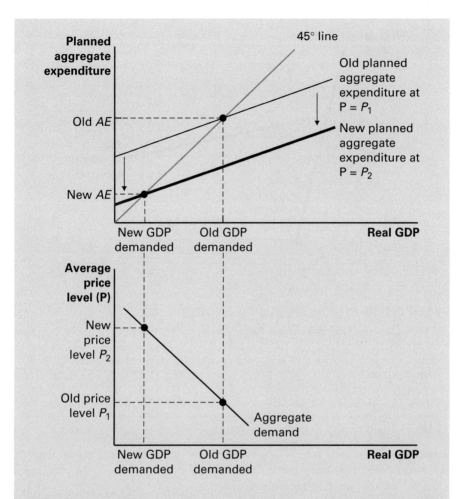

Figure 14.1 The Aggregate Demand Curve.

The aggregate demand curve shows how the amount of goods and services demanded (GDP demanded) responds to a change in the average price level. At a higher price level, the planned aggregate expenditure line shifts down due to the interest rate, wealth, and foreign trade effects. The new amount of goods and services demanded (GDP demanded) falls by even more than the initial drop in planned aggregate expenditure due to the spending multiplier.

Shifts of the Aggregate Demand Curve

A change in prices moves us along an existing aggregate demand curve. When anything *other than* a change in prices causes planned aggregate expenditure to change, the aggregate demand curve will shift. An increase in planned aggregate expenditure due to an event *other than* a change in output prices shifts the *AD* curve to the right. A decrease in planned aggregate expenditure due to an event *other than* a change in output prices shifts the *AD* curve to the left.

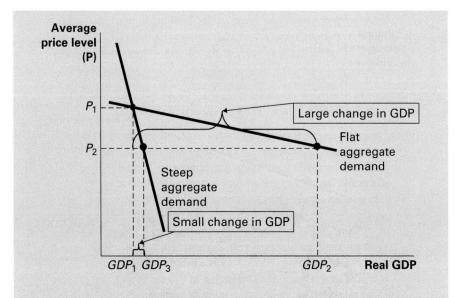

Figure 14.2 The Slope of the Aggregate Demand Curve.
When the aggregate demand curve is flat, a change in price from P_1 to P_2 results in a large change in GDP demanded from GDP_1 to GDP_2. When the aggregate demand curve is steep, a change in price from P_1 to P_2 results in a small change in GDP demanded from GDP_1 to GDP_3.

TIP

Remember the general rule: if it's measured on one of the axes and it changes, we *move along* an existing curve. If it's not measured on one of the axes and it changes, we *shift* an existing curve.

The list of events that shift the aggregate demand curve is almost as long as the list of events that shift the planned aggregate expenditure line in the Keynesian cross diagram. There's a reason for that: with the exception of a change in output prices, anything that shifts the planned aggregate expenditure line also shifts the aggregate demand curve.

Figure 14.3 illustrates the connection between shifts of the planned aggregate expenditure line and the aggregate demand curve. When the planned aggregate expenditure line shifts down due to an initial decrease in spending, the amount of GDP demanded decreases. The change in GDP demanded is greater than the initial change in planned aggregate expenditure because of the spending multiplier. Had the downward shift of the planned aggregate expenditure line been due to a change in the average price level, we would have moved along an existing aggregate demand curve as shown in Figure 14.1. But if the downward shift of the planned aggregate expenditure line is due to any other event, the aggregate demand curve

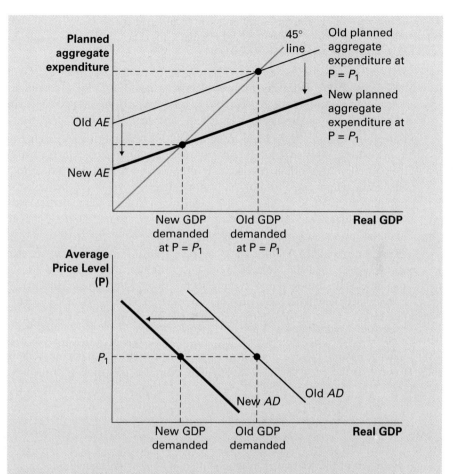

Figure 14.3 Shifts of the Aggregate Demand Curve.

The price level is unchanged, and there is an initial decrease in planned aggregate expenditure. Multiplier effects determine the total drop in GDP demanded. One point on the new aggregate demand curve is the combination of price level P_1 and the new level of GDP demanded. Because the drop in planned aggregate expenditure is due to an event *other than* a change in the average price level, the entire aggregate demand curve shifts to the left.

will shift to the left. An upward shift of the planned aggregate expenditure line due to any event other than a change in the average price level causes the aggregate demand curve to shift to the right.

What can shift the aggregate demand curve? The list of events includes

- *Fiscal Policy:* Expansionary fiscal policy (increase in G, increase in TR, or decrease in TA) will shift the AD curve to the right. Contractionary fiscal policy (decrease in G, decrease in TR, or increase in TA) will shift the AD curve to the left.

- *Monetary Policy:* Expansionary monetary policy (increase in *MS*) will shift the *AD* curve to the right. Contractionary monetary policy (decrease in *MS*) will shift the *AD* curve to the left.
- *Shift in Household Saving Preferences:* A shift in cultural attitudes in favor of saving (thrift) and away from consumption could decrease autonomous consumption, shifting the *AD* curve to the left. A shift in attitudes in favor of consumption and away from thrift will shift the *AD* curve to the right.
- *Change in Wealth:* A decrease in household wealth—not due to a change in prices of goods and services—can lower consumption spending and shift the *AD* curve to the left. (A decrease in household wealth that is due to a change in output prices simply moves us along an *AD* curve because the initiating event is the change in prices, which is measured on the vertical axis when graphing *AD*.) An increase in household wealth not due to a change in output prices shifts the *AD* curve to the right.
- *Change in Expected Future Sales:* More optimism among businesspeople will increase what they expect to sell in the future, increasing investment spending and shifting the *AD* curve to the right. More pessimism among businesspeople will decrease what they expect to sell in the future, decreasing investment spending and shifting the *AD* curve to the left.

The list could go on. The important thing to remember is that if the event *begins* with a change in the average price level, then it is shown as a movement along the *AD* curve. If the event begins with anything else, it is shown as a shift of the *AD* curve.

TRY

7. For each of the following events, is it shown as a movement along or a shift of the *AD* curve?
   a. Household access to credit is restricted, limiting households' ability to consume.
   b. Output prices fall 2%.
   c. Businesses become more optimistic about future sales opportunities.
   d. The federal government implements expansionary fiscal policy, increasing government spending and decreasing taxes.
   e. A "buy domestic" advertising campaign is successful, leading consumers to switch their purchases from imports to domestically-produced goods and services.
   f. The Fed increases the money supply.

AGGREGATE SUPPLY

Aggregate supply focuses on the production side of the economy, or what is sometimes called the **supply side** of the economy. How much output people, businesses, and government agencies want to *purchase* is irrelevant. What matters is the relationship between output prices and how much output businesses want to *produce*.

Warning! There is no consensus among economists when it comes to aggregate supply. Different textbooks have different explanations for the aggregate supply curve. Some even draw it differently. Be sure you know how your textbook explains the aggregate supply curve.

Some Clues from Microeconomics

Some of the principles learned in microeconomics are helpful in understanding the macroeconomic relationship between prices and amount of GDP supplied.

- Firms produce an amount of output that maximizes profit. When output's price goes up, all else constant, profit-maximizing firms will produce more output. "All else constant" is important, though: this microeconomic result depends upon assuming that wage rates and the per-unit cost of other inputs are constant.
- When firms buy inputs, they are the purchasers who constitute the demand for those inputs. Increased demand for inputs will increase the per-unit price of inputs. When firms use those same inputs in the production process, that higher per-unit "price" is called a higher per-unit "cost" of production.
- Excess supply in a market means that the current price is below the equilibrium price. In that case, increased demand simply decreases the gap between quantity demanded and quantity supplied, and does not trigger a higher price.

Long-Run Aggregate Supply Curve

The long run is defined in this context as a period of time long enough that all wages and prices are fully flexible. Prices are said to be fully flexible when there are no institutional or other constraints preventing prices from changing. If wages were fully flexible, then wages would rise when output prices rise. If what you are producing starts selling for $10 rather than $8 (a 25% increase), the wages you are paid should also rise by 25%. Of course, the reverse is also true: if what you are producing starts selling for $6 rather than $8 (a 25% decrease), then with fully flexible wages and prices, the wages you are paid would also fall by 25%.

TIP

Economists have several different definitions of "long run." For economic growth, "long run" means decade-to-decade changes. For microeconomics, "long run" means a long enough period of time for all inputs to vary. For this part of macroeconomics, "long run" means a long enough period of time so that all wages and prices can change.

In the long run, when all wages and prices are fully flexible, prices of output and prices of inputs move together. Higher output prices trigger higher input prices. Lower output prices trigger lower input prices.

Businesses change output in response to changes in profit. But if input prices change when output prices change, then there is no change in profit. If there is no change in profit, there is no incentive for firms to change the amount of output they are producing.

So, in the long run, the amount of output that firms want to produce does not change in response to movements in the average level of output prices. Instead, the amount of output that firms produce in the long run is simply equal to the potential output of the economy. **Potential output** (also called **potential GDP, potential income, or full-employment GDP**) is the amount of output that the economy's firms can produce when all inputs are fully employed.

TIP

The production possibilities frontier first taught us about potential output. The amount of output produced when the economy is on the PPF is its potential output.

Graphically, the **long-run aggregate supply curve** is just a vertical line. Figure 14.4 illustrates. The usual notation for the long-run aggregate supply curve is **LRAS**. Regardless of the price level, in the long run, the economy will produce an amount of output equal to $GDP_{potential}$. If the economy grows—if there is an increase in the quantity of inputs or in their productivity—then the LRAS shifts to the right.

TRY

8. For each of the following events, what is its effect on the long-run aggregate supply curve, LRAS?
   a. Population growth increases the labor force.
   b. Business investment spending increases the nation's capital stock.
   c. A natural disaster destroys buildings, equipment, and physical infrastructure, and kills thousands of people.
   d. Technological change increases labor productivity.
   e. Educational attainment of the labor force increases.
   f. Financial institutions are developed that more efficiently channel funds from savers to borrowers.

Short-Run Aggregate Supply Curve

The question addressed with the short-run aggregate supply curve is: What is the relationship, in the short run, between the average level of output prices and the

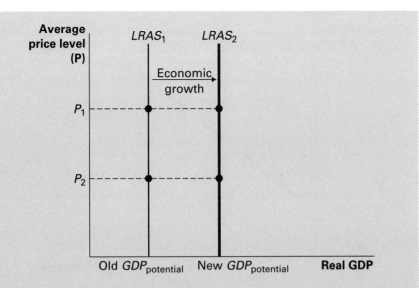

Figure 14.4 Long-Run Aggregate Supply Curve.

In the long run, when prices and wages and other input costs are all fully flexible, changes in the average level of output prices (P) do not change the amount of GDP firms will produce. The long-run aggregate supply curve is vertical and is located at the economy's potential output level. Economic growth—an increase in the quantity of inputs or in their productivity—will increase the economy's potential output, shifting LRAS to the right.

amount of final goods and services that firms want to produce? In this context, the short run refers to a period of time short enough that some wages and other input costs are not fully flexible. Economists refer to this as the assumption of **sticky wages**. Wages may change, but they change more slowly than output prices.

For most workers, wages are indeed sticky. Wages may change eventually—in the long run—but they don't change right away. For some workers, wages are set by a contract that is revisited no more than once a year. For workers without a contract, wages are also not changed frequently. Wage cuts are particularly bad for morale and worker productivity. Employers usually try to avoid implementing a wage cut until it's absolutely necessary. For these and other reasons, wages and some input costs tend to be sticky in the short run.

TIP

In explaining short-run aggregate supply, we encounter the least amount of consensus. The explanation here draws from several sources.

The relationship between the average level of output prices and the amount of GDP produced in the short run goes in both directions: from prices to output, and from output to prices.

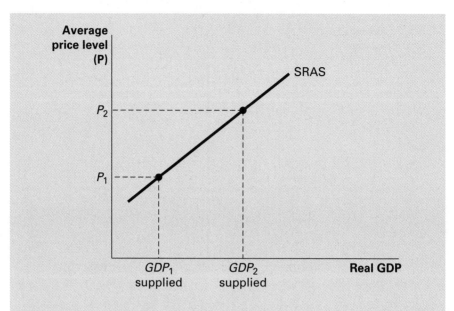

Figure 14.5 A Short-Run Aggregate Supply Curve.

In the short run, higher prices of output will lead profit-maximizing firms to produce more output if some input costs are fixed. When the average price level rises from P_1 to P_2, the amount of output supplied rises from GDP_1 to GDP_2.

From P to GDP

If some input prices are fixed in the short run, then when output prices rise, profit rises. Profit-maximizing firms will want to increase the amount of output they are producing. In the aggregate, the total amount of GDP produced will rise. On the other hand, if output prices fall and some input prices are fixed in the short run, profit falls. Profit-maximizing firms will want to decrease the amount of output they are producing. In the aggregate, the total amount of GDP produced will fall.

The **short-run aggregate supply curve** or **SRAS** will therefore slope up. Figure 14.5 illustrates. At higher output prices, more output is produced if some input costs are fixed in the short run. At lower output prices, less output is produced if some input costs are fixed in the short run.

The slope of the short-run aggregate supply curve depends upon how much output changes in response to a change in the average price level. The more flexible wages and other input costs are, the smaller the change in profit will be when output prices change. Thus, the more flexible wages and other input costs are, the smaller the change in output will be in response to a change in output prices.

Employers are much more hesitant to cut a worker's pay than they are to increase it. Wages therefore tend to be stickier when they are going down than they are when they are going up. The change in GDP will thus be larger when the average price level falls below its current level than when the average price

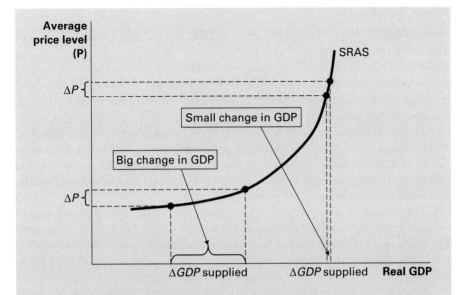

Figure 14.6 A Nonlinear Short-Run Aggregate Supply Curve.

When output prices fall below current levels and are relatively low, wages and other input costs are particularly sticky. The change in GDP supplied is quite large, so the SRAS curve is relatively flat. When output prices rise above current levels and are relatively high, wages and other input costs tend to be relatively flexible. The change in GDP supplied is quite small, so the SRAS curve is relatively steep.

level rises above its current level. The resulting short-run aggregate supply curve shown in Figure 14.6 will be nonlinear. At prices below current prices, the SRAS is relatively flat. At prices above current prices, the SRAS is relatively steep.

TIP

Notice that the aggregate supply story told so far discusses the effects of a change in output prices, but not the sources of any change in output prices.

TRY

9. Why does a drop in output prices lead to a drop in the amount of GDP supplied in the short run?

10. Why is the SRAS curve flatter below current output levels than it is above current output levels?

From GDP to P

How do output prices change in reaction to how much output is being produced? That is the question answered with this second set of stories that explain why the SRAS curve is upward-sloping. Rather than start from an assertion of changing prices without a word as to the source of the change, this set of stories starts with a change in how much output is being produced and examines the effect on the average level of prices of output.

The general idea is this: When businesses produce more output, doing so requires more inputs. Their increased demand for inputs—a shift in the demand for inputs—drives up the per-unit costs of the inputs. Higher costs of production lead businesses to increase what they are charging for output. Output prices therefore rise when the amount of output produced increases.

The reverse is also true. When businesses produce less output, doing so requires fewer inputs. Their decreased demand for inputs—a shift in the demand for inputs—drives down the per-unit costs of the inputs. Lower costs of production lead businesses to decrease what they are charging for output. Output prices therefore fall when the amount of output produced decreases.

Showing the relationship graphically gives us the same short-run aggregate supply curve we saw in Figure 14.5. At higher levels of GDP supplied, output prices are higher. At lower levels of GDP supplied, output prices are lower. The SRAS curve slopes up.

How much output prices change when output is changing may depend upon the gap between how much is being produced and the economy's potential GDP. At very low levels of output, there are many underutilized inputs. Workers are unemployed. Factories are idled. Equipment is not being used to its capacity. At very low levels of output, then, when businesses increase how much output they are producing, their increased demand for inputs may be satisfied with little or no increase in input costs. Unemployed workers can be hired without having to offer them higher wages. Idled factories can be restarted. Equipment can be used full time rather than just a few hours per day. Because the increased demand for inputs causes little or no increase in input costs, businesses can produce more output without having to increase output prices much, if at all. At very low levels of output, increases in output yield little or no increases in output prices. The SRAS curve is relatively flat. Figure 14.7 illustrates.

At very high levels of output—at or beyond potential output—inputs are being used to capacity. Workers have jobs. Factories are being operated 40 hours per week. Equipment is used full time as well. At very high levels of output, then, when businesses try to increase how much output they are producing, their increased demand for inputs will trigger large increases in input costs. Workers can work overtime, but will be paid 1.5 times their usual wage. Factories and equipment can be operated more than 40 hours per week, but maintenance costs on overworked equipment will soar. Because increased demand for inputs causes large increases in input costs, businesses will increase output prices a great deal. At very high levels of output, increases in output trigger large increases in output prices. The SRAS is relatively steep.

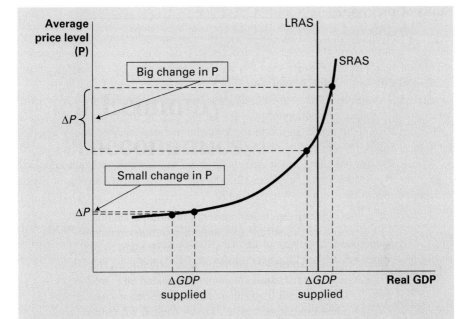

Figure 14.7 The SRAS and LRAS Curves.

The LRAS curve shows the economy's potential GDP. When output is well below potential, there is a lot of slack in the economy. Increases in GDP trigger very small increases in output prices. On the other hand, when output is near or beyond potential GDP, increases in GDP trigger very large increases in output prices. The SRAS curve is upward-sloping and nonlinear.

Can the economy produce beyond full employment, beyond the potential GDP? Yes, but only for short periods of time. Producing beyond potential GDP requires that workers work overtime, that people who would not normally be in the labor force be put to work, and that factories operate more than their usual number of hours. The U.S. economy can be thought of as producing beyond potential GDP in the last years of World War II, and perhaps during the Vietnam War. During World War II, government-mandated wage and price controls prevented input costs and output prices from rapidly increasing. During the Vietnam War, producing beyond capacity brought the unemployment rate down below 4% and led to increases in input costs and output prices.

TRY

11. Why does an increase in the amount of output produced lead to an increase in output prices in the short run?

12. Why is the SRAS curve flatter when the economy is far below its potential than when the economy is near or above its potential?

Shifts of the Aggregate Supply Curve

A change in output prices moves us along an existing aggregate supply curve. A change in the amount of output produced moves us along an existing aggregate supply curve. Any other event that affects the combination of output prices and amount of GDP supplied will shift the aggregate supply curve.

The LRAS curve shifts to the right when there is long-run economic growth. What are the causes of economic growth? Think back to the discussions of economic growth in Chapters 2 and 5. In the long run, the economy grows—potential GDP increases—if there are more inputs or higher productivity of inputs.

The LRAS curve shifts to the left when there is long-run economic decline. Potential GDP declines and the LRAS shifts to the left when there are fewer inputs or when productivity declines. What can cause a decrease in potential GDP? Natural disaster is a leading candidate.

An increase in aggregate supply in the short run is shown as a rightward shift of the SRAS curve. We can think of this as either "at every price level, firms want to produce more output" or "for every level of GDP supplied, firms will charge lower prices."

A decrease in aggregate supply in the short run is shown as a leftward shift of the SRAS curve. We can think of this as either "at every price level, firms want to produce less output" or "for every level of GDP supplied, firms will charge higher prices."

The SRAS curve shifts when the LRAS curve shifts. And the SRAS curve can shift when input costs change. Economists use the phrase **supply shock** or **cost shock** to refer to the effect of higher input costs. So the three events that shift the SRAS are as follows:

- Quantity of inputs changes
- Input productivity changes
- Input costs change*

Why is there an asterisk (*) after "input costs change"? Because the interpretation of the effect of input costs depends upon which aggregate supply story we are telling: from prices to GDP, or from GDP to prices.

If we explain the upward slope of the SRAS curve by examining how a change in the average level of output prices causes a change in output supplied, $\Delta P \rightarrow \Delta GDP_{supplied}$, then any change in input costs will shift the SRAS curve. The source of the change in input costs is irrelevant. For any level of output prices, if input costs rise, then profits are smaller. Profit-maximizing businesses will produce less output. So for any level of output prices, when input costs rise, GDP supplied falls: the SRAS curve shifts to the left. Higher input costs reduce short-run aggregate supply.

On the other hand, if we explain the upward slope of the SRAS curve by examining how a change in the amount of output supplied causes a change in the average level of output prices, $\Delta GDP_{supplied} \rightarrow \Delta P$, then some changes in input costs move us along the SRAS curve and other changes in input costs shift the SRAS curve. When more output is produced and demand for inputs increases, input costs rise, causing businesses to increase output prices. Here, higher input costs move us along the SRAS curve; input costs increased because more *output* was supplied.

But when input costs rise because of restricted supplies of *inputs*, the SRAS curve shifts. Again, higher input costs would lead businesses to raise output prices. But here, higher input costs are due to decreased supplies of inputs. For any level of output supplied, higher input costs would cause output prices to rise. Higher input costs *due to decreased supply of inputs* shifts the SRAS curve up.

Shifts of the aggregate supply curve are illustrated in Figure 14.8. To summarize the factors that can shift aggregate supply:

↑*Quantities of inputs* → *shift LRAS and SRAS to the right*

↓*Quantities of inputs* → *shift LRAS and SRAS to the left*

↑*Productivity of inputs* → *shift LRAS and SRAS to the right*

↓*Productivity of inputs* → *shift LRAS and SRAS to the left*

↑*Costs of inputs* → *shift SRAS up (equivalently, to the left)*

↓*Costs of inputs* → *shift SRAS down (equivalently, to the right)*

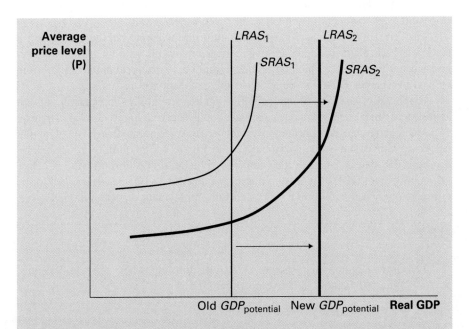

Figure 14.8 Shifts of the Aggregate Supply Curves.

A change in the average level of output prices or in GDP supplied moves us along an existing SRAS curve. An increase in quantities of inputs or in the productivity of inputs shifts both the LRAS and the SRAS curves to the right.

13. For each of the following events, what is its effect on the LRAS and SRAS curves?

    a. Labor force grows
    b. Amount of capital in the economy increases
    c. Labor productivity rises
    d. The price of energy rises

AS/AD EQUILIBRIUM

Aggregate demand is the set of combinations of average price level and planned aggregate expenditure, $C + I + G + NX$. At a higher average price level, planned aggregate expenditure is lower due to the interest rate, wealth, and foreign trade effects. The aggregate demand curve slopes down.

Aggregate supply is the set of combinations of average price level and amount of output businesses want to produce, GDP supplied. At a higher average price level, firms produce more output in the short run. And when firms produce more output in the short run, output prices rise. The short-run aggregate supply curve slopes up.

The economy is in macroeconomic equilibrium when it is at the average price level at which planned aggregate expenditure equals the amount of output businesses want to produce. This is the same definition of macroeconomic equilibrium we had in Chapter 6. All we've added is the connection to prices.

Graphically, macroeconomic equilibrium occurs at the intersection of the aggregate demand and short-run aggregate supply curves. Figure 14.9 illustrates.

Macroeconomic equilibrium in the short run can occur at a level of output below (or above) the economy's potential. In Figure 14.9, equilibrium occurs at a level of GDP that is less than the economy's potential. Equilibrium GDP is below full-employment GDP. There is an output gap that, as in Chapter 9, is equal to the difference between equilibrium GDP and full-employment or potential GDP.

14. Draw a graph that shows *AS/AD* equilibrium when the equilibrium amount of output is above potential GDP.

Changes of Macroeconomic Equilibrium

In the short run, the macroeconomic equilibrium can change. A shift of the aggregate demand curve or a shift of the short-run aggregate supply curve will take the economy to a new equilibrium combination of average level of output prices and GDP.

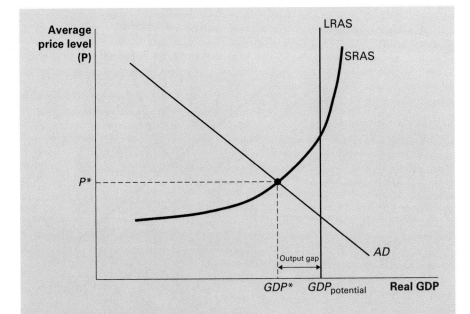

Figure 14.9 Macroeconomic Equilibrium.

The economy is in short-run macroeconomic equilibrium at price level P^* and output level GDP*. At P^*, planned aggregate expenditure equals the amount of output firms wish to produce. Because the equilibrium amount of output is below potential output, there is an output gap, and the economy is experiencing unemployment.

If aggregate demand increases, the *AD* curve shifts to the right. In short-run equilibrium, GDP and prices will both be higher. Figure 14.10 illustrates. Economists call the increase in prices due to an increase in aggregate demand **demand-pull inflation**: prices are being pulled higher by greater demand.

If aggregate demand decreases, the *AD* curve shifts to the left. In short-run equilibrium, GDP and prices will both be lower.

If short-run aggregate supply increases, the SRAS curve shifts to the right. In short-run equilibrium, GDP will be higher, and prices will be lower.

If short-run aggregate supply decreases, the SRAS curve shifts to the left. In short-run equilibrium, GDP will be lower, and prices will be higher. Figure 14.11 illustrates. Economists call the increase in prices due to a decrease in aggregate supply **cost-push inflation**: prices are being pushed up by higher costs.

TRY

15. For each of the following events, what is its effect on prices and output in the short run?
    a. Prices of houses fall
    b. Businesses become more optimistic

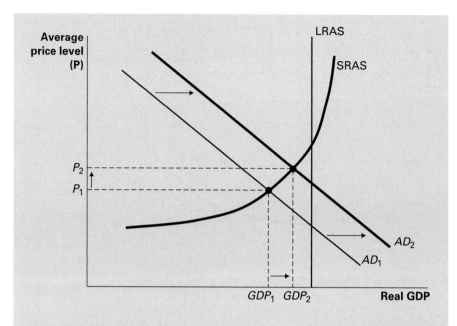

Figure 14.10 Demand-Pull Inflation.

When aggregate demand increases, the *AD* curve shifts to the right. In equilibrium, GDP increases and prices increase.

c. The government undertakes expansionary fiscal policy
d. Price of energy rises
e. The labor force increases
f. Taxes are increased

DYNAMIC *AS/AD* MODEL

The *AS/AD* model seems to tell us that when aggregate demand falls, prices fall. Put another way: when people and businesses spend less, there is price deflation. An income tax increase causes people to spend less. So the *AS/AD* model seems to tell us that an income tax increase causes price deflation. Really?

No. Interpreting the *AS/AD* model correctly requires us to pay careful attention to the *ceteris paribus*, or "all else constant," assumption. The correct statement is this: the *AS/AD* model tells us that when aggregate demand falls due to a tax increase, prices will be lower *than they would have been* had taxes not been increased. That's quite a mouthful.

The *AS/AD* model presents us with a counterfactual—a way of comparing the world after some event has occurred with how the world would have been had the event not occurred. When we look at the effect of a tax increase, should we

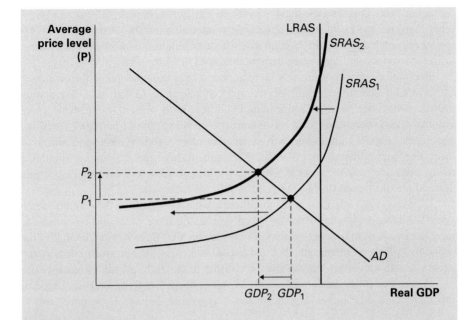

Figure 14.11 Cost-Push Inflation.
When aggregate supply decreases, the SRAS curve shifts to the left. There is stagflation: in equilibrium, GDP decreases and prices increase.

really expect to see price deflation? No. But we should expect to see that prices are lower than they would have been. When we look at a tax cut, should we necessarily expect to see unemployment fall? No. But we should expect to see that the unemployment rate is lower than it would have been without the tax cut.

Imagine it this way. Suppose we could rewind history, have a global "redo." We can look up what actually happened in the U.S. economy between December 2007 and December 2009: the unemployment rate rose from 5.0 to 10.0%, real GDP fell from $13.4 to $12.9 trillion per year, and the GDP deflator rose from 107.1 to 109.9. But what *would have happened* had income taxes been cut even further than they were cut in the 2009 American Recovery and Reinvestment Act (ARRA)? The *AS/AD* model tells us that lower income taxes, which are shown as a rightward shift of the *AD* curve, would increase output and raise prices.

Would real GDP have increased above $13.4 trillion? We can't say. But we can say that an income tax cut would have increased real GDP above $12.9 trillion. Would unemployment have fallen back to 5.0%? We can't say. But we can say that an income tax cut would have left the unemployment rate below 10.0%. Would the GDP deflator have risen above 109.9? Yes. An income tax cut would have further increased prices.

One way of trying to capture these ideas graphically is with a graph called the **dynamic *AS/AD* model**. Dynamic means "in motion." The contrast is with a **static *AS/AD* model**, in which things are not changing. The *AS/AD* model presented throughout this chapter is a static *AS/AD* model; we assumed "all else constant" other than the one event whose effects we wanted to examine. A dynamic *AS/AD* model acknowledges that in an economy whose population is increasing over time, aggregate supply and aggregate demand are always increasing.

Population growth means that there are constantly more people in the economy. Consumption spending should be rising from one year to the next. Population growth means that there are more school children, more drivers, more roads, more criminals, and more court cases. Government spending should be rising from one year to the next. Population growth means that more goods are being produced to meet demand, requiring more plants and equipment. Investment spending should be rising from one year to the next. Overall, population growth means that aggregate demand should be shifting to the right a little bit each year.

Population growth also means that there are more workers in the economy each year. The labor supply is increasing. And purchasing more plant and equipment to meet the needs of a growing population also means that there is more capital in the economy each year. Increased labor and capital mean that the long-run and short-run aggregate supply curves should also be shifting to the right a little bit each year.

Figure 14.12 illustrates a dynamic *AS/AD* model. If nothing unusual happens, real GDP should be increasing each year. If aggregate demand rises more quickly

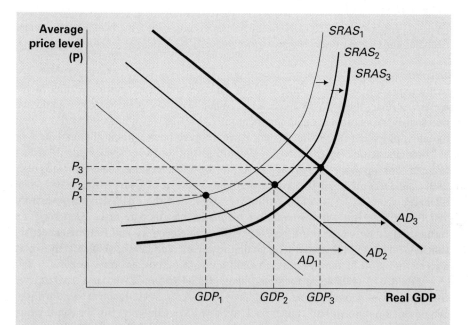

Figure 14.12 A Dynamic *AS/AD* Model.

Each year, aggregate demand increases and aggregate supply increases. In year 1, aggregate demand is AD_1 and aggregate supply is $SRAS_1$. In year 2, aggregate demand is AD_2 and aggregate supply is $SRAS_2$. In year 3, aggregate demand is AD_3 and aggregate supply is $SRAS_3$. Real GDP rises from one year to the next, as do prices.

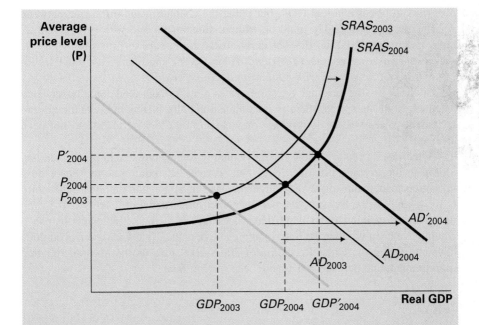

Figure 14.13 A Change in Aggregate Demand in a Dynamic *AS/AD* Model.

Due to population growth, *AS* and *AD* are constantly shifting to the right. If nothing unusual happens in 2004, GDP will increase from GDP_{2003} to GDP_{2004}, and prices will rise from P_{2003} to P_{2004}. But if aggregate demand increases more in 2004 than normal, shifting to AD'_{2004}, then GDP will increase from GDP_{2003} to GDP'_{2004}, and prices will rise from P_{2003} to P'_{2004}.

than aggregate supply, prices should be a little bit higher each year than they were in the previous year.

What if wealth rises rapidly in 2004 due to, say, rapid increases in housing prices? Then the increase in consumption would make aggregate demand in 2004 shift further to the right than it would have had wealth not risen so rapidly. Real GDP in 2004 would be greater than it would have been in 2004 had wealth not risen so rapidly. Output prices would be higher in 2004 than they would have been had wealth not risen so rapidly.

Trying to graph all this creates a bit of a mess. We could have AD_{2003} and AD_{2004} and then AD'_{2004}, where AD_{2004} is the aggregate demand curve without the rapid wealth increase and AD'_{2004} is the aggregate demand curve with the rapid wealth increase. Then we'd have GDP_{2003} and GDP_{2004} and GDP'_{2004}, where GDP_{2004} is what GDP would have been without the rapid wealth increase and GDP'_{2004} is what GDP would have been with the rapid wealth increase. Figure 14.13 illustrates.

Alternatively, we could just remember—and repeat often—that the standard *AS/AD* model we drew earlier in this chapter is showing us not the difference *over time* in prices and real GDP, but rather the counterfactual difference between what prices and real GDP would be without some event and with some event. A rapid rise in wealth shifts the *AD* curve to the right, raising prices *above where they would have been without the rapid rise in wealth* and raising real GDP *above where it would have been without the rapid rise in wealth*.

So back to the original question: Does the AS/AD model really say that when taxes are increased, there is price deflation? No. It says that when taxes are increased, prices will be lower *than they would have been* if taxes had not been changed.

What does it require, then, for the economy to generate actual price deflation, a drop in the average price of goods and services? It requires a very large drop in aggregate demand, or a very large increase in aggregate supply. If the norm is for prices to rise by, say, 2% per year, then price deflation occurs if the drop in aggregate demand is so large that prices are more than 2% lower than they would have been without the drop in aggregate demand. That we experienced price deflation during the Great Recession of 2007–2009 tells us that the precipitating drop in aggregate demand must have been mighty large.

TRY

16. Draw a dynamic *AS/AD* model for two years, year 1 and year 2. In year 2, taxes are increased. The tax increase slows but does not eliminate growth in GDP.

WHAT'S AHEAD

We assumed the Fed had a money supply target when we derived the aggregate demand curve. What if, instead, the Fed had an interest rate target? That possibility is explored in Chapter 15, which takes a different approach to studying the macroeconomic connections between prices and output.

Chapter 15

Inflation and Output: The Monetary Policy Approach

Chapter 14 examined the links between output and prices when the Fed targets the money supply. In this chapter we ask: What is the link between output and inflation when, rather than the money supply, the Fed targets an interest rate?

The Fed chooses a target for the federal funds rate in response to current and future expected levels of inflation and GDP growth. The federal funds rate influences all other interest rates. Interest rates affect aggregate demand, the sum of consumption, investment, government, and net export spending. Aggregate demand determines how much output is produced. How much output is produced influences the inflation rate. Monetary policy is a potent force in fighting rising inflation or recession if the economy's troubles are due to shifts in aggregate demand. But monetary policy cannot simultaneously fight both a recession and rising inflation.

KEY TERMS AND CONCEPTS

- Phillips curve
- Stagflation
- Inflationary expectations
- Supply shock
- Productivity
- Beige Book
- Taylor Rule
- Inflation hawk
- Inflation dove

KEY EQUATION

- Taylor Rule: interest rate target = neutral interest rate + A (actual − goal inflation rate) + B (actual − goal GDP growth rate)

KEY GRAPH

- Phillips curve

COMPARING THE *AS/AD* AND MONETARY POLICY APPROACHES

The Federal Reserve sets monetary policy in the United States. It faces a choice, as we noted in Chapter 12: the Fed can target a particular interest rate and let the money supply change as need be to achieve that interest rate target, or it can target a particular level of the money supply and let the interest rate change as need be to achieve that money supply target. If our money demand never changed, the Fed would not have to choose between interest rate and money supply targets. But for any number of reasons, our money demand changes from month to month, quarter to quarter, year to year, and so the Fed must choose between a money supply and an interest rate target.

In Chapter 14, we used the *AS/AD* model to look at the connection between output and prices when the Fed targets the money supply. Here in Chapter 15, we look at the connection between output and inflation when the Fed targets the interest rate. Even though our starting point differs—an interest rate target rather than a money supply target—many of the principles introduced in Chapter 14 still apply.

What is the same, and what is different? These principles apply whether we assume the Fed targets the money supply or interest rates:

- We need to consider both the demand side and the supply side. The demand side is spending. The supply side is production.
- Planned aggregate expenditure is the sum of consumption, investment, government, and net export spending. $AE = C + I + G + NX$.
- When aggregate demand increases, firms produce more output. When aggregate demand falls, firms produce less output. GDP therefore depends on $C + I + G + NX$.
- When firms produce more output, their demand for inputs rises, increasing the cost of inputs, which increases prices charged for output. $\Delta GDP \rightarrow \Delta P$
- The supply-side relationship between output and prices can shift if there are changes in productivity or in the supplies of inputs.

The key differences between the *AS/AD* approach and the monetary policy approach are the following:

- Instead of assuming that the Fed targets the money supply and lets interest rates fluctuate in response to a change in money demand, we assume that the Fed targets interest rates and lets the money supply fluctuate.
- Instead of focusing on changes in the price *level*, the monetary policy approach focuses on changes in the *rate of change* of prices, the inflation rate.
- Because there is an interest rate target, a change in prices doesn't change interest rates, so there's no interest rate effect on aggregate expenditure.
- The wealth effect and foreign trade effect, which gave us the downward-sloping aggregate demand line of the *AS/AD* model, are assumed to be inconsequential. This is not an outlandish assumption. Most wealth is held

in assets whose real value doesn't change when output prices change, thus minimizing any impact of the wealth effect. And most economies are integrated to some degree or another internationally, so price movements in one country are typically mirrored in another country, minimizing any impact of the foreign trade effect.

- Instead of a graph with two lines intersecting, we summarize the monetary approach with one graph (the Phillips curve) and one equation (the Taylor Rule).

TRY   *(Answers to all "TRY" questions are at the back of the book.)*

1. The key difference between the monetary policy approach and the *AS/AD* approach is the Fed's choice of target. What variable does the Fed target in the *AS/AD* approach? In the monetary policy approach?

THE FED'S CHOICE: MONEY SUPPLY OR INTEREST RATE TARGET

Over its history, the Fed has moved back and forth between a money supply and an interest rate target. Their most recent use of a money supply target began October 6, 1979, when the Fed was fighting very high inflation. Controlling money supply growth meant letting interest rates soar. The federal funds rate peaked in June 1981, at 21.7%.

The sharp rise in interest rates had the desired effect. Inflation had hit double digits in the late 1970s and peaked at over 13% in 1979. The Fed's willingness to hold the reins on money growth even as interest rates soared brought the inflation rate down to below 4% by 1982.

The Fed shifted its focus once again in the early 1980s. Since then, the Federal Reserve has pursued an interest rate target.

Using an Interest Rate Target: An Overview

The Fed observes and projects near-term values for inflation and for the growth rate of GDP. In response to where the economy is and where it seems to be heading, the FOMC sets the target for the federal funds rate—the rate banks charge other banks on overnight loans of reserves.

When inflation is too high or is projected to go too high, the Fed raises its target for the federal funds rate. When GDP is growing too slowly or projected to grow too slowly, the Fed lowers its target for the federal funds rate. At the conclusion of each FOMC meeting, the target federal funds rate is announced. Other interest rates change in response to the Fed's announcement.

A change in interest rates affects investment spending and net export spending. Through the spending multiplier, consumption and import spending change as well. The total change in aggregate demand in response to a change in interest rates triggers a change in how much output is produced (GDP).

When businesses change how much they are producing, their demand for inputs changes, which leads to changes in input prices. In response, businesses change the prices of their output. The inflation rate changes.

In the rest of this chapter, we'll take this story apart and then put it back together again. Our first step: How does the Fed change interest rates?

TRY

2. Why does the Fed have to choose between a money supply target and an interest rate target? (You may want to review Chapter 12).

3. What two economic variables does the Fed consider when setting its interest rate target?

THE FED TARGETS THE FEDERAL FUNDS RATE

When the Fed targets interest rates, the interest rate it targets is the federal funds rate, the interest rate that banks charge each other on overnight loans to cover reserve requirements. As we first discussed in Chapter 12, the Fed can influence the federal funds rate because with open market operations, the Fed can change how much reserves the banks have to lend each other.

TIP

Reminder: The name "federal funds rate" is a bit of a misnomer: *federal* funds are not associated with the *federal* government in any way, but are funds held in a bank's reserve account at a *Federal* Reserve Bank.

To lower the federal funds rate, the Fed will inject reserves into the banking system by purchasing government bonds. Its purchases drive up the price of existing government bonds, driving down their rate of return.

To raise the federal funds rate, the Fed will remove reserves from the banking system by selling government bonds. The Fed's sales of bonds drive down the price of existing government bonds, driving up their rate of return.

Other interest rates move with the federal funds rate. The prime rate—the rate banks charge their best business customers—changes within hours of a Fed announcement of a change in its target for the federal funds rate. Many consumer loans—home equity loans, credit cards, some mortgage loans—are tied to the prime rate, so those interest rates jump, too.

Long-term rates on fixed-rate home mortgages and on 10-, 20-, and 30-year government bonds change, too, but not by much. Remember Chapter 13: Long-term rates are influenced not just by today's short-term rates, but also by our expectations of tomorrow's short-term rates.

The Fed has generally done a good job of hitting its target for the federal funds rate since 2000; the difference between the target and the actual rate is usually within a few basis points. But the Fed has more difficulty hitting its target during periods of extreme financial stress. When the global financial meltdown began in August 2007 and when financial markets imploded in fall 2008, the target and actual rates diverged by as much as 3 percentage points (300 basis points).

TRY

4. If the Fed wants to increase the federal funds rate, what does it do? Do all interest rates change?

INTEREST RATES AFFECT AGGREGATE DEMAND

When the Fed changes interest rates, aggregate demand (or planned aggregate expenditure) changes. We covered the details in Chapters 7 and 13. Here's a brief review: An increase in interest rates lowers investment and net export spending. A decrease in interest rates raises investment and net export spending. Consumer spending may also respond to a change in interest rates, but there the evidence is mixed. And then there are multiplier effects, which further change aggregate spending.

TIP

We can again use "planned aggregate expenditure" and "aggregate demand" interchangeably. We needed to make the distinction between *AE* and *AD* only in Chapter 14.

Investment and interest rates are inversely related because interest rates affect the cost of investment. We first discussed this relationship in Chapter 7. Investment spending—business purchases of equipment, construction of new residential and nonresidential structures, and changes in the value of inventory holding—is undertaken by businesses aiming to earn profit. The higher the cost of investment, the less profitable investment will be, and thus businesses will do less investment spending.

$$\uparrow interest\ rates \rightarrow \downarrow investment\ spending$$
$$\downarrow interest\ rates \rightarrow \uparrow investment\ spending$$

Net exports and interest rates are also inversely related. When U.S. interest rates rise, U.S. wealth holders move some of their wealth out of international financial assets, and foreign wealth holders put more of their wealth in U.S. financial assets. The movements of wealth across borders cause the dollar price of one unit of foreign currency to fall. Goods and services produced abroad become less expensive within the United States, increasing U.S. imports. Goods and services produced in the United States become more expensive to foreigners, decreasing U.S. exports. U.S. net exports fall.

$$\uparrow interest\ rates \rightarrow \downarrow Price\ of\ foreign\ currency \rightarrow \uparrow IM\ \&\ \downarrow EX \rightarrow \downarrow NX$$

$$\downarrow interest\ rates \rightarrow \uparrow Price\ of\ foreign\ currency \rightarrow \downarrow IM\ \&\ \uparrow EX \rightarrow \uparrow NX$$

The initial effect on aggregate consumption spending is ambiguous. Durable goods purchases tend to fall when interest rates rise. But higher rates of return on assets encourage more consumer spending.

The changes in aggregate demand kick off multiplier effects, leading to round after round of changes in output, income, and spending. (The spending multiplier was covered in Chapter 8.) Because of the multiplier, real GDP and income ultimately change by more than just the initial change in spending. For instance, if investment and net export spending fall by $100 billion per year—perhaps running at a pace of $1,900 billion per year rather than $2,000 billion per year—and the spending multiplier has a value of 1.8, real GDP will ultimately decline by $180 billion per year—perhaps falling from $14,000 billion per year to $13,820 billion per year.

TRY

5. Why does investment spending rise when interest rates fall?

6. Why does net export spending rise when interest rates fall?

7. In which case would the effect of interest rates be greater: when the marginal propensity to consume is 0.4, or when the marginal propensity to consume is 0.9? Why?

THE (USUAL) TRADE-OFFS BETWEEN UNEMPLOYMENT AND INFLATION: PHILLIPS CURVE

Output changes when aggregate demand changes. When more output is produced, there is more employment in the economy. (We discussed the connection between GDP, employment, and unemployment in Chapter 6.) If the additional employment is greater than the rise in the labor force, then the unemployment rate will decline as GDP rises.

What is the connection between unemployment and inflation? An economic concept called the "Phillips curve" helps us understand why there is—and sometimes isn't—a trade-off between unemployment and inflation.

The Phillips Curve, Unadorned

In 1958, economist A. W. Phillips depicted an apparently stable relationship between the rate of change of money (nominal) wages and unemployment in the United Kingdom over the period 1861 to 1957. Phillips suggested the logic behind this relationship:

> When the demand for labour is high and there are very few unemployed we should expect employers to bid wage rates up quite rapidly, each firm and each industry being continually tempted to offer a little above the prevailing rates to attract the most suitable labour from other firms and industries. On the other hand it appears that workers are reluctant to offer their services at less than the prevailing rates when the demand for labour is low and unemployment is high so that wage rates fall only very slowly.[1]

The question immediately arose: Is there a similar relationship for the United States? American economists examined the relationship between unemployment and *price* inflation (not wage inflation) in the United States. The move from wage to price inflation was quite logical: if wages are increasing more rapidly this year than last year, businesses will pass these increased costs on to their customers, so prices will also be rising more rapidly this year than last year.

The stable trade-off between wages and unemployment that Phillips had found for the United Kingdom appeared to exist between consumer prices and unemployment in the United States. Higher unemployment was associated with lower inflation. Lower unemployment meant higher inflation.

The **Phillips curve** came to mean this relationship between unemployment and price inflation. Comparing consumer price inflation and unemployment for 1955 to 1968 yields Figure 15.1 on page 270.

But even as some economists were starting to suggest using the Phillips curve as a menu for policy choices—"Choose a point on the Phillips curve, Mr. President, and we your policy advisors will fine-tune the economy and move it there"—others were urging caution. Surely, they argued, factors other than unemployment contribute to the inflation rate. They were right.

"The Phillips Curve Is Dead"

Even without economists urging caution on theoretical grounds, the events of the next several years gave everyone pause. Between 1969 and 1970, as seen in Figure 15.2, both the unemployment rate and the inflation rate increased. From 1970 to 1973, the U.S. economy again seemed to be moving along a stable Phillips curve, but one up and to the right from the first Phillips curve. Then again between 1973 and 1974, both the unemployment rate and the inflation rate increased. By now economists had coined a name for this unfortunate coincidence of events: **stagflation** meant simultaneous increases in both the unemployment and inflation

---

[1] A. W. Phillips, "The Relation between Unemployment and the Rate of Change of Money Wage Rates in the United Kingdom, 1861–1957," *Economica*, New Series, Vol. 25, No. 100 (Nov. 1958), pp. 283–299.

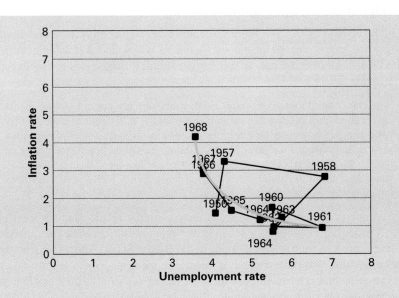

Figure 15.1 Phillips Curve for the United States, 1955–1968.

Using data for the U.S. economy from 1955 to 1968, there appears to be a smooth, stable Phillips curve showing the relationship between the unemployment rate and the price inflation rate. At higher unemployment rates, the inflation rate is lower. At lower unemployment rates, the inflation rate is higher.

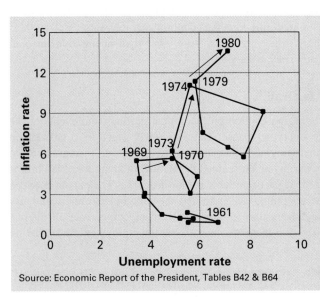

Source: Economic Report of the President, Tables B42 & B64

Figure 15.2 Spiraling Inflation, 1969–1980.

The smooth and stable relationship between unemployment and inflation that seemed to exist in the 1960s shifted three times in the next decade. Between 1969 and 1970, between 1973 and 1974, and between 1979 and 1980, both unemployment and inflation increased; inflation seemed to be spiraling out of control.

rates. From 1974 to 1979, again the U.S. economy seemed to move along a stable Phillips curve—but, again, one up and to the right from the second curve! And then again it happened: between 1979 and 1980 both unemployment and inflation increased. Inflation appeared to be spiraling out of control.

Yet soon events seemed to turn around. Figure 15.3 shows the data for the U.S. economy after 1980. The economy moved along yet a fourth Phillips curve between 1980 and 1983, far to the right of the original 1960s Phillips curve. But between 1983 and 1986, both unemployment and inflation fell. From 1987 to 1992, we seemed to be moving along a curve in about the same position as in 1970 to 1973. And then, from 1992 to 1998, the Phillips curve shifted in yet again, returning by the late 1990s to the combinations of unemployment and inflation evident in the 1960s U.S. economy.

In the 1970s it was common to hear economists say, "The Phillips curve is dead." But the Phillips curve was not dead, not even in the 1970s. It was shifting, and shifting rapidly. That's a far cry from dead.

When economists said, "The Phillips curve is dead," they usually meant that there was no consistent trade-off between unemployment and inflation. For evidence, they pointed to three periods when both unemployment and inflation increased: 1969–1970, 1973–1974, and ultimately 1979–1980.

But economists would never look at the market for, say, 6-ounce cups of chocolate-flavored frozen yogurt and claim, "The demand curve is dead," even though there are times when both prices and quantities demanded increase. The inverse relationship between price and quantity demanded in a market is not "dead" when the demand curve shifts; that inverse relationship exists "*all else constant*." What other factors, the economist will ask, could be causing the entire relationship between prices and quantity demanded to shift?

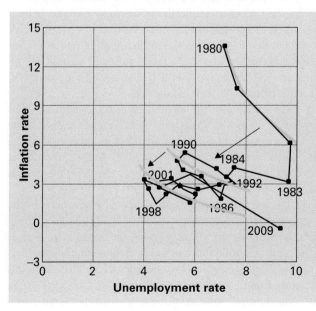

Figure 15.3 Phillips Curve, 1980–2009.

After the early 1980s, the Phillips curve seemed to shift back in several times. The unemployment and inflation rates in the early 1990s centered around one trade-off. By the late 1990s, the trade-offs between unemployment seemed even more favorable, with the Phillips curve having shifted back to its 1960s position.

The same logic applies to the Phillips curve. When the unemployment rate and the inflation rate change in the same direction, the inverse relationship isn't "dead"; that inverse relationship between unemployment and inflation exists "*all else constant.*" Instead, we need to ask: What factors could be causing the entire relationship between unemployment and inflation to shift?

Shifts of the Phillips Curve

By focusing on labor relations, Phillips had captured an explanation for why an economy might move along an existing trade-off between unemployment and inflation. But what was important as well was that the terms of the trade-off might shift. We need to remember the important lesson taught when we studied supply and demand: some events *move us along* an existing curve; other events *shift* a curve.

So what events can shift the Phillips curve? Three events have been particularly important over the last 40 years:

- Changes in inflationary expectations
- Supply shocks that change input prices
- Changes in productivity growth

Change in Inflationary Expectations

The Phillips curve must take into account our expectations of inflation, or what economists call our **inflationary expectations**. Think about how workers and bosses behave. Suppose everyone—workers and bosses alike—believes the inflation rate will be 2% next year. The workers are likely to be content with a 3% raise because it at least beats the rate of inflation; the bosses may even be willing to offer a 3% raise because they can probably raise their customer prices to cover most of it. Now suppose instead that everyone believes the inflation rate next year will be 10%. Workers will not be happy with a 3% raise; they will want at least a 10% raise. Bosses will, perhaps begrudgingly, offer a 10% raise, figuring they will be able to cover it with a 10% increase in their final prices.

Increased inflationary expectations—a higher expected inflation rate—does not mean that everyone in the economy sits down with an economics textbook, the business news, the latest Fed reports, and forms an equation to predict what the inflation rate will be next year. It simply means that you and I and the librarian at the desk all have an answer to the question: "So, how much do you think prices will go up next year?"

When the inflation rate has been stable for some years, as it has been in the United States since the early 1990s, then our answer is typically the same from one year to the next: "Oh, I don't know, probably about the same as this year: about 2, maybe $2\frac{1}{2}\%$." But when the inflation rate has been changing, as it did in the United States in the early 1970s after nearly two decades of stability, then our answer changes, too: "Oh, gosh, I don't know, last year I thought prices were going to rise about 2 or 3% this year but they went up a lot more than that; I guess I'd

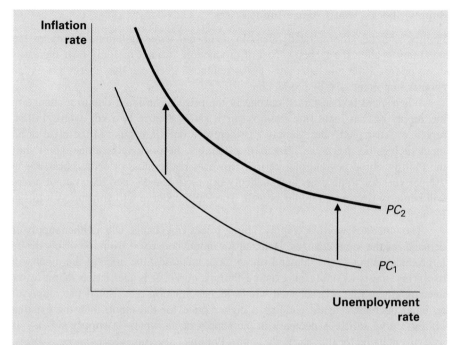

Figure 15.4 A Shift Up of the Phillips Curve.

When inflationary expectations rise, there will be higher wage and price inflation at every possible unemployment rate. The entire Phillips curve shifts up.

say about 4, maybe 5%." All we need in order to form an expectation is our daily experience in the marketplace: Gas used to be $1.90 a gallon and now fluctuates around $3.00 a gallon: inflation. Rent went up 10%: inflation. A Snickers bar used to cost 69¢ but now it's 79¢ (and smaller to boot!): inflation.

When everyone thinks next year's inflation rate will be higher than this year's, workers will want, and employers will provide, higher wage increases. Higher wage increases raise production costs and are passed on to consumers in the form of higher prices. The inflation rate rises.

At every possible unemployment rate, wage and price inflation are higher when inflationary expectations rise. As seen in Figure 15.4, increased inflationary expectations shift the Phillips curve up. When inflationary expectations fall, the Phillips curve shifts down.

The 1950s and 1960s were years of stable inflation and unchanging inflationary expectations. But by the late 1960s prices had started rising more rapidly. The expected inflation rate rose, too, and the Phillips curve shifted up—not just once, but several times. The Fed's "monetary experiment" of 1979–1982 broke the back of inflation, and the inflation rate fell quickly from over 10% in 1981 to around 4% throughout the mid- and late-1980s. The expected inflation rate fell, too, and the Phillips curve shifted down.

Supply Shocks That Change Input Prices

Phillips's initial story related unemployment and *wage* inflation. Wages are an important—often the largest—cost of production, but not the only one. Increases in oil prices in the mid- and late- 1970s reminded everyone that energy prices are another important cost of production.

When there is a sustained change in the price of an input due to a change in the supply of that input, the Phillips curve shifts. Notice two key words in that sentence: "sustained" and "supply." If there is a one-time spike in the price of an input such as oil, prices will rise in reaction, but the price spike alone won't shift the Phillips curve beyond that period. However if the input price had been rising 2% per year for some years and suddenly begins to rise 6% per year, output prices will begin to rise more rapidly as well. The Phillips curve will shift up as it did in Figure 15.4.

The other key word is "supply." Input prices can change when either supply or demand for the input changes. Demand for inputs is derived from the firm's desire to produce output. If the demand for an input increases, the price of the input will rise. This *moves us along* an existing Phillips curve. It is the reason that a lower unemployment rate is associated with a higher inflation rate. But if the supply of an input decreases, again yielding a higher price for the input, then the existing Phillips curve *shifts*. A decrease in the supply of an input—a **supply shock**—is an exogenous factor that shifts the entire Phillips curve up.

Supply shocks tend to produce very short-term shifts of the Phillips curve precisely because they are *shocks*; they rarely produce *sustained* increases in input prices. Input price shocks that increase the inflation rate even for a short time can, however, make our expectations of inflation rise. And those increased expectations can sustain a shift up of the Phillips curve.

Changes in Productivity Growth

A third factor that shifts the Phillips curve is a change in the productivity growth rate. **Productivity** is the amount of output a worker can produce per hour. When productivity rises, firms can produce the same quantity of output at lower cost. Lower costs of production can lead businesses to reduce their output prices.

Over time, productivity tends to rise. But sometimes productivity rises quickly; other times it grows slowly. When the productivity growth rate is higher than usual, the Phillips curve shifts down as in Figure 15.5. When the productivity growth rate is lower than usual, the Phillips curve shifts up.

Changes in productivity growth rates benefited the economy in the 1990s. After two decades of slowdown in productivity growth rates, labor productivity growth rates started to rise in the early 1990s. The strong growth in productivity allowed the economy to enjoy ever lower unemployment rates without any acceleration of the inflation rate. In the 1990s, the Phillips curve shifted down several times until by the turn of the century it had returned to its 1960s position.

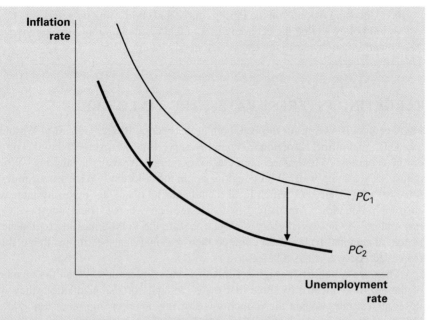

Figure 15.5 A Shift Down of the Phillips Curve.

When the productivity growth rate rises, the Phillips curve shifts down. Notice that a shift down and a shift to the left of the Phillips curve produce the same result: a more favorable trade-off between unemployment and inflation.

Inflation Can Change for Several Reasons

To summarize: the inflation rate can change for many reasons. An increase in demand for output can raise the inflation rate; a drop in demand can reduce inflation. These changes would move us along an existing Phillips curve.

Or the Phillips curve can shift. A rise in inflationary expectations can increase the inflation rate; a drop in the expected inflation rate can lower inflation. A decrease in the supply of inputs can raise the inflation rate; an increase in supply can lower inflation. A slowdown in productivity growth can raise the inflation rate; a rise in the productivity growth rate can lower inflation.

TRY

8. Why can there be a trade-off between unemployment and inflation?
9. For each of the following, what is its effect on the Phillips curve?
   a. Inflationary expectations fall.
   b. The supply of a major input to production increases.
   c. Labor productivity growth rates rise.

10. "Choosing a point" on the Phillips curve and conducting monetary and fiscal policy so that the economy gets to that combination of unemployment and inflation rates is not always a good strategy. Why?

TARGETING INTEREST RATES: THE TAYLOR RULE

Many economists work for the Fed, both at the Federal Reserve Board in Washington, D.C., and at the 12 regional Federal Reserve Banks. Together, they keep tabs on the economy: Where is economic activity rising? Where is it faltering? Which industries are doing well? Which regions are in the doldrums? What's happening to prices of raw materials? Which local manufacturing plants are reporting increased costs of production? Are there labor shortages anywhere? These questions, and many more, are answered every six weeks before the FOMC meeting by the staffs of the 12 regional banks, who compile their regional analyses in the **Beige Book** (so called because it has a beige cover).

They are watching for signs of inflation and of recession. When the members of the FOMC collectively agree that there are signs of rising inflation, they will raise interest rates. When the economy is slowing down or in a recession, and the inflation rate tends to be relatively low, the Fed will stimulate the economy through lowering interest rates.

To Fight Inflation, Raise Interest Rates

When the Fed raises interest rates to fight inflation, it sets a series of events in motion. World financial markets react immediately—indeed sometimes they react before the Fed even announces their next interest rate move—and the dollar rises slightly, eventually reducing net exports. Investment spending is curtailed somewhat. The resulting drop in income for businesses and workers in export, business equipment, and construction industries kicks off a multiplier effect that gradually winds its way through the consumer sector. GDP will be lower than it would have been had the Fed not acted. Greater slack in labor markets alleviates some of the pressure on wages, which diminishes some of the pressure on prices. The Fed has fought the inflation, though at the cost of slower GDP and employment growth than would have otherwise been. Their actions move the economy along a Phillips curve toward higher unemployment and lower inflation.

To Fight a Recession, Lower Interest Rates

When the Fed reduces interest rates to fight a recession, the same set of events are set in motion, but in reverse. The dollar falls, and net exports rise. Investment spending rises. Through the multiplier, consumption also rises. At each point, more spending means businesses are producing more output, increasing income for the employees and business owners. If the existing labor force can't produce the additional output, employees are added. The unemployment rate falls. This puts additional pressure on wages and prices. The Fed will have fought the slowdown, allowing the inflation rate to rise as unemployment fell. Again, the Fed's actions move the economy along a Phillips curve, this time toward lower unemployment and higher inflation.

When the Fight Is Over, Everyone Returns to Their Corner

The Fed also has a sense of a neutral interest rate. If it has been fighting inflation with higher rates, then once the fight is won, the Fed will lower interest rates back to that neutral rate. If it has fought a recession by lowering interest rates and achieved their goal of stimulating the economy, it will want to raise the interest rate back to that neutral rate.

The Fed's notion of a neutral federal funds rate seems to be a rate that is about 2 percentage points above the inflation rate. So if the inflation rate is 1%, the neutral federal funds rate is 3%. If the inflation rate is 6%, the neutral federal funds rate is 8%.

Because the Fed returns interest rates to a neutral level, we can't look just at the Fed's change in interest rates and conclude, "Ah, the Fed is fighting inflation" or "Oh, the Fed is trying to stimulate the economy." If the Fed increases interest rates by 25 basis points, it could be raising rates above the neutral rate to fight inflation, or just raising them *back* to the neutral rate to ready for the next fight. Conversely, if the Fed decreases interest rates by 25 basis points, it could be lowering rates below the neutral rate to fight recession or just taking them *back down* to the neutral rate to ready for the next fight. To properly interpret an interest rate move, we also need to know the state of the macroeconomy.

The Taylor Rule

We have described here the **Taylor Rule**, whereby the interest rate target chosen by the Fed depends on inflation and GDP growth. The Taylor Rule is an equation that captures the Fed's behavior:

$$\text{interest rate target} = \text{neutral interest rate}$$
$$+ A(\text{actual} - \text{goal inflation rate})$$
$$+ B(\text{actual} - \text{goal GDP growth rate})$$

where A and B are constants that measure the weight the FOMC members put on fighting inflation versus fighting slow GDP growth.

The Fed sets an inflation rate goal—commonly believed to be about 2–2.5%—and then undertakes monetary policy to try to achieve that goal. When the inflation rate is above or heading above the Fed's goal rate, the Fed will increase interest rates. When the inflation rate is below or heading below the Fed's goal rate, the Fed will decrease interest rates.

The Fed also has a goal for GDP growth. In the U.S. economy, GDP needs to increase by about 2 to 3% each year just to absorb the new workers in the labor force and keep the unemployment rate constant. When GDP growth is below or heading below the Fed's goal growth rate, the Fed will decrease interest rates.

When GDP growth is above or heading above their goal growth rate, the Fed will increase interest rates.

The Fed's monetary policy is set by the members of the Federal Open Market Committee—the chairman of the Fed, the other six members of the Federal Reserve Board, and 5 of the 12 regional Federal Reserve Bank presidents. These individuals are generally from the banking and academic communities. They bring with them a wealth of understanding of the economy. But they are not necessarily of one mind insofar as the relative costs of high inflation and low GDP growth are concerned.

Borrowing from the language of war, the phrases "inflation hawk" and "inflation dove" have come to describe two extremes. Hawks fight; doves don't. An **inflation hawk** is someone who puts heavy weight on the importance of fighting inflation and is not as concerned about the costs of low GDP growth. An **inflation dove** is someone who is willing to accept higher inflation if the alternative is a big increase in the unemployment rate.

If the FOMC is dominated by inflation hawks, the value of A will be large relative to that of B. Deviations of inflation from its goal will generate bigger changes in interest rates than deviations of GDP growth from its goal. If the FOMC is dominated by inflation doves, B will be large relative to A. Deviations of inflation from its goal will generate smaller changes in interest rates than deviations of GDP growth from its goal.

The members of the FOMC don't literally know what their values of A and B are. The debates at the FOMC meetings are not couched in terms of coefficients of an equation. But thinking about their deliberations this way does help us to see what is at stake.

TRY

11. What does the Fed do to its interest rate target if inflation is rising? If inflation is falling? If the growth rate of GDP is rising? If the growth rate of GDP is falling?

12. The Fed announces a $1/4$ percentage point increase in the federal funds rate target. Does that necessarily mean the Fed is fighting inflation? Explain.

13. What is the Taylor Rule? Do members of the FOMC literally use the Taylor Rule to make their decisions?

14. Suppose that the Taylor Rule is

$$\text{interest rate target} = 0.04 + \tfrac{1}{2}(\text{actual inflation rate} - 0.02)$$
$$+ \tfrac{1}{4}(\text{actual GDP growth rate} - 0.03)$$

   a. According to this Taylor Rule, what is the Fed's goal for the inflation rate? What is the Fed's goal for the GDP growth rate?

   b. For each of the following combinations of inflation and GDP growth rates, calculate the value of the interest rate target.

      i. inflation rate = 2% (0.02), GDP growth rate = 3% (0.03)

      ii. inflation rate = 6% (0.06), GDP growth rate = 3% (0.03)

iii. inflation rate = 2% (0.02), GDP growth rate = 0%

15. What does it mean to be an inflation hawk? An inflation dove? If the Taylor Rule in question 14 describes the Fed, would you characterize the FOMC as dominated by hawks, or by doves?

SOME FIGHTS ARE EASIER THAN OTHERS

Some fights the Fed faces are easier than others. When inflation begins to rise because aggregate demand is rising, the Fed can fight back by raising interest rates. Net export and investment spending will fall, offsetting some of the earlier rise in spending. But when inflation begins to rise because of price disruptions due to supply shocks or because of increased inflationary expectations, the Fed's fight is tougher.

An Increase in Aggregate Demand

Suppose that initially the inflation rate and GDP growth rate are near the Fed's goal, and that the federal funds rate is near its neutral rate. Now government spending rises. If the Fed does nothing, the economy will move along the Phillips curve in Figure 15.6 from point A to point B. Inflation will rise to $infl_B$ and unemployment will fall to u_B.

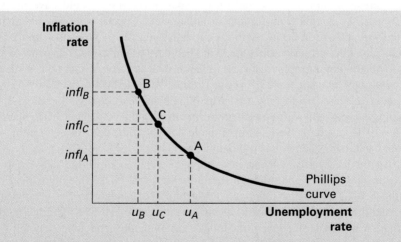

Figure 15.6 The Fed Fights an Increase in Aggregate Demand.

Increased government spending would move the economy from A to B. The Fed reacts by increasing interest rates, so the economy only moves from A to C. As a result of the combination of higher government spending and higher interest rates, the inflation rate rises and the unemployment rate falls. In the extreme, the Fed could raise interest rates so high that the economy would simply remain at point A despite the increase in government spending.

But if the Fed does nothing, it risks more than just inflation rising to $infl_B$. The Fed risks letting inflationary expectations rise. Rising expectations of inflation are especially bad; they shift the Phillips curve up and worsen any trade-off between unemployment and inflation. So the Fed fights the inflation by raising interest rates.

Perhaps the Fed raises rates enough that the economy stays at point A. In this case, higher interest rates lower investment and net export spending by the same amount as the government initially increased its spending.

Or perhaps the Fed will raise rates to dampen but not eliminate the effect of expansionary fiscal policy. The economy will wind up at some point C between A and B. The inflation rate will be lower than it would have been had the Fed done nothing ($infl_C < infl_B$) but is higher than it was initially ($infl_C > infl_A$). The unemployment rate will be higher than it would have been had the Fed done nothing ($u_C > u_B$) but is lower than it was initially ($u_C < u_A$). The Fed's inflation fighting behavior, when coupled with an increase in aggregate demand, can leave the economy no worse off than it was before aggregate demand rose.

A Supply Shock or Increase in Inflationary Expectations

When rising inflation is due to a supply shock or to rising inflationary expectations, the Fed's choices are the same: the Fed can do nothing, or it can change its interest rate target. But this time the decision is tougher.

Again suppose that initially the inflation and GDP growth rates are near the Fed's goals, and the federal funds rate is near its neutral rate. But this time, suppose that there is a supply shock that raises input prices. (We would have the same analysis if we started from a jump in inflationary expectations.) The economy is initially at point A on the first Phillips curve in Figure 15.7. When the supply shock occurs, the Phillips curve shifts up. If the Fed does nothing, the economy moves to a combination of unemployment and inflation such as point B, with higher inflation.

But the Fed can't stand by; it must react. Were the Fed to stand idly by while inflation increased from $infl_A$ to $infl_B$, inflationary expectations would rise. The Phillips curve would shift up yet again. And then again. And again. The experience of the 1970s taught the Fed an important lesson about the costs of not fighting soon enough and hard enough when inflation rises.

So the Fed raises interest rates to fight inflation, lowering net export and investment spending and, through the multiplier, real GDP. Unemployment rises. If the Fed fights all the inflation, the unemployment rate rises a great deal, to u_D, and the inflation rate remains at $infl_A$. Perhaps the Fed will fight that hard. Or perhaps it will fight off some of the inflation, moving the economy to a point like C. The inflation rate will be lower than it would have been had the Fed done nothing ($infl_C < infl_B$), but higher than it was initially ($infl_C > infl_A$). The unemployment rate will be higher than it would have been had the Fed done nothing ($u_C > u_A$), and also higher than it was initially ($u_C > u_A$).

There's nothing satisfying at all about this fight against inflation. The economy winds up with more people out of work and higher prices: stagflation. The inflation

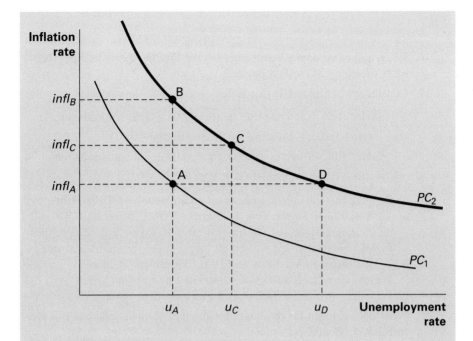

Figure 15.7 The Fed Fights an Adverse Supply Shock.

A supply shock would move the economy from A to B. The Fed reacts by increasing inter-est rates. If the Fed eliminates the inflation problem, then the economy moves to point D with very high unemployment. If the Fed fights the inflation problem but doesn't eliminate it, the economy moves from A to C. The Fed has no way to bring the economy back to point A.

isn't as bad as it would have been had the Fed done nothing. But all most people know is what they experience, not what might have been in some alternate universe. And what they know is bad: higher unemployment and higher inflation.

The Zero Lower Bound

In its efforts to fight the Great Recession of 2007–2009, the Fed in December 2008 lowered the target for the federal funds rate essentially to 0. (The official target was a range, $0-1/4\%$.) The economy continued to worsen through 2009. According to the Taylor Rule, as the economy worsened, the target federal funds rate should have continued to fall, becoming negative. But nominal interest rates can't go below zero. So even though events suggested that the FOMC should lower the federal funds target rate further, the Fed could not do so. It was at the zero lower bound.

TRY

16. When aggregate demand decreases but the Phillips curve does not shift, what strategy will the Fed pursue?

17. Consider two different Taylor Rules:

   > Taylor Rule 1: interest rate target $= 0.04 + 1$(actual inflation rate $- 0.02) + \frac{1}{4}$(actual GDP growth rate $- 0.03$)

   > Taylor Rule 2: interest rate target $= 0.04 + \frac{1}{4}$(actual inflation rate $- 0.02) + 1$(actual GDP growth rate $- 0.03$)

   a. Suppose that the inflation rate is 6% (0.06) and that GDP is falling by 1% (-0.01). If Taylor Rule 1 describes FOMC behavior, what will be the target value for the interest rate? If Taylor Rule 2 describes FOMC behavior, what will be the target value for the interest rate?

   b. Which Taylor Rule reflects an FOMC dominated by inflation hawks? Which one reflects an FOMC dominated by inflation doves?

   c. Why does the mix of inflation hawks and doves on the Fed matter?

18. What does it mean for the target for the federal funds rate to be at the zero lower bound?

CONCLUSION

To fight inflation or slow GDP growth, the Fed changes interest rates. The Taylor Rule captures how much the Fed changes rates in reaction to changes in inflation and the GDP growth rate. Aggregate demand—$C + I + G + NX$—changes in response. Firms change how much output they are producing, which changes the unemployment rate.

The economy moves along a Phillips curve. So long as the Phillips curve doesn't shift, fighting inflation comes at the cost of higher unemployment than would otherwise exist, and fighting recession comes at the cost of higher inflation than would otherwise exist. But if the Phillips curve *does* shift, the Fed faces difficult choices. The more the Phillips curve shifts, the higher unemployment must go in order to defeat inflation.

PART VI

The Open Economy

Chapter 16

Open Economy Macroeconomics

Modern economies live on an international stage. Trade of goods and services produces long-run economic gains but is nevertheless sometimes restricted by various barriers to trade. International purchases and sales of goods and services and of assets are recorded in an accounting system called the balance of payments system. The balance of payments impacts exchange rates, the rate at which one country's currency can be exchanged for another. International trade provides a channel for interest rates to affect output and employment, and affects the spending multiplier.

KEY TERMS AND CONCEPTS

- Free trade
- Trade promotion policy
- Trade protection policy
- Export subsidy
- Infant industries
- Barriers to trade
- Embargo
- Quota
- Tariff
- Retaliatory tariffs
- International trade agreements
- Balance of payments
- Balance on current account
- Balance on financial account
- Trade balance
- Trade surplus
- Trade deficit
- Merchandise trade balance
- Payments for factor incomes
- International transfer payments
- Remittances

- Current account surplus
- Current account deficit
- Financial inflows
- Financial outflows
- Financial account surplus
- Financial account deficit
- Reserve account
- Official reserve transaction (ORT)
- Statistical discrepancy
- Balance of payments surplus
- Balance of payments deficit
- Exchange rate
- Foreign currency or foreign exchange
- Floating exchange rates
- Exchange rate regime
- Fixed exchange rates
- Peg
- Managed (dirty) float

KEY EQUATIONS

- Trade balance = exports of goods and services − imports of goods and services
- Balance on current account = trade balance + net factor income + net international transfer payments
- Balance on financial account = financial inflows − financial outflows
- Balance of payments = balance on current account + balance on financial account

KEY GRAPH

- Exchange rate

INTERNATIONAL TRADE POLICIES

When one country can produce a good relatively well and another country can produce a different good relatively well, there are economic incentives for the two countries to specialize and trade. This is the idea of the gains from trade that we first covered in Chapter 2. When one country has the comparative advantage in the production of a good because its opportunity cost of producing the good is lower than another country's opportunity cost of producing the same good, the country should specialize in producing the good in which it has the comparative advantage in production. The other country can produce a good in which it has the comparative advantage in production. The two countries then trade. Total worldwide production and consumption of the goods increase. International trade can therefore benefit a country, because there are long-run gains: the country can end up with more output than it would have without trade.

Some countries want to increase their exports for more immediate gains. Producing goods and services for export means that people are employed in the economy's export-producing sector. Increasing exports will boost a country's national income and employment in the short run.

When there are no government promotions or restrictions on purchases and sales of goods and services across international boundaries, economists say there is **free trade**. But both economic and non-economic incentives may lead a country to impose policies that promote or restrict trade. Policy designed to increase international trade is called **trade promotion policy**. Policy designed to reduce international trade is called **trade protection policy**.

Because of the long-run gains from trade and the short-run employment benefits of greater exports, some countries implement trade promotion policies. One common example is an **export subsidy**: a government policy that encourages production for export. Export subsidies can take a variety of forms: tax breaks, cheap loans, government-paid marketing, and more. All export subsidies either decrease production costs or increase export revenue, encouraging producers of exported goods and services to increase the amount of output produced.

Despite the economic gains from trade, not all trade is viewed positively. Remember from Chapter 2 that pursuing the gains from trade is a long-run strategy. The short-run adjustment process can be difficult for the industry that loses employment and output. For instance, some might argue that the United States does not have a comparative advantage in car production but does have a comparative advantage in higher education. Pursuing the gains from trade would mean shifting resources from car production toward the production of college degrees. In blunt terms: pursuing the gains from trade would mean firing car workers and shutting car manufacturing plants while hiring professors and building more colleges and universities. The job losses in the declining industry are—in the long run—offset by job gains in the growing industry. But there is no guarantee that the fellow laid off from the GM plant will find a job at a state college. Because the costs of specializing and trading are not evenly borne by all in an economy, some people view free trade negatively.

What if an industry is relatively new? Here again, some may oppose free trade. An economy may eventually have a comparative advantage in the production of that industry's goods, but not initially. The industry may need time to develop, establish networks, refine production methods, and locate efficiencies. For so-called **infant industries**, trade could prevent the industry from developing and growing to the point where it can compete on a global scale. Until an industry is past its infancy, it could benefit from trade protection.

Others may oppose trade because it conflicts with national security. History is rife with examples of opposition to trade for national security interests. Neither Spain nor England wanted to be without its own ship-building industry in the sixteenth century; each country's national security depended upon the nation's ability to defend itself at sea. Environmental protection, labor protection, and other interests also underlie trade opposition.

Some countries therefore erect **barriers to trade**. Such protectionist policies can take a variety of forms. An **embargo** is a ban on some or all trade with another country. The United States began an embargo on trade with Cuba in 1962. A **quota** establishes a limit to the number of imports of a particular good from a particular country over some time period. The U.S. quota for imports of raw sugar from Australia is 87.4 million kg per year. A **tariff** is a tax placed on imports. The U.S. assesses a 4.4% tariff on cotton thread imported from a long list of countries.

Because one country's imposition of a tariff will hurt its trading partners' economies, it is not uncommon for the trading partner to retaliate by imposing its own tariffs. The threat of such **retaliatory tariffs** may prevent a legislature from slapping on a tariff in a heated moment. The Smoot-Hawley tariff imposed by the United States in 1930 in an effort to fight the Great Depression led to a series of retaliatory tariffs that many argue reduced U.S. exports.

Protectionist trade policies may protect economies in the short run, but many economists believe they are harmful in the long run, because they can prevent the pursuit of the economic gains from trade. Several **international trade agreements** have been struck over the years in efforts to limit protectionism and encourage free trade. There are agreements that involve just a few countries, such as the North American Free Trade Agreement (NAFTA), which seeks to eliminate trade barriers between Mexico, the United States, and Canada; and the United States–Dominican Republic–Central America Free Trade Agreement (CAFTA), which does the same between the United States, the Dominican Republic, and countries of Central America. There are also agreements that involve many countries from several continents. The General Agreement on Tariffs and Trades (GATT) was formed in 1947. Under GATT, many nations, including the United States, agreed to reduce tariffs. The World Trade Organization (WTO) was founded in 1994 as a successor to GATT. Over 150 countries are members of the WTO, whose purpose is to resolve trade disputes between countries and liberalize trade through facilitating trade agreements.

TRY   (*Answers to all "TRY" questions are at the back of the book.*)

1. What is meant by the "gains from trade"?
2. What is the definition of "free trade"?
3. What are some of the reasons for opposition to international trade?
4. What are the differences between an embargo, a quota, and a tariff?

BALANCE OF PAYMENTS

The accounting system used to keep track of transactions between countries is called the **balance of payments** system. You can think of the balance of payments system as tracking the flows of currency between two countries.

There are two types of transactions tracked within the balance of payments system: purchases and sales of goods and services, and purchases and sales of assets. Goods and services transactions are part of the **balance on current account**. Asset transactions are part of the **balance on financial account**.

Each balance can be in surplus, in deficit, or balanced. Rather than memorizing a series of definitions, keep this one idea in mind:

If money coming in > money going out, there is a surplus.
If money going out > money coming in, there is a deficit.
If money coming in = money going out, the account is balanced.

These definitions are always true, whether we are talking about your own personal finances, the government's budget, or the balance of international payments.

TIP

Watch for the difference between balance and balanced. Each of the differences we are about to define is called a "balance." A "balance" can be greater than, less than, or equal to 0. The balance is balanced if the balance equals zero.

Balance on Current Account

The difference between exports of goods and services and imports of goods and services is called the **trade balance**.

Trade balance = exports of goods & services − imports of goods & services

The balance of trade in goods and services is the same as net exports, *NX*.

Trade balance = NX = EX − IM

When exports exceed imports, there is more money coming into the country to pay for exports than is leaving the country to pay for imports. The trade balance is positive, and there is a **trade surplus**. When imports are greater than exports, the trade balance is negative and there is a **trade deficit**.

A distinction is sometimes made between trade in goods and trade in services. The balance of trade in goods (also called the **merchandise trade balance**) equals exports of goods minus imports of goods. The balance of trade in services equals exports of services minus imports of services.

The balance on current account measures the flow of funds in goods and services transactions, plus payments for factor incomes, plus international transfer payments. **Payments for factor incomes** include wages paid to someone working in a foreign country and rent, interest income, or dividends paid to someone whose assets are being used in a foreign country. Wages paid to a U.S. resident working in Canada represent a flow of funds out of Canada and into the United States. Dividends paid to a Mexican resident who owns stock in a U.S. corporation represent a flow of funds from the United States to Mexico. Net factor income in the United States equals factor income received by U.S. residents from foreign sources minus factor income paid by U.S. sources to foreign residents.

The third and final component of the balance on current account is **international transfer payments**—payments between individuals in two different countries for which nothing but gratitude is received in exchange. Many international transfer payments are **remittances**: money sent by a worker to family or others living in another country.

The balance on current account is thus money flowing in for three purposes—to pay for goods and services, to pay factors of production, and for transfer payments received from abroad—minus money flowing out for the same three purposes. Equivalently, the balance on current account is the trade balance plus net factor income plus net international transfer payments.

Balance on current account = trade balance + net factor income

+ net international transfer payments

When the balance on current account is positive, there is a **current account surplus**. When the balance on current account is negative, there is a **current account deficit**.

TRY

5. The data below are for international transactions between the United States and China in 2005.

Exports of goods from the United States	$41.1 billion
Exports of services from the United States	$9.0 billion
Imports of goods into the United States	$243.9 billion
Imports of services into the United States	$6.7 billion
Factor income paid by the United States	$21.4 billion
Factor income paid by China	$4.9 billion
Net transfer payments from the United States to China	$2.2 billion

a. What was the value of the U.S. merchandise trade balance with China in 2005? Which country had a merchandise trade deficit? Which one had a merchandise trade surplus?

b. What was the value of the U.S. balance of trade in goods and services with China in 2005? Which country had a deficit in trade of goods and services? Which one had a surplus in trade of goods and services?

c. What was the value of the U.S. balance on current account with China in 2005? Which country had a current account deficit? Which one had a current account surplus?

Balance on Financial Account

The financial account measures purchases and sales of assets. One way to think about the difference between the current account and the financial account is to think back to GDP. Transactions that are counted in GDP are in the current account. The purchase and sale of assets, on the other hand, does not directly contribute to a country's GDP. Purchasing shares of stock in a Dutch company or buying a seventeenth-century villa in Tuscany does not alter U.S. GDP. Purchases and sales of assets are thus recorded separately in the financial accounts.

TIP

Confusion alert! Terminology is changing. For many years, the phrase "capital account" was used instead of "financial account" to describe purchases and sales of assets. But recently "capital account" was redefined. Some textbooks still use the old terminology; some use the new.

The balance on the financial account measures the flow of money into the country minus the flow of money out of the country. Money flows into the United States when foreigners purchase U.S. assets. Foreign purchases of U.S. assets are called **financial inflows**.

Money flows out of the country when U.S. residents purchase foreign assets. U.S. purchases of foreign assets are called **financial outflows**.

The balance on financial account is the difference between money flowing in and money flowing out. So the balance on financial account is financial inflows minus financial outflows.

Balance on financial account = financial inflows − financial outflows

= foreign purchases of U.S. assets − U.S. purchases of foreign assets

When more money is flowing in than is flowing out, the balance on financial account is positive. Financial inflows are more than financial outflows. There is a **financial account surplus**.

When more money is flowing out than is flowing in, the balance on financial account is negative. Financial outflows are more than financial inflows. There is a **financial account deficit**.

TRY

6. In 2005, U.S. purchases of Chinese assets totaled $5.4 billion, and Chinese purchases of U.S. assets totaled $224.7 billion. What was the U.S. balance on financial account with China in 2005? Which country had a financial account surplus? Which one had a financial account deficit?

Is the Overall Balance of Payments Balanced?

The overall balance of payments is the sum of the balance on the current account and the balance on the financial account.

Balance of payments = balance on current account

+ balance on financial account

Is the overall balance always balanced? Alas, the answer depends on what transactions are included in the financial account. And that in turn depends upon which textbook you are using.

If the financial account includes the **reserve account**, then the balance of payments is always balanced. The reserve account is a central bank's holding of foreign currency. **Official reserve transactions (ORTs)** are purchases or sales of foreign currency by the central bank. When official reserve transactions are measured as part of the financial account, then the balance of payments is always balanced. (Caveat: there are always errors and omissions causing measurement errors, so the balance of payments is balanced once a **statistical discrepancy** item is included to account for any remaining discrepancy or difference.)

TIP

Another confusion alert! The "reserve account" held at the central bank for official reserve transactions has nothing to do with bank reserves held at the central bank. It is simply an unfortunate reuse of the same phrase we first saw in Chapter 11.

Because the balance of payments is balanced when official reserve transactions are counted as part of financial flows, the sum of the balance on current account and the balance on financial account equals zero.

Balance on current account + balance on financial account (including ORT) = 0

Manipulating that equation slightly yields

Balance on current account = −balance on financial account (including ORT)

If a country's current account balance is positive, its financial account balance will be negative. That is, a country running a current account surplus will also have a financial account deficit. Conversely, if a country's current account balance is negative, its financial account balance will be positive. That is, a country running a current account deficit will also have a financial account surplus.

What if the reserve account is not counted as part of the financial account? In that case, the overall balance of payments can be in surplus or in deficit. If the total flow of funds into the country is greater than the total flow of funds out of the country, then there is a **balance of payments surplus**. A balance of payments surplus exists when either the current account surplus is larger (in absolute value) than the financial account deficit or the financial account surplus is larger (in absolute value) than the current account deficit. A balance of payments surplus leads to an accumulation of foreign currency. The central bank's holdings of foreign currency will rise.

If the reserve account is not counted as part of the financial account and the total flow of funds into the country is less than the total flow of funds out of the country, then there is a **balance of payments deficit**. A balance of payments deficit exists when either the current account deficit is larger (in absolute value) than the financial account surplus or the financial account deficit is larger (in absolute value) than the current account deficit. A balance of payments deficit leads to a loss of foreign currency. The central bank's holdings of foreign currency—its reserve account balance—will fall.

The United States has a current account deficit measured in the hundreds of billions of dollars per year. The current account deficit for 2009 was over $400 billion, or about 3% of GDP. The United States runs a financial account surplus also measured in the hundreds of billions of dollars per year. The financial account surplus for 2009 was also over $400 billion, including about $50 billion increase in official reserves and a statistical discrepancy of over $200 billion. The statistical discrepancy increased a great deal in 2008 and 2009, presumably due to the global financial disturbances associated with the Great Recession.

TRY

7. When the U.S. financial account is in deficit, are U.S. people, businesses, and government agencies borrowing more, or borrowing less, from foreigners than they are lending?

8. The United States' total international transactions with all other countries in 2005 were

U.S. balance on current account	−$748.7 billion
Financial inflows	$1,295.2 billion
Financial outflows	$532.6 billion

   Was the U.S. balance on current account in surplus or deficit? Was the U.S. balance on financial account in surplus or deficit? Was the U.S. overall balance of payments in surplus or deficit? Did U.S. reserve accounts of foreign currency increase or decrease?

9. The U.S. balance on current account was consistently positive from 1890 until 1970. Since 1975, the annual U.S. balance on current account has been negative. In which period was the U.S. financial account in surplus? When was the U.S. financial account in deficit?

EXCHANGE RATES

The flow of funds between countries determines the rate at which one country's currency exchanges for another, or what economists call the **exchange rate**. The language of exchange rates and their determinants is new, but the ideas are simply supply and demand—the same supply and demand model we covered in Chapter 3.

Dollars are the currency of the United States. Other countries and regions have their own currency: the European euro, Mexican peso, Japanese yen, Chinese yuan, Indian rupee, British pound, and so on. Economists use the phrases **foreign currency** or **foreign exchange** to refer generally to other countries' currencies.

An exchange rate is simply a price. It is the price of one currency in terms of another. For instance, if 1 euro (the currency of much of Europe) can be purchased for $1.25, the dollar price of 1 euro is $1.25. Rather than "price," we use the phrase "exchange rate": the exchange rate between the dollar and the euro is $1.25 per euro.

What about the euro price of 1 dollar? It is simply the reciprocal of the dollar price of 1 euro. If 1 euro costs $1.25, then 1 dollar costs $1/1.25 = €0.80$.

TIP

Is the exchange rate between the dollar and the euro equal to the dollar price of 1 euro, or the euro price of $1? It depends. For some currencies, the convention is to express the exchange rate as dollars per unit of the foreign currency; for others, we state the amount of foreign currency per dollar. In this book, we always use "exchange rate" to mean the dollar price of 1 unit of foreign currency.

Prices are determined in markets. The price of a product—say, the egg you had for breakfast—depends upon the demand for eggs and the supply of eggs. This is the essence of the supply and demand model of Chapter 3. The demand for eggs represents the behavior of people with dollars who wish to trade those dollars for eggs. The supply of eggs represents the behavior of people with eggs who wish to exchange those eggs for dollars. The equilibrium price of eggs is the number of dollars that trade for each egg, and is the price at which the quantity demanded equals the quantity supplied. If the equilibrium price of eggs is 20¢, we could say that the dollar price of 1 egg is $0.20, or that 5 eggs ($1/0.20 = 5$) can be traded for $1.

Instead of eggs, simply reread the previous paragraph and say "euro" instead of "eggs." The price of a euro depends upon the demand for euros and the supply of euros. The demand for euros represents the behavior of people with dollars who wish to trade those dollars for euros. The supply of euros represents the behavior of people with euros who wish to exchange those euros for dollars. The equilibrium price of euros is the number of dollars that trade for each euro, and is the price at which the quantity demanded equals the quantity supplied. If the equilibrium price of euros is $1.25, we could say that the dollar price of 1 euro is $1.25, or that 0.80 euros ($1/1.25 = 0.80$) can be traded for $1.

The determination of an exchange rate is depicted in Figure 16.1. The demand curve represents people with dollars who want euros. As the price of euros rises, the quantity of euros demanded falls. The demand curve slopes down. The supply curve represents people with euros who want dollars. As the price of euros rises, the quantity of euros supplied rises. The supply curve slopes up. The equilibrium price of euros—the exchange rate between dollars and euros—is the price where demand and supply intersect.

The demand for foreign currency (foreign exchange) represents the behavior of people who have dollars and want foreign currency. People with dollars would want foreign currency either because they want to purchase foreign goods and services, or because they want to purchase foreign assets. Purchases of foreign goods and services are imports. Purchases of foreign assets are financial outflows. Demand for foreign currency therefore depends upon

- Imports of goods and services into the United States
- Financial outflows out of the United States

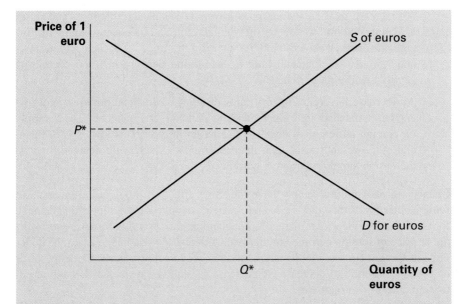

Figure 16.1 The Exchange Rate between Dollars and Euros.

The demand for euros slopes down; as the price of a euro rises, fewer people want to trade dollars for euros. The supply of the euro slopes up; as the price of a euro rises, more people want to trade euros for dollars. The equilibrium dollar price of euros is the price where demand and supply intersect.

The supply of foreign currency (foreign exchange) represents the behavior of people who have foreign currency and want dollars. People with foreign currency would want dollars either because they want to purchase U.S. goods and services, or because they want to purchase U.S. assets. Foreign purchases of U.S. goods and services are U.S. exports. Foreign purchases of U.S. assets are financial inflows. Supply of foreign currency therefore depends upon

- Exports of goods and services from the United States
- Financial inflows into the United States

Changes in demand and supply emanate from changes in imports, exports, and financial flows, which are themselves most often due to changes in domestic income, foreign income, domestic interest rates, and foreign interest rates.

- An increase in U.S. income increases U.S. imports, increasing demand for foreign currency. A decrease in U.S. income decreases U.S. imports, decreasing demand for foreign currency.
- An increase in foreign income increases U.S. exports, increasing supply of foreign currency. A decrease in foreign income decreases U.S. exports, decreasing supply of foreign currency.

- An increase in U.S. interest rates lowers U.S. financial outflows and raises U.S. financial inflows, decreasing demand for, and increasing supply of, foreign currency. A decrease in U.S. interest rates raises U.S. financial outflows and lowers U.S. financial inflows, increasing demand for, and decreasing supply of, foreign currency.

- An increase in foreign interest rates raises U.S. financial outflows and lowers U.S. financial inflows, increasing demand for, and decreasing supply of, foreign currency. A decrease in foreign interest rates lowers U.S. financial outflows and raises U.S. financial inflows, decreasing demand for, and increasing supply of, foreign currency.

Changes in demand and supply have the same effect on the equilibrium price of foreign currency as they did in Chapter 3 when we looked at the supply and demand for goods and services. An increase in demand as shown in Figure 16.2 causes the dollar price of foreign currency to increase. A decrease in demand causes the dollar price of foreign currency to decrease. An increase in supply causes the dollar price of foreign currency to decrease. A decrease in supply causes the dollar price of foreign currency to increase.

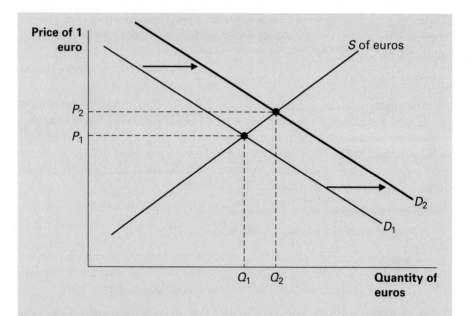

Figure 16.2 Effect of a Shift in Demand.
An increase in imports or an increase in financial outflows requires that those who have dollars exchange more dollars for foreign currency. The demand for foreign currency increases, shifting the demand curve to the right. As a result, the dollar price of foreign currency rises.

TRY

10. For each of the following events, what are the effects on the supply of foreign currency, the demand for foreign currency, and the dollar price of foreign currency? Does the dollar rise or fall?

    a. A recession occurs in the United States, lowering U.S. income.
    b. An economic boom increases income in China.
    c. U.S. interest rates decrease.
    d. Interest rates decrease in all countries.
    e. Interest rates rise in Europe and Asia, but not in the United States.

Exchange Rate Regimes

The process of determining exchange rates that we have just described—with changes in demand for or supply of foreign currency causing a change in the exchange rate—occurs when there are no government interventions in the market for foreign currency. In that case, the price is allowed to move in response to changes in demand or supply, and we have what are called **floating exchange rates**.

But there are also times in history when countries have intervened in their exchange rate markets; indeed, some countries still do today. Economists use the phrase **exchange rate regime** to describe the degree and type of government intervention in foreign currency markets.

When the government sets the price for foreign currency and does not allow market forces to change the rate, economists say there are **fixed exchange rates**. Fixed exchange rates usually occur as a result of a bilateral (two-country) agreement in which both governments agree to intervene as necessary to keep the exchange rate at a constant value.

When one country decides unilaterally to fix its exchange rate with another currency, the country is often said to **peg** its exchange rate. For example, the Cayman Islands currency, also called the dollar, has been pegged since 1974 to the U.S. dollar. The official exchange rate has been constant: 1 Cayman Islands dollar = 1.20 U.S. dollars.

Finally, a **managed float** or **dirty float** exchange rate regime is one in which the exchange rate is allowed to float within a prespecified range. It is a mix of floating and fixed exchange rate regimes. The government will intervene only if the price rises above the preset price ceiling or falls below the preset price floor.

How does a government manipulate exchange rates? By buying or selling currency, and thus becoming part of the demand for or supply of foreign currency. In Figure 16.3, we depict a country that has fixed its exchange rate. Suppose the demand for foreign currency rises—something that, without government intervention, would increase the market price of foreign currency. If the government is committed to maintaining the fixed exchange rate, it will intervene in the market by selling the foreign currency. Doing so shifts the supply curve to the right,

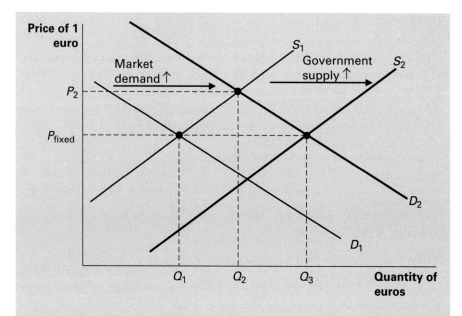

Figure 16.3 Maintaining a Fixed Exchange Rate.

The government wants to keep the price of foreign currency at price P_{fixed}. When market forces drive up the demand for foreign currency, the government must respond by increasing the supply of foreign currency. The government thus sells part of its official reserves of the foreign currency. The equilibrium price remains at P_{fixed} rather than rising to P_2.

keeping the equilibrium price constant. The government will have sold some of its official reserves of foreign currency in order to maintain the fixed exchange rate.

What if the market forces were pushing the exchange rate down, below the fixed exchange rate? In that case a government that wants to maintain a fixed exchange rate would intervene by purchasing foreign currency, shifting the demand for foreign currency to the right until the equilibrium price is once again at the fixed exchange rate.

TRY

11. A country has pegged its currency to the U.S. dollar. There is a great deal of trade between the U.S. and this country. Consider what happens when the U.S. economy enters a recession.

   a. If the other country does not maintain the peg, what will happen to the U.S. dollar price of its currency?
   b. If the other country does not maintain the peg, what will happen to U.S. imports from, and exports to, that country?
   c. If the other country does maintain the peg, what must its government do in the foreign exchange market in order to maintain the peg?

    d. In which case will the U.S. recession have a larger effect on U.S. imports from the other country: when the other country does not maintain the peg, or when it does? In which case will the U.S. recession have a larger effect on U.S. exports to the other country: when the other country does not maintain the peg, or when it does?

    e. Based on your answer to (d), does maintaining the peg help, or hurt, the other country's GDP when the U.S. economy enters a recession?

OPEN ECONOMY MACRO

In a closed economy, exports and imports are zero. All goods and services are produced domestically and consumed domestically. There is no international trade. In an open economy, exports and imports are positive. Some of the goods and services produced domestically are sold abroad, and some of the goods and services purchased domestically were produced abroad.

Exports and imports, as first noted in Chapter 7, are part of aggregate demand. An increase in exports or a decrease in imports, all else constant, will increase aggregate demand. A decrease in exports or an increase in imports, all else constant, will decrease aggregate demand.

Incorporating international transactions amends two of the macro stories we've told in previous chapters:

- Interest rates affect exchange rates, changing net exports.
- Income affects imports, changing the value of the spending multiplier.

These relationships have been covered in previous chapters, so we will simply review them here.

Incorporating international transactions enhances the effect of interest rates. We first covered this material in Chapter 13.

When U.S. interest rates are increased, U.S. financial inflows rise and U.S. financial outflows fall. Supply of foreign currency rises and demand for foreign currency falls, both of which cause the dollar price of foreign currency to fall. Imported goods and services cost less, so imports increase. U.S. exports cost more, so exports decrease. The combination of higher imports and lower exports both decrease net exports.

The reverse is also true. When U.S. interest rates are decreased, U.S. financial inflows fall and U.S. financial outflows rise. Supply of foreign currency falls and demand for foreign currency rises, both of which cause the dollar price of foreign currency to rise. Imported goods and services cost more, so imports decrease. U.S. exports cost less, so exports increase. The combination of lower imports and higher exports both increase net exports.

Incorporating international transactions reduces the size of the spending multiplier. We first covered this material at the end of Chapter 8.

In an open economy, an increase in income generates increases in both consumption and imports. Take the difference between the two, and you have the increase in purchases of *domestically-produced* goods and services. The more we import in each round of the multiplier process, the smaller will be the changes in purchases of *domestically-produced* goods and services, the smaller will be the total change in GDP, and the smaller will be the multiplier.

The effect of any initial drop in spending is therefore smaller in an open economy than in a closed economy. In each round of the multiplier process, only part of the drop in spending is for domestically-produced goods and services. Only that part of spending will cause further job losses and income decreases in the domestic economy. In essence, part of the downturn is exported abroad.

In a recovery, when spending is rising, the effect of an initial increase in spending is again smaller in an open economy than in a closed economy. In each round of the multiplier process, only the part of spending that is for domestically-produced goods and services will create jobs and increase income in the domestic economy. Part of the recovery is shared with other economies.

TRY

12. When is the initial effect of monetary policy on planned aggregate expenditure greater: in an open economy, or in a closed economy? Why?

13. Compare two economies. Economy O is an open economy. Economy C is a closed economy.

    a. Which economy has the greater change in GDP following a drop in investment spending?

    b. Which economy has the greater change in GDP after expansionary monetary policy?

    c. Which economy has the greater change in GDP after expansionary fiscal policy?

Answers to "TRY" Questions

CHAPTER 1: ECONOMICS TOOLS—MATH AND GRAPHING

1. $Y = 500$

2. Rate of change
$= (110 - 100)/100 = 10\%$

3. Rate of change
$= (100 - 110)/110 = -9.1\%$

4. Slope = rise/run $= -2/2 = -1$.

5. Quantity demanded decreases as price increases, so this is a downward-sloping curve.

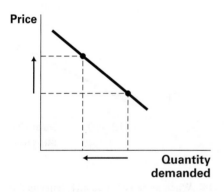

6. Spending increases as wealth increases, but the increases in spending get smaller and smaller as wealth gets larger and larger, so this is a curve with a positive and decreasing slope.

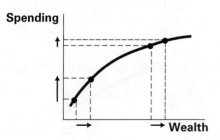

7. As the number of workers increases, their marginal product first increases but then later decreases, so this is a curve that first increases and then decreases.

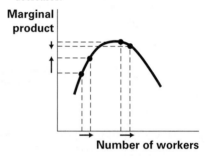

8. Income always equals aggregate spending, so this is a curve with a slope of 1.

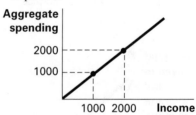

9. When the unemployment rate is low, the inflation rate is high, but when the unemployment rate is high, the inflation rate is low, so this is a downward-sloping curve.

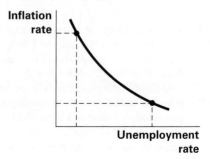

10. Quantity supplied increases as price increases, so this is an upward-sloping curve.

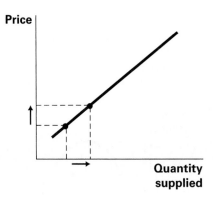

Price

Quantity supplied

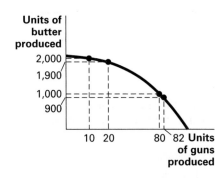

Units of butter produced

2,000
1,900
1,000
900

10 20   80 82 **Units of guns produced**

13. Quantity supplied is 13 when price is 5. But when price is 8, quantity supplied is 19. This is an upward-sloping curve.

11. For a monopolist, as quantity increases, marginal revenue has a steeper negative slope than average revenue, so we need two curves, both with a negative slope. The marginal revenue curve will be steeper than the average revenue curve.

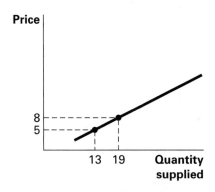

Price

8
5

13 19   **Quantity supplied**

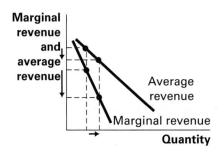

Marginal revenue and average revenue

Average revenue

Marginal revenue

Quantity

14. When price is 5, quantity demanded is 40. But when price is 10, quantity demanded is 30. This is a downward-sloping curve.

12. When the amount of butter produced is decreased from 2,000 units to 1,900, the number of guns produced increases from 10 units to 20. But when the amount of butter produced is decreased from 1,000 units to 900, the number of guns produced increases from 80 to just 82, so this is a curve with a negative and increasing slope (concave to the origin).

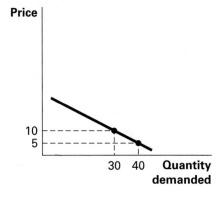

Price

10
5

30 40   **Quantity demanded**

CHAPTER 2: PRODUCTION POSSIBILITIES FRONTIER, ECONOMIC GROWTH, AND GAINS FROM TRADE

1. Opportunity cost is 30,000 pounds of butter.

2. Opportunity cost is 5,000 guns.

3.

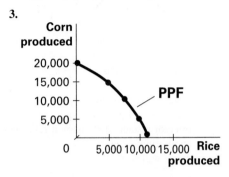

4. Yes, these numbers illustrate the law of increasing opportunity cost. The opportunity cost of increasing rice production rises as the amount of rice that is being produced increases. And the opportunity cost of increasing corn production also rises as the amount of corn that is being produced increases.

5.

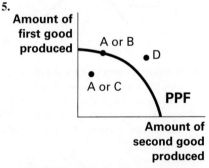

a. An attainable combination of output is any point on the PPF or inside of the PPF.

b. An efficient combination of output is any point on the PPF.

c. An inefficient combination of output is any point inside of the PPF.

d. An unattainable combination of output is any point above and to the right of the PPF.

6. No, a combination cannot be simultaneously efficient (using all available resources) and unattainable (impossible to produce with all available resources).

7. Kern County has the absolute advantage in corn production; 200 bushels of corn can be produced per acre in Kern County whereas just 100 bushels per acre can be produced in Taft County.

8. Kern County also has the absolute advantage in wheat production; 150 bushels of wheat can be produced per acre in Kern County whereas just 50 bushels per acre can be produced in Taft County.

9. The "gain from trade" is more output.

10. Yes, Robin and Marian will gain from trading. It does not matter that Robin is better at everything. Robin and Marian will together have a healthier garden and better meals—gains from trade—if they each specialize in their comparative advantage. Robin should cook and Marian should garden.

CHAPTER 3: DEMAND AND SUPPLY

1. When buyer income rises, demand for normal goods increases. The entire demand curve shifts to the right. The equilibrium price of laptops will rise. The equilibrium quantity of laptops will also rise.

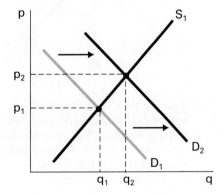

2. When the wages of pen manufacturers rise, this increase in input costs decreases supply of pens. The supply curve shifts to the left. The equilibrium price of pens rises. The equilibrium quantity of pens falls.

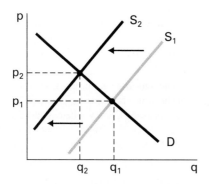

3. When buyer preferences shift toward hybrids, demand for hybrid cars increases. The entire demand curve shifts to the right. The equilibrium price of hybrid cars will rise. The equilibrium quantity of hybrid cars will also rise.

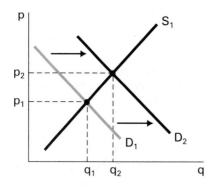

4. When the price of gasoline rises, demand for complementary goods such as SUVs decreases. The entire demand curve shifts to the left. The equilibrium price of SUVs will fall. The equilibrium quantity of SUVs will also fall.

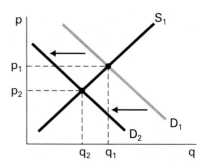

5. When more restaurants open in town, the supply of restaurant meals increases. The entire supply curve shifts to the right. The equilibrium price of restaurant meals will fall. The equilibrium quantity of restaurant meals will rise.

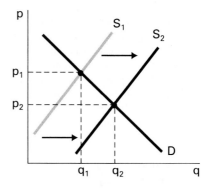

6. When hurricanes destroy dozens of oil rigs, the supply of crude oil decreases. The supply curve shifts to the left. The equilibrium price of crude oil rises. The equilibrium quantity of crude oil falls.

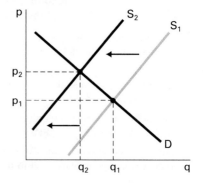

7. When a town's population increases, the demand for rental apartment increases. The entire demand curve shifts to the right. The equilibrium price of rental apartments will rise. The equilibrium quantity of rental apartments will also rise.

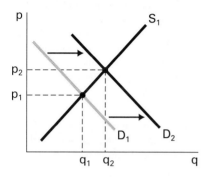

8. When the price of chocolate truffle cookies increases, the supply of brownies decreases. Brownies are substitutes in production for chocolate truffle cookies. The supply curve shifts to the left. The equilibrium price of brownies rises. The equilibrium quantity of brownies falls.

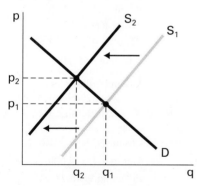

CHAPTER 4: MEASURING THE MACROECONOMY

1. Output refers to the goods and services that are produced. Output is things—books, pens, attorney's services. Income is what we receive for producing those goods and services. Income is money.

2. John Maynard Keynes wrote *The General Theory*.

3. The Great Depression was in the 1930s.

4. Nondurable goods are tangible goods that have a relatively short life. Food and clothing are good examples. Services are intangible. Shelter (rent), concerts, and medical services are all good examples. Durable goods are tangible goods that last at least three years. Cars and furniture are good examples.

5. Something is "output" if someone has a paying job producing it.

6. The underground economy is not counted in GDP because it is not reported and thus not measured. Illegal activity is not reported. Cash transactions may be legal, but if they are not reported they are not counted in GDP.

7. Excluding the underground economy, about $3.5 trillion in output was actually produced between April 1 and June 30, 2007.

8. GDP focuses on where output is produced. GNP focuses on who owns the resources being used to produce the output.

9. Nominal GDP is calculated using current-year prices. Real GDP is calculated using base-year prices.

10. Prices have risen, but the quantity of output has remained constant.

11. Between 1981 and 1982, real GDP fell 1.9%. Between 1982 and 1983, real GDP rose 4.5%.

12. "Long run" refers to changes that occur decade to decade or generation to generation. Short run refers to changes that occur year to year or quarter to quarter.

13. Decline—long run; depression—short run; growth—long run; growth recession—short run; peak—short run; recession—short run; recovery—short run; trough—short run.

14. The unemployment rate was $10.7/(10.7 + 99.5) = 9.7\%$. The labor force participation rate was $(10.7 + 99.5)/(10.7 + 99.5 + 62.1) = 64.0\%$.

15. a. A new college grad: frictional

b. A ski lift operator: seasonal

c. Wal-Mart sales clerk: cyclical

d. A worker in San Francisco: structural

16. There is more than one definition of the natural rate of unemployment. It can mean the unemployment rate consistent with being on the production possibilities frontier, the unemployment rate that occurs in a healthy economy with full employment, or the lowest rate of unemployment consistent with a low and stable inflation rate.

17. The consumer price index focuses just on consumer goods, uses a market basket that is the same from year to year, and is reported monthly by the BLS. The GDP deflator (GDP price index) focuses on all goods and services produced, uses actual quantities produced, which can change from year to year, and is reported quarterly by the BEA.

18. Inflation rate $= (177.1 - 172.2)/172.2 = 2.8\%$.

CHAPTER 5: LONG-RUN ECONOMIC GROWTH

1. a. 33.3% between 1998 and 1999; 5.0% between 1999 and 2000; 2.4% between 2000 and 2001; 4.7% between 2001 and 2002.

b. The average annual rate of change is 11.4%.

2. a. The value of real GDP per capita (the standard of living) in each year is $15,000 in 1998, $19,277 in 1999, $19,765 in 2000, $20,000 in 2001 and $20,690 in 2002.

b. The average annual rate of change in real GDP per capita is 8.4%.

3. If the standard of living is increasing 8.4% per year, it will take 8.3 years for the standard of living to double. If, instead, the standard of living is increasing 2.0% per year, it will take 35 years for the standard of living to double. If, instead, the standard of living is increasing just 1.0% per year, it will take 70 years for the standard of living to double.

4. Inputs are labor (L), capital (K), and, sometimes, but not in every textbook, natural resources (NR).

5. Output $= A^*F(K,L)$

6. "Capital" (K) includes machinery or equipment, and buildings or structures. Capital does not include money, stocks and bonds, or other financial assets.

7. $K = 100, L = 1,000,$

so Output $= 948.7$

$K = 100, L = 2,000,$

so Output $= 1,341.6$

$K = 100,$

$L = 3,000,$

so Output $= 1,643.2$

The example illustrates diminishing marginal returns. Holding constant K, and increasing L by 1,000 each time, the increase in output decreases from 392.9 to 301.6.

8. $K = 100, L = 4,000,$

so Output $= 46,784.3$

$K = 200,$

$L = 8,000,$

so Output $= 93,568.6$

$K = 360,$

$L = 14,400,$

so Output $= 168,423.3$

The example illustrates economies of scale. There are constant returns to scale. Doubling the inputs capital and labor results in a doubling of output. An increase of inputs by a factor of 1.8 results in an increase in output by a factor of 1.8

9. Increases in output and in output per worker are caused by increases in the quantity of inputs, and increases in total factor productivity or knowledge (A).

10. Increases in L are caused by increases in the labor force participation rate or in population. Increases in population are in turn caused by natural population growth or by immigration.

11. Increases in K are caused by increased investment or decreased depreciation.

12. Increases in NR are caused by land acquisition, mining, and discoveries.

13. Increases in A are caused by improvements in education, research and development, financial institutions, transportation networks, political institutions, property rights laws, and judicial systems.

14. During the productivity growth slowdown, productivity was not falling. Productivity was rising, but at a slower pace than previously.

15. There is not one widely accepted explanation for the productivity growth slowdown. There is a widely accepted explanation for the productivity growth resurgence: developments in information technology.

CHAPTER 6: KEYNESIAN CROSS

1. When employment falls, unemployment usually rises.

2. One reason that a drop in employment sometimes does *not* lead to a rise in unemployment is that laid-off workers may leave the labor force rather than search for new jobs.

3. When output falls, employment usually falls.

4. One reason that a drop in output sometimes does *not* cause employment to fall is that businesses may be hesitant to lay off workers until they are sure the drop in output will be long-lasting. Workers have less to do but do not initially lose their jobs when output of their firm falls.

5. When aggregate spending falls, output usually falls.

6. One reason that a drop in aggregate spending sometimes does *not* cause output to fall is that sometimes firms will lower prices rather than reduce output.

7. Inventories are accumulating. The change in inventory holdings is $200 billion. Businesses will not produce $3 trillion ($3,000 billion) worth of output in the next quarter, because when they produced $3 trillion in output, inventories accumulated. Therefore $3 trillion is not the equilibrium level of output.

8. Inventories are being depleted. The change in inventory holdings is $400 billion. Businesses will not produce $3 trillion worth of output in the next quarter, because when they produced just $3 trillion in output, inventories were depleted. Therefore $3 trillion is not the equilibrium level of output.

9. Inventories are neither accumulating nor being depleted. The change in inventory holdings is 0. Businesses will produce $3 trillion worth of output in the next quarter, because inventories neither accumulated nor were depleted when they produced $3 trillion in output. Therefore $3 trillion is the equilibrium level of output.

10. Households have two roles: suppliers of inputs, and purchasers of output. Firms also have two roles: suppliers of output, and purchasers of inputs. Households sell inputs to firms. Firms sell output to households.

11. a. Doctor's appointment is output.

b. Interest income earned on savings account is income.

c. Missile is output

d. A physician's annual salary is income.

e. Rent received by the landlord is income to the landlord.

f. Restaurant meal is output.

g. A sales clerk's hourly wages are income.

h. Shelter provided by an apartment is output.

i. Soybeans are output.

j. A textbook is output.

k. A tip received by a waitress is income.

12. When the macroeconomy is in equilibrium, $Y = AD$.

13. a. When $Y = 1,000, AD = 300 + 0.8(1,000) = 1,100$. Because $AD > Y$, 1,000 is not the equilibrium value of output

b. When $Y = 3,000$, $AD = 300 + 0.8(3,000) = 2,700$. Because $AD < Y$, 3,000 is not the equilibrium value of output

14. When $AD = 300 + 0.8Y$, equilibrium output $= 300/(1 - 0.8) = 1,500$.

15.

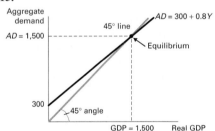

16. The 45° line is a quick way to find the equilibrium point on the AD line. Every point on the 45° line is a point where $Y = AD$, which is the equilibrium condition. The one point

that is *the* equilibrium is the point that is on both the 45° line and the AD line—the point where the two lines intersect.

17. Net taxes, $T = 4,000 - 3,000 = 1,000$. Disposable income, YD $= 10,000 + 3,000 - 4,000 = 9,000$.

18. Disposable income, $YD = \$5,000 - \$2,000$ billion $= \$3,000$ billion per year. Personal saving, $S = \$3,000 - \$2,500$ billion $= \$500$ billion per year.

CHAPTER 7: AGGREGATE DEMAND

1. Consumption spending: households. Investment spending: businesses. Government spending: government agencies (federal, state, and local). Net exports: exports are purchased by households, businesses, and government agencies in the rest of the world; imports are purchased by domestic households, businesses, and government agencies.

2. A common error is to equate "investment" with purchases of stocks and bonds. But "investment" means business purchases of machinery, construction of buildings, and changes in business inventory holdings.

3. a. Doctor's appointment: consumption

b. Government pays V.A. doctor's salary: government

c. U.S. Army buys a domestically-manufactured missile: government

d. U.S. Army buys Chilean-grown fruit: government, imports

e. Monthly rent on your apartment: consumption

f. Chase Bank buys new desks: investment

g. Buy a shirt manufactured in India: consumption, imports

h. Canadian companies purchase U.S.-grown fruit: exports

i. Public library buys new books: government

j. Buy a new book: consumption

k. Law office buys new books: investment

4. Consumption plus investment plus government spending add up to more than 100% of total spending for domestically-produced goods and services, because C, I, and G include spending for both domestically and foreign-produced goods and services.

5. Imports and exports are now a larger share of GDP than in the 1950s and 1960s.

6. Wealth refers to the total value of what we own, and is determined as of a particular day: wealth as of December 31, 2010. Income refers to what we earn for producing goods and services, and is determined over some time period: income for the month December 2010.

7. When disposable income falls, consumption spending falls. When wealth falls, consumption spending falls.

8. Disposable income (increase). Wealth (increase). Interest rates (perhaps decrease; depends on mix of borrowers and savers in total population). Availability of credit (increase). Expectations of the future (increase or improve).

9. Today's tax cut raises disposable income which should raise consumption. But next year's tax increase will lower next year's disposable income—thus lowering expected future disposable income—which should lower consumption. The two effects may fully offset each other.

10. a. When $YD = 2,000, C = 1,000 + 0.75 \cdot (2,000) = 2,500$. Consumption spending is $2,500 billion, or $2.5 trillion, per quarter.

b. If instead $YD = 3,000$, then $C = 1,000 + 0.75 \cdot (3,000) = 3,250$. Consumption spending is $3,250 billion, or $3.25 trillion, per quarter.

c. When disposable income increased by $1,000 billion per quarter, consumption spending per quarter increased by $750 billion per quarter.

d. The vertical intercept is $1,000 billion. The slope of the consumption function is 0.75.

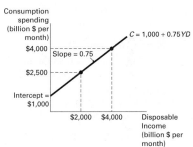

11. a. When $YD = 2,000, C = 1,000 + 0.75 \cdot (2,000) = 2,500$. So $S = YD - C = 2,000 - 2,500 = -500$. Saving is negative; $S = -\$500$ billion per quarter.

b. If, instead, $YD = 3,000$, then $C = 3,250$. So $S = YD - C = 3,000 - 3,250 = -250$. Saving is still negative; $S = -\$250$ billion per quarter.

c. When disposable income increased by $1,000 billion per quarter, saving per quarter rose by $250 billion, from $-\$500$ to $-\$250$ billion.

12. The saving function is $S = -1,000 + 0.25YD$. The vertical intercept is $-1,000$. The slope is 0.25.

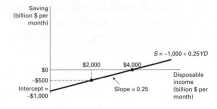

13. Paying off debt is "saving" because it is a use of disposable income that is *not* a current purchase of a final good or service. Saving is essentially "not consumption"—it is any use of disposable income other than current consumption spending. When we pay off debt, we are paying off a loan we took out in some previous period when we purchased something. The consumption was recorded in the year the item was purchased, not in the year the loan was repaid.

14. a. The *mpc* = 0.75. The *mps* = 1 − 0.75 = 0.25

b. From #10, when *YD* = 2,000, *C* = 2,500, so the *apc* = 2,500/2,000 = 1.25 = 125%. From #11, when *YD* = 2000, *S* = −500, so the *aps* = −0.25 = −25%.

c. If instead *YD* = 3,000, *C* = 3,250, and *S* = −250. So the *apc* = 1.083 = 108.3%, and the *aps* = −0.083 = −8.3%.

d. The *apc* decreases as disposable income increases, because the *mpc* is less than 1. Every additional dollar of disposable income generates less than a dollar of consumption. So the ratio of consumption to disposable income gradually becomes smaller as disposable income becomes larger.

15. a. Pay cuts: Movement along *C*, to the left, as income falls

b. Tax cut: Shift up of *C*

c. Stock prices fall: Shift down of *C*

d. Interest rates rise: Would shift *C*. Whether *C* shifts up or down depends upon the mix of borrowers (who lower consumption when interest rates rise) and savers (who raise consumption when interest rates rise).

e. Credit availability is restricted: Shift down of *C*

f. Consumer expectations turn optimistic: Shift down of *C*

g. Consumers expect a decrease in future income: Shift down of *C*

16. "Capital" refers to buildings (structures) and machines (equipment).

17. Buy the equipment if interest rates are 10% or lower.

18. Investment projects with an expected rate of return of 4% or greater are profitable and should be undertaken.

19. a. Interest rates rise: Movement up and to the left along the investment demand curve

b. Businesses' expectations for future sales improve: Shift of investment demand curve to the right

c. The price of producer durable equipment falls: Shift of investment demand curve to the right

20. a. European incomes fall: Decrease U.S. exports to Europe; decrease U.S. net exports.

b. U.S. incomes fall: Decrease U.S. imports; increase U.S. net exports

c. The dollar depreciates relative to the euro: increase U.S. exports to Europe; decrease U.S. imports from Europe; increase U.S. net exports.

CHAPTER 8: THE SPENDING MULTIPLIER

1. Initial change in spending: Government spending rises as local communities pay paving companies to fill potholes and repave roads. Multiplier effects: On payday, the new employees buy new appliances for their homes, and enjoy dinner at a local restaurant.

2. Initial change in spending: Government spending falls as teachers and aides at local schools are laid off. Multiplier effects: Because they have just lost their jobs, the laid-off school employees cancel their annual vacation plans and stop eating out.... The restaurants lay off some of their employees, who subsequently spend far less than usual on holiday gift shopping.

3. a. Equilibrium GDP = 500. See graph in (b).

   b. New equilibrium GDP = 1,250.

   c. The initial change in spending is +150. The total change in GDP is +750.

   d. ...the multiplier effect.

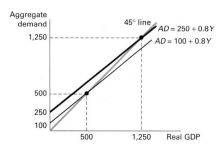

4. The value of the multiplier is 4 ($400 billion/$100 billion).

5. The value of the multiplier is 2.5 (−$500 billion/−$200 billion).

6.

Round #	Δspending (billions of $)	$\Delta Y = \Delta YD$ (billions of $)
1	Initial Δspending = −$1,000	$\Delta Y = \Delta YD = -\$1,000$
2	$\Delta C = -\$750$	$\Delta Y = \Delta YD = -\$750$
3	$\Delta C = -\$562.5$	$\Delta Y = \Delta YD = -\$562.5$

7. When $mpc = 0.75$, multiplier $= 4$. When the initial Δspending $= -1,000$, the total change in output and income is − 4,000.

8. When $mpc = 0.4$, multiplier $= 1.67$. When the initial Δspending $= +200$, the total change in output and income is +333.

9. When mpc equals 0, multiplier $= 1$. An mpc of 0 means that consumers spend nothing when their income changes, so the total change in output and income will simply equal the initial change in spending.

10. When $mpc = 1$, the value of the multiplier is infinite. An mpc of 1 means that consumers change their spending by the full amount of a change in income. In every round, the change in spending will equal the change in income that generated the spending. Every round is the same; the process does not converge; the multiplier is infinitely large.

11. When the mpc increases, the value of the multiplier increases. A larger mpc means that consumers are spending more out of any increase in income (or cutting spending by more when there is a drop in income). Because there is a larger change in spending in each round of the multiplier process, the total change in output and income due to an initial change in spending will be larger, too.

12. Taxes increase by $200 billion. Disposable income increases by $800 billion.

13. Taxes decrease by $150 billion. Disposable income decreases by $350 billion.

14.

Round #	Δspending (billions of $)	ΔY (billions of $)	ΔT (billions of $)	ΔYD (billions of $)
1	Initial Δspending $= -\$1,000$	$\Delta Y = -\$1,000$	$\Delta T = -\$200$	$\Delta YD = -\$800$
2	$\Delta C = -\$600$	$\Delta Y = -\$600$	$\Delta T = -\$120$	$\Delta YD = -\$480$
3	$\Delta C = -\$360$	$\Delta Y = -\$360$	$\Delta T = -\$72$	$\Delta YD = -\$288$

15. If $mpc = 0.75$ and tax rate $= 0.2$, multiplier $= 2.5$. When the initial Δspending $= -1,000$, the total change in output and income is $-2,500$.

16. If $mpc = 0.4$ and tax rate $= 0.1$, multiplier $= 1.5625$. When the initial Δspending $= +200$, the total change in output and income is $+312.5$.

17. If tax rate $= 1$, multiplier $= 1$. When tax rate $= 1$, any change in income equals the change in taxes; there is no change in disposable income. Because there is no change in disposable income, there is no change in consumption spending. So the total change in output and income simply equals the initial change in spending. Multiplier $= 1$.

18. When the tax rate increases, the value of the multiplier decreases. With a higher tax rate, more taxes are withheld from an increase in income, so the increase in disposable income is smaller. Or, if income is falling, with a higher tax rate, the drop in taxes is larger, so the drop in disposable income is smaller. Because the change in disposable income is smaller (for a given change in income), the changes in spending in each round will be smaller, too, than they would be with a lower tax rate. So the multiplier will be smaller when the tax rate is larger.

19. When income increases by $1,000 billion per year and the mpm is 15%, the annual change in imports is +$150 billion.

20. When income decreases by $500 billion per year and the mpm is 20%, the annual change in imports is $-$100 billion.

21.

Round #	Δspending (billions of $)	$\Delta Y = \Delta YD$ (billions of $)	ΔC (billions of $)	ΔIM (billions of $)
1	Initial Δspending $= -\$1,000$	$\Delta Y = \Delta YD$ $= -\$1,000$	$\Delta C = 0.75 \cdot \Delta YD$ $= -\$750$	$\Delta IM = 0.25 \cdot \Delta Y$ $= -\$250$
2	$\Delta C - \Delta IM$ $= -\$750 - (-\$250)$ $= -\$500$	$-\$500$	$-\$375$	$-\$125$
3	$\Delta C - \Delta IM$ $= -\$375 - (-\$125)$ $= -\$250$	$-\$250$	$-\$187.5$	$-\$62.5$

22. If $mpc = 0.75$ and $mpm = 0.25$, multiplier = 2. When initial $\Delta spending = -1,000$, total change in output and income $= -2,000$.

23. If $mpc = 0.4$ and $mpm = 0.1$, multiplier = 1.43. When initial $\Delta spending = +200$, total change in output and income $= +285.7$.

24. If $mpm = mpc$, multiplier = 1. When $mpm = mpc$, every dollar spent by consumers is for goods and services produced in other countries. So when income changes, there is no change in purchases of domestically produced goods and services. The total change in output and income will simply equal the initial change in spending.

25. When the marginal propensity to import increases, the value of the multiplier decreases. With a higher mpm, a greater share of changes in domestic income is used to purchase imported goods and services, generating income for the producers of those imports—people and businesses in other countries. A smaller share of domestic income is used to purchase domestically produced goods and services. So in each round of the multiplier process, there is less domestic spending. The total change in output and income for an initial change in spending is smaller. The multiplier is smaller.

CHAPTER 9: MACROECONOMIC POLICY: THE OVERVIEW

1.

2. There is an output gap. The unemployment rate is above the full-employment rate of unemployment.

3. Direct fiscal policy is an action that immediately and directly changes aggregate demand $= C + I + G + NX$. Indirect fiscal policy is an action that ultimately affects aggregate demand, but its first effect is on something other than C, I, G, or NX.

4. "The Fed" refers to the Federal Reserve System: the Board of Governors, located in Washington, D.C., and the twelve regional Federal Reserve Banks located across the United States.

5. If you borrow $10,000 from ABC Loans and pay back $10,500 in one year, the interest is $500 and the rate is $500/$10,000 = 5%. The interest rate is a cost to you, the borrower, and is a rate of return to ABC Loans, the lender.

6. A tax increase is contractionary fiscal policy. Transfer payment increases are expansionary fiscal policy. Here, the simultaneous implementation of both policies is a decrease in net taxes ($T = TA - TR$) of $20 billion, so it is expansionary fiscal policy.

7. Expansionary monetary policy refers to increases in money supply or decreases in interest rates that expand (or increase) aggregate demand. Contractionary monetary policy refers to decreases in money supply or increases in interest rates that contract (or decrease) aggregate demand.

8. Recognition lag: amount of time it takes to recognize the existence of a problem. Implementation lag: amount of time it takes to write and pass a bill, and to implement the resulting policy. Response lag: amount of time it takes for the economy to change in response to the policy.

9. Answers to this question can vary. The factors to keep in mind are how long it takes for the spending to first enter the economy, and how long it takes for the multiplier effects to kick in.

10. The "zero lower bound" refers to the inability of the Fed to push nominal interest rates below zero. In 2009, after the Fed hit the zero lower bound, it implemented new and creative policies, all designed to inject liquidity (reserves) into banks and financial institutions.

11. The counterfactual value of the unemployment rate is a hypothetical value: what the unemployment rate would be, had the policy action not been implemented.

12. If the actual unemployment rate is less than the counterfactual unemployment rate, then the policy was successful in lowering the unemployment rate below where it would have been without the policy.

CHAPTER 10: FISCAL POLICY

1. When $mpc = 0.8$ and $\Delta G = +\$100$ billion, the total change in income and output will be $500 billion. When $mpc = 0.8$ and $\Delta TA = -\$100$ billion, the total change in income and output is $400 billion.

2. When $mpc = 0.8$ and $\Delta G = -\$400$ billion per year, GDP falls by $2,000 billion per year. If instead $\Delta TR = -\$400$ billion per year when $mpc = 0.8$, GDP falls by $1,600 billion per year.

3. If $mpc = 0.75$, an increase in government spending of $0.5 trillion ($500 billion) or a tax cut of $0.67 trillion ($667 billion) would be required to close a $2 trillion output gap.

4. If $mpc = 0.5$, a *drop* in government spending of $100 billion or a decrease in transfer payments of $200 billion would be required to close a $200 billion inflationary gap.

5. Proportional taxes are called an "automatic stabilizer" because the automatic changes in taxes collected when income changes reduce the size

of the change in disposable income, reducing the size of subsequent changes in spending. The changes in taxes are automatic because no additional act of Congress or a state legislature is required to change the tax collections; taxes collected by the government are a proportion (a percentage) of the base. Spending, income, and GDP are being stabilized.

6. No, a decrease in lump-sum taxes is not an example of an automatic stabilizer. Automatic stabilizers are taxes and transfers that change automatically as income changes.

7. If $G = \$2,000$ billion, $TR = \$1,400$ billion, and $TA = \$3,000$ billion per year, then budget balance $= -\$400$ billion per year—a budget deficit.

8. The budget deficit increases when a recession begins because taxes and transfers change automatically as income falls and unemployment rises. Lower income means lower income tax revenue, increasing a budget deficit. Higher unemployment means higher transfer payments, also increasing a budget deficit.

9. When the federal government runs a deficit, it must borrow the money it uses to pay the bills that it can't pay with tax revenues.

10. The "structural deficit" is a hypothetical value of the budget deficit, calculated based on the assumption that the economy is at full employment. Because ARRA was temporary discretionary fiscal policy implemented in response to the economic recession, it did not add directly to the structural deficit.

11. Three concerns about increased government borrowing are expressed: that it will drive up interest rates and crowd out investment spending, that repayment will drain financial resources from the economy, and that lenders will decide the government has exceeded its ability to repay and will cease lending.

CHAPTER 11: MONEY CREATION

1. Money is a medium of exchange (it is accepted in exchange for goods and services), a unit of account (used for expressing prices), and a store of value (an asset that does not physically lose its value over time). Credit cards are not money, because they are not a store of value.

2. a. Shells in eighteenth-century societies in western Africa were commodity money because in eighteenth-century western African societies, they met the three characteristics of money.

   b. Bus or subway tokens are not money, because they are not a medium of exchange. They are not accepted widely in exchange for goods and services, but only for bus or subway rides.

   c. Euros (the currency of Europe) are not money when used in Chicago, Illinois, because they are neither a medium of exchange nor a unit of account. Prices in Chicago are not expressed in euros, and euros are not accepted in exchange for goods and services.

3. M1 includes coins, paper currency, traveler's checks, and balances in checking accounts. M2 includes M1 plus savings deposits, "small"-time deposits (under $100,000), and balances in money market mutual funds. M2 has increased more rapidly in the last half-century.

4. a. Gross monthly salary is income.

   b. The paycheck itself is money.

   c. Being worth a million dollars describes wealth.

   d. $900 in my checking account is money.

   e. Revenue from selling artwork is income.

   f. A retirement fund is wealth.

5. A check is an instruction from the check-writer to the individual's bank to transfer some of the check-writer's money to the payee of the check. There is no essential difference between a check and an online bill payment.

6. HONEY deposits the check at Hive Bank. Hive Bank electronically instructs its Federal Reserve Bank to transfer $100 from Tree Bank to it. The information is also sent to Tree Bank, which deducts $100 from your checking account.

7. a. Your money holdings fell by $100.

   b. HONEYS money holdings rose by $100.

   c. Total deposits in the banking system were unchanged.

   d. Tree Bank's reserve balance at the Fed fell by $100.

   e. Hive Bank's reserve balance at the Fed rose by $100.

   f. Total reserves in the banking system were unchanged.

8. Banks have an incentive to hold a relatively low level of reserves because they earn a very low rate of interest on reserves and can earn much more in interest by making loans. The Fed sets a minimum required level of reserves because it is important that banks hold enough reserves to be able to meet not just regular but even extraordinary daily withdrawals.

9. Required reserves = $54.5 million. Excess reserves = $5.5 million.

10. Required reserves = $54.5 million. The bank can borrow from the Fed at the discount window, or it can borrow reserves from another bank.

11. Printing (and distributing) paper currency simply replaces previously issued paper currency that is ready for the shredder or that is given out in exchange for a lower checking account balance. Neither action increases the amount of money in the economy.

12. Tree Bank might loan the excess reserves because it earns more profit from a consumer loan than from holding onto the reserves. If there is a lot of economic uncertainty, Tree Bank may decide that it is safer to hold the excess reserves rather than lend them.

13. Money is created when the bursar deposits the check into your college's checking account.

14. A bank with no excess reserves cannot make any loans. Making loans creates money in the form of deposits. If the bank has no excess reserves, it will not be able to cover its reserve requirement on the newly created deposits.

15. a. Your checking account balance: your asset and Tree Bank's liability.

b. Tree Bank's reserve account balance: Tree Bank's asset and the Fed's liability.

c. A $5 bill in your wallet: your asset and the Fed's liability.

d. A $5 bill in Tree Bank's vault: Tree Bank's asset and the Fed's liability.

16.

Your Bank (Tree Bank)	
A	L
Reserves at Fed +500	Your checking account balance +500

Boss's Bank (Hive Bank)	
A	L
Reserves at Fed −500	Boss's checking account balance −500

Fed Reserve Bank	
A	L
	Tree Bank reserves +500
	Hive Bank reserves −500

17.

Tree Bank	
A	L
Reserves at Fed −100	Your checking account balance −100

Hive Bank	
A	L
Reserves at Fed +100	Honey's checking account balance +100

Fed Reserve Bank	
A	L
	Tree Bank reserves −100
	Hive Bank reserves +100

18. Bank A has not lent out all of its excess reserves. Because the contractor deposits the check back into Bank A, $90,000 is still at Bank A, only now in the contractor's account. Bank A must hold 10% of that amount in required reserves. So the bank's remaining excess reserves are now $81,000.

19. a. The money multiplier is 10. $4,000,000 will be created.

   b. The money multiplier is 8.33. $3,333,333 will be created.

   c. The money multiplier is 10. $2,000,000 will be destroyed.

20. If banks decide to hold some excess reserves, they will not lend as much, and thus the money multiplier will be smaller than 1/(required reserve ratio).

CHAPTER 12: THE MONEY MARKET

1. We hold our wealth as money or as bonds (non-money assets).

2. Money demand refers to how much of our wealth we want in money rather than in bonds. The money market refers to the supply of money from banks and the demand for money from people, businesses, and government institutions.

3. Money: can be used to pay for transactions, but earns a zero rate of return. Non-money assets (bonds): earns a positive rate of return, but cannot be used to pay for transactions.

4. a. Increased income: increases money demand; shifts *MD* curve to the right

   b. Increased interest rates: decreases money demand; movement along the *MD* curve down and to the right

   c. Increased prices: increases money demand; shifts *MD* curve to the right

5. We draw the money supply as a vertical line because we are assuming that the Fed sets the money supply at some level.

6. Banks actually determine the amount of money in the economy, but the Fed determines how many excess reserves are available to them to lend.

7. Money demand increases, indicating that people and businesses want more of their wealth in money. They sell bonds, which increases the supply of bonds, lowering the price of bonds, and increasing their rate of return. The higher rate of return on bonds lowers money demand. People and businesses will continue selling bonds, raising interest rates, until their money demand falls back to its original level.

8.

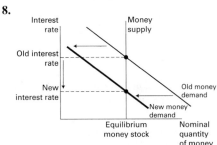

9. Excess reserves and the money supply both fall when the required reserve ratio is increased.

10. a. You: Assets the same, but $98,000 more in bonds and $98,000 less in checking. Your bank: $98,000 less in liabilities (your checking account balance) and $98,000 less in assets (balance in Fed reserve account). Fed: $98,000 less in assets (bonds) and $98,000 less in liabilities (your bank's reserve account balance).

   b. Excess reserves and the money supply both decline.

11. When the Fed buys bonds from the public, the Fed gets the bond and the public gets paid with a check (money!). The check is deposited into a bank, increasing the bank's required and excess reserves, allowing it to make loans and create even more money. Interest rates have decreased, because the Fed's actions represent an increase in demand for bonds, increasing the price on bonds and thus decreasing their interest rate.

12.

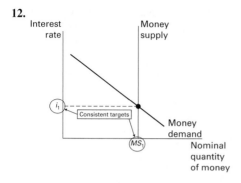

13. Money demand falls when income falls. If the money supply is unchanged at MS_1, then interest rates will fall to i_2. The Fed can't simultaneously achieve its original money supply target of MS_1 and interest rate target of i_1.

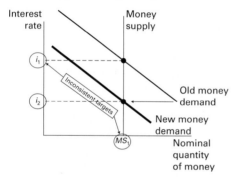

14. When prices fall, money demand falls, which lowers interest rates. If instead the Fed has an interest rate target, then the money supply will be decreased when prices fall.

CHAPTER 13: MONETARY POLICY AND INTEREST RATES

1. The FOMC is the Federal Open Market Committee, a committee of the Federal Reserve that determines monetary policy.

2. a. The Fed's target inflation rate is 2–3%: objective

   b. The Fed's target money supply growth rate is 4%: strategy

   c. The Fed's target interest rate is 1%: strategy

3. The Fed can't just tell banks to change the federal funds rate because the federal funds rate is a market rate determined by banks.

4. When the Fed sells bonds, the money supply decreases, because reserves are decreased as people and institutions pay for the bonds they purchase from the Fed. Interest rates rise because the Fed's action increases the supply of bonds, lowering their price and raising their rate of return.

5. Answers will vary.

6. a. Today's 3-year interest rate will be at least 4%. Due to the risk premium, the 3-year rate will probably be more than 4%.

   b. Today's 3-year interest rate should increase when there's an increase in future expected short-term rates.

   c. When the yield curve is inverted, future expected short-term rates are expected to be lower than current short-term rates.

7. Real interest rate = 5% − 6% = −1%.

8. Real interest rate falls when the inflation rate rises. All else constant, investment spending increases.

9. "The" interest rate is a problematic simplification when the slope or shape of the yield curve changes.

10. Contractionary monetary policy means an increase in interest rates. Investment spending falls, because fewer potential projects will have an expected rate of return greater than the now-higher interest rate. Net export spending falls because the dollar rises when interest rates rise. Consumption spending might fall; it depends on whether the drop in durable goods consumption exceeds the rise in spending by savers. Each of these initial changes in aggregate demand kick off multiplier effects, causing further drops in spending.

11. If only short-term rates and not long-term rates change, then contractionary monetary policy will not have as large an effect on the economy. Investment spending in particular responds primarily to changes in long-term, not short-term, interest rates.

12. Inflation rate $= 3 + 4 - 2 = 5\%$.

13. The inflation rate will be approximately 400%. Small changes in the growth rates of velocity or real GDP might make the inflation rate a few points above or below that, but it will round to 400%.

14. If a higher money growth rate is offset by a lower velocity growth rate, then the inflation rate won't increase when money growth rate increases.

15. Rules are a prescribed course of action. Discretion means allowing the policymaking authorities to determine the course of action at any time. The advantage to rules is predictability. The advantage to discretion is flexibility.

16. Our inflationary expectations can fluctuate a lot in reaction to economic events and rumors if the Fed's commitment to fighting inflation is not credible.

17. Bank: Total assets are unchanged but mix is changed; fewer MBS and more reserves at the Fed. Fed: Assets are greater (more MBS) and liabilities are greater (greater balance in bank reserve accounts); money supply will increase.

CHAPTER 14: INFLATION AND OUTPUT: THE AS/AD APPROACH

1. When interest rates increase, investment spending and net exports both fall. (Consumption spending might initially fall too; it depends on the mix of borrowers and savers in the economy.) Multiplier effects kick in, further decreasing planned aggregate expenditure.

2. When real wealth increases, savers don't need to save as much in order to achieve the same wealth goal. Consumption spending rises. Multiplier

effects kick in, further increasing planned aggregate expenditure.

3. Prices of houses and of stock are not included in the GDP deflator, because houses and stock are not output that is currently produced.

4. When output prices fall in the United States but not in the rest of the world, exports from the United States rise and imports into the United States fall; both these things increase net exports. Multiplier effects kick in, further increasing planned aggregate expenditure.

5. Planned aggregate expenditure would decrease when output prices increase, even if the spending multiplier equaled 1, because the initial changes in exports and imports would still occur.

6. When prices fall, planned aggregate expenditure rises. See figure at top of page 320.

7. a. Household access to credit restricted: shift AD left
   b. Output prices fall: move down and to the right along AD curve
   c. Businesses more optimistic: shift AD right
   d. Increased government spending and decreased taxes: shift AD right
   e. Consumers switch from imports to domestically produced goods and services: shift AD right
   f. The Fed increases the money supply: shift AD right

8. a. Increase labor force: shift LRAS right
   b. Increase nation's capital stock: shift LRAS right
   c. Natural disaster: shift LRAS left
   d. Increase labor productivity: shift LRAS right
   e. Educational attainment increases: shift LRAS right
   f. Financial institutions developed: shift LRAS right

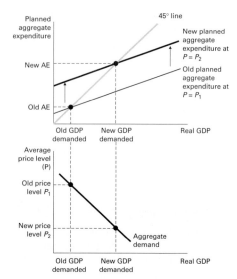

9. When output prices fall and some input costs are fixed, profit decreases, which leads profit-maximizing firms to decrease how much they produce. GDP supplied decreases.

10. The SRAS curve is flatter below current output levels than it is above them, because employers are much more hesitant to cut wages than they are to raise them. So a drop in prices below the current level results in a bigger drop in profit than does an equal-sized increase in prices. Because the change in profit is larger, the change in output produced is larger when prices fall than when prices rise.

11. In order to produce more output, firms increase their demand for inputs, raising the price of inputs. The increased cost of production is passed on to consumers in the form of higher output prices.

12. When the economy is far below its potential, the increased demand for inputs can be satisfied with little or no change in input prices, so there will be little or no increase in output prices. But when the labor force is fully employed, greater demand for workers

primarily increases wages rather than increasing employment. Prices rise, but there is very little change in how much output is produced.

13. a. Labor force increases: LRAS and SRAS both shift right

b. Capital increases: LRAS and SRAS both shift right

c. Labor productivity rises: LRAS and SRAS both shift right

d. Energy price rises: LRAS unchanged; SRAS shifts up (left)

14.

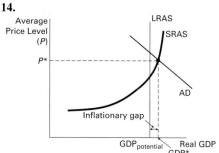

15. a. House prices fall: *AD* shifts left; *P* falls and real GDP falls.

b. Businesses more optimistic: *AD* shifts right; *P* rises and real GDP rises. (More complex answer also includes effect on *AS*. More investment spending raises the capital stock, shifting SRAS and LRAS to the right. Net effect on prices depends upon the relative sizes of the shifts in *AD* and SRAS. Real GDP increases further.)

c. Expansionary fiscal policy: *AD* shifts right; *P* rises, and real GDP rises.

d. Price of energy rises: SRAS shifts up; *P* rises, and real GDP falls.

e. Labor force increases: SRAS and LRAS shift right; *P* falls, and real GDP rises.

f. Increased taxes: *AD* shifts left; *P* falls, and real GDP falls.

16.

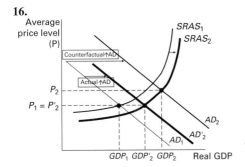

CHAPTER 15: INFLATION AND OUTPUT: THE MONETARY POLICY APPROACH

1. *AS/AD* approach: money supply target. Monetary policy approach: interest rate target.

2. When income or prices rise, money demand rises. The Fed can keep the money supply constant, but then interest rates will rise. Or the Fed can keep interest rates constant, but then the money supply will rise. The Fed can't simultaneously keep both money supply and interest rates constant after a change in money demand.

3. The inflation rate and the real GDP growth rate.

4. To increase the federal funds rate, the Fed sells T-bills to the public. As payments to the Fed for the T-bills clear, bank reserves drop, lowering the supply of federal funds and increasing the demand for federal funds. Banks raise the federal funds rate. Most interest rates then also increase as wealth holders substitute between assets. But long-term rates typically do not change as much as short-term rates.

5. Investment spending rises when interest rates fall, because some previously unprofitable investment projects are now profitable (their rates of return are now more than prevailing interest rates) and thus will be undertaken.

6. Net export spending rises when U.S. interest rates fall because wealth-holders move some of their wealth out of the United States, decreasing supply of, and increasing demand for, foreign currency. The resulting higher price of foreign currency (weaker dollar) makes imports more expensive and U.S. exports less expensive. Imports fall and exports rise; both these things raise net exports.

7. The effect of interest rates is greater when *mpc* = 0.9 than it is when *mpc* = 0.4. The multiplier increases as *mpc* increases (see Chapter 8), making the total change in output greater for any initial change in spending.

8. As unemployment falls, higher demand for labor raises wages, which increases costs of production. Businesses pass higher costs on to customers by increasing output prices. A faster increase in output prices is a higher inflation rate.

9. a. Inflationary expectations fall: Phillips curve shifts down

   b. Increased supply of a major input: Phillips curve shifts down

   c. Labor productivity growth rates rise: Phillips curve shifts down

10. Events other than fiscal and monetary policy can shift the Phillips curve, making any "point" impossible to achieve.

11. Inflation rising: raise interest rates. Inflation falling: lower interest rates. Growth rate of GDP rising: raise interest rates. Growth rate of GDP falling: lower interest rates.

12. An increase in the federal funds rate target could mean that the Fed is fighting inflation, or it could mean that the Fed is returning the federal funds rate to its neutral level after having successfully fought a recession.

13. The Taylor Rule describes how the interest rate target responds to changes in the inflation rate and the GDP growth rate. FOMC members don't

literally use the Taylor Rule to make their decisions, but their complex deliberations are captured reasonably well by that one equation.

14. a. Inflation rate goal = 2%; GDP growth rate goal = 3%

 b. i. interest rate target = $0.04 + 1/2(0) + 1/4(0) = 4\%$
  ii. interest rate target = $0.04 + 1/2(0.04) + 1/4(0) = 6\%$
  iii. interest rate target = $0.04 + 1/2(0) + 1/4(0.03) = 3.25\%$

15. An inflation hawk is very aggressive in fighting inflation, even though the cost is higher unemployment. An inflation dove fights inflation, but not as aggressively, because of the unemployment costs. The Taylor Rule in question 14 probably characterizes an FOMC dominated by hawks.

16. Decreased aggregate demand: Fed will decrease interest rates to fight the recession.

17. a. Taylor Rule 1: interest rate target = 7%. Taylor Rule 2: interest rate target = 1%.

 b. Inflation hawks: Taylor Rule 1. Inflation doves: Taylor Rule 2.

 c. The mix of inflation hawks and doves on the Fed matters when the economy is experiencing both rising inflation and falling output (stagflation) and the FOMC has to decide which problem to fight more aggressively.

18. When the target predicted by the Taylor Rule is negative, the target for the federal funds rate will be at the zero lower bound.

CHAPTER 16: OPEN ECONOMY MACROECONOMICS

1. The "gains from trade" are the increases in total worldwide output due to specialization and trade.

2. Free trade refers to trade unencumbered by trade promotion or trade restriction policies.

3. Trade is opposed because the costs of specializing are not borne evenly, because infant industries sometimes cannot compete, and because of national security concerns, as well as for other reasons.

4. Embargo: total ban on trade with a specific country. Quota: numerical limit to imports of particular product from specific country. Tariff: tax placed on imported products.

5. a. 2005 U.S. merchandise trade balance with China = $41.1 - 243.9 = -\$202.8$ billion. Merchandise trade deficit: United States. Merchandise trade surplus: China.

 b. 2005 U.S. balance of trade in goods and services with China = $(41.1 + 9.0) - (243.9 + 6.7) = -\$200.5$ billion. Deficit in trade of goods and services: United States. Surplus in trade of goods and services: China.

 c. 2005 U.S. balance on current account with China = $(41.1 + 9.0 + 4.9) - (243.9 + 6.7 + 21.4 + 2.2) = -\$219.2$ billion. Current account deficit: United States. Current account surplus: China.

6. 2005 U.S. balance on financial account with China = $224.7 - 5.4 = \$219.3$ billion. Financial account surplus: United States. Financial account deficit: China.

7. When the U.S. financial account is in deficit, U.S. people, businesses, and government agencies are borrowing less from foreigners than they are lending.

8. There was a U.S. current account deficit and U.S. financial account surplus. U.S. overall balance of payments = $-748.7 + (1295.2 - 532.6) = +\$13.9$ billion, a balance of

payments surplus. U.S. reserve accounts of foreign currency decreased.

9. The U.S. financial account was in deficit from 1890 until 1970, and in surplus since 1975.

10. a. A U.S. recession: supply of foreign currency, no effect; demand for foreign currency, decrease; dollar price of foreign currency, decrease. The dollar rises.

    b. Economic boom in China: supply of foreign currency, increase; demand for foreign currency, no effect; dollar price of foreign currency, decrease. The dollar rises.

    c. U.S. interest rates decrease: supply of foreign currency, decrease; demand for foreign currency, increase; dollar price of foreign currency, increase. The dollar falls.

    d. Interest rates decrease in all countries: supply of foreign currency, no effect; demand for foreign currency, no effect; dollar price of foreign currency, no effect. The dollar does not change.

    e. Interest rates rise in Europe and Asia, but not in the United States: supply of foreign currency, decrease; demand for foreign currency, increase; dollar price of foreign currency, increase. The dollar falls.

11. a. When the U.S. economy enters a recession, U.S. demand for foreign currency will decrease. If the other country does *not* maintain the peg, the U.S. dollar price of its currency will fall. The dollar rises.

    b. If the other country does not maintain the peg, U.S. imports from the country will first fall (because of the drop in income) and then recover somewhat (because of the rise of the dollar). U.S. exports to that country will fall (because of the rise of the dollar).

    c. If the other country does maintain the peg, its government must buy its own currency and sell dollars in order to maintain the peg. The demand curve returns to its original position.

    d. The U.S. recession has a larger effect on U.S. imports when the other country *does* maintain the peg. There is no rise of the dollar that offsets the initial recession-driven drop in imports into the United States. The U.S. recession has a larger effect on U.S. exports when the other country *does not* maintain the peg; with the peg, there's no change in U.S. exports.

    e. Maintaining the peg hurts the other country's GDP when the U.S. economy enters a recession. Their imports fall more than would be the case if the currency was allowed to float.

12. Monetary policy has a larger initial effect on planned aggregate expenditure in an open economy, because net exports also respond to interest rates.

13. Compare two economies. Economy O is an open economy. Economy C is a closed economy.

    a. Economy C has a larger spending multiplier, so it has the greater change in GDP following a drop in investment spending.

    b. This is ambiguous. Economy C has a larger spending multiplier, so the effect of an initial change in spending is greater in Economy C than in Economy O. But Economy O has a larger initial change in spending, because both investment and net export spending change in response to expansionary monetary policy.

    c. Economy C has the greater change in GDP after expansionary fiscal policy, because it has a larger spending multiplier. (The answer assumes that interest rates are held constant.)

Index